GEOFF
HAMILTON'S
PARADISE GARDENS

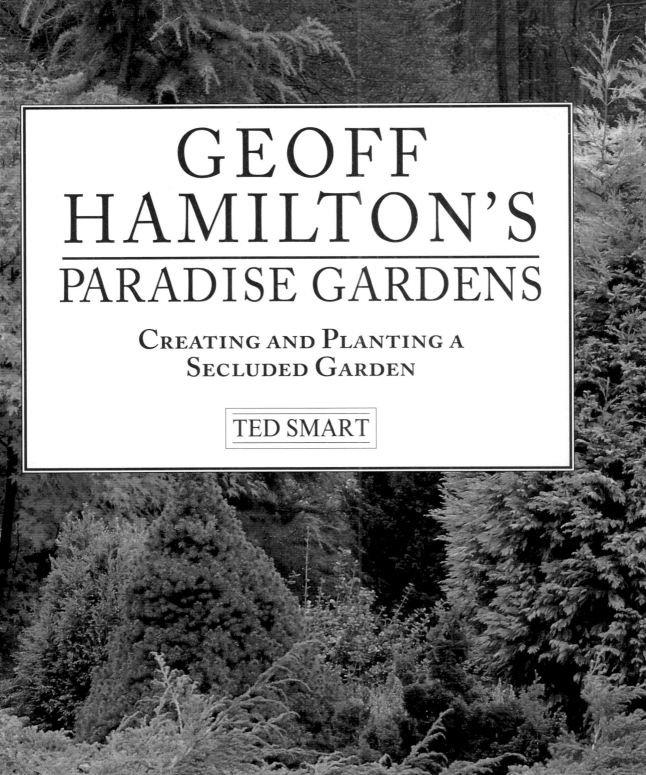

GEOFF HAMILTON'S
PARADISE GARDENS

CREATING AND PLANTING A
SECLUDED GARDEN

TED SMART

Geoff Hamilton died shortly after he had finished writing Paradise Gardens.
As always with Geoff, his enthusiasm and passion for gardening are captured in his words.
This book is dedicated to his memory

This book is published to accompany the television series entitled *Geoff Hamilton's Paradise Gardens* which was first broadcast in 1997. The series was produced by Catalyst Television for the BBC
Executive Producer: Tony Laryea
Producer and director: Ray Hough
BBC Books would like to thank Gay Search for her help with this project

This edition produced for The Book People Ltd,
Hall Wood Avenue, Haydock, St. Helens WA11 9UL
by BBC Books, an imprint of BBC Worldwide Publishing.
BBC Worldwide Limited, Woodlands, 80 Wood Lane, London W12 0TT

First published 1997
This printing 1997
© Geoff Hamilton 1997
The moral right of the author has been asserted
ISBN 0 563 38732 7

Illustrations by Jane Cradock-Watson
Photographs by Stephen Hamilton
Set in Palatino
Printed in Great Britain by Cambus Litho Ltd, East Kilbride
Bound in Great Britain by Hunter and Foulis Ltd, Edinburgh
Colour separations by Radstock Reproductions Ltd, Midsomer Norton
Jacket printed by Lawrence Allen Ltd, Weston-super-Mare

CONTENTS

INTRODUCTION

If asked to define our own idea of a personal paradise, I think most of us would visualize rolling green hills, shady trees and flower-studded meadows, all orchestrated with the song of birds and the buzzing of insects: in other words, the countryside. In reality, few of us have the good fortune to live in this kind of Arcadian situation, but we still yearn for the beauty and simplicity of a life lived close to nature.

I can see my own theoretical paradise now. The good earth delivering up its bounty to us brown-skinned, smiling peasants, brimming with health and well-being on our diet of good, wholesome, home-produced food and relaxing in flowery arbours surrounded by our laughing and only slightly grubby children as they play happily together.

Of course, it can be no more than a dream. To be in paradise we would have to be guaranteed sunshine, rain only at night, crops that never failed, animals that never succumbed to disease and a complete absence of aggression from our fellow men. In any case few of us these days would admit to wanting the hardships that went with the simple, old-fashioned country life our grandparents knew. Leaky thatch, no running water or electricity, trudging to work at first

light in the snow and hail, and endless, unremitting toil – who needs it?

Nonetheless I'm convinced that we all need some kind of escape from the complexity, the pressure and the ever-accelerating speed of modern life, a life just about as far removed from the one for which our minds and bodies were originally designed as it's possible to get. I'm certain too that most of us are desperate for a philosophy that counters our current passion for materialism and the shallow values of 'sophisticated society'. Well I think that it is possible to have our cake and eat it too.

I firmly believe that the garden presents us with a controlled situation where we can have the best of the rural existence without any of the drawbacks. And, fanciful though it may seem, I do believe that most of us have a straightforward, biological need to live at least part of our lives a little closer to the soil, a little more in touch with nature.

It doesn't take much to prove it. Find a quiet place in the countryside where you can be alone and surrounded by nothing but the natural world. Then just sit and contemplate your navel. Within minutes your body will relax and your mind and spirit will soar away to other planes of thought. You'll come down to earth refreshed, relaxed and more sure than ever that there are better things in life than cable television and the national lottery.

In this book I aim to show you how you can recreate that quiet country glade right there in your own back yard, wherever it happens to be. How you can surround yourself with flowers and share your garden with a benevolent natural world that will fill your life with pleasure. How you can escape from the nightmare of constant noise, traffic, shopping malls, canned entertainment, muzac, low-flying aircraft, intrusive neighbours and all the other horrors of modern existence and get right back to living the simple life, when you want to do it and without any of the hardships. In other words how to create, just for yourself, your own personal private paradise.

I can't guarantee that the sun will always shine there, but I can promise that it will always seem that way.

Chapter one

INSPIRATION FROM HISTORY

When Arab armies conquered much of Spain in the eighth century, they brought with them a reverence for plants and a love of gardens. It's interesting to note that a directive to advancing soldiers included instructions that no palm trees were to be cut down, orchards destroyed or cornfields burnt. The Koran taught that it was man's duty to conserve plant life which had a divine creator. Gardens were looked upon as a recreation of heaven on earth. They called them *paradeisoi* – paradises.

The most notable remaining example of Islamic garden art in Europe is the Alhambra and Generalife in Granada and the buildings and gardens are filled with symbolism. As far as I know, it isn't possible to visit this inspiring complex without being constantly jostled by a thousand tourists. Yet, if you stand or sit quietly in the gardens, surrounded by antiquity and with the sights, sounds and smells of a man-made natural world, it's still impossible to escape the power of that ancient philosophy.

Fanciful it may seem, but the combination of the miracle of nature that's beyond our understanding and the art and artifice of the most talented of ancient craftsmen, employed to the glory of that natural force, somehow enters the soul. The feeling of continuity and connection with the past through an abiding love of gardens is as inspiring as the knowledge of the minute scale of our own contribution is humbling.

Mind you, life in those turbulent times was tough and far more so for people not fortunate enough to be able to use their gardens for contemplation and pleasure. Most of the population had no time for flowers and fine thoughts. They were too busy scratching a very meagre living from the soil. So I don't think I could bring myself to recommend a return to those conditions. But we would be foolish to overlook the lessons we can learn from those far-off days.

Until the industrial revolution, when the lure of instant fortune and the evil magic of

Heaven on earth. The world-famous Islamic paradise garden at the Alhambra in Granada still retains today a remarkable sense of stillness and spirituality.

materialism changed our lives for ever, life in Britain was lived at a different pace and with very different values. Religion ruled people's existence and the belief in pagan magic – what we now call superstition – was also very much alive. All religions, races and classes of people revered the natural world as a creation of the Almighty and they valued quiet, planted places as conducive to higher thoughts. Every monastery, for example, had its garden, used for prayer, contemplation and study, and even pleasure gardens were designed as a tribute to a power greater than ourselves.

Today, as we've learned to control, even if only temporarily, a part of the power of nature with chemicals and technology, most of us have lost that reverence for the things that have always been beyond our understanding. Because few of us make our living from the soil, we've lost touch with the natural world and we no longer live in awe of the wonder of nature.

Our children are taught that material wealth is an end rather than a means and we adults are wont to rush about mindlessly chasing our tails, spending so much of our lives endeavouring to 'better ourselves' by making money that we never have the time to spend it.

It's a crazy world and I believe that we have never needed that ancient philosophy more than we do now. Nature is and always will be a greater force than all man's ingenuity could ever control. When we respect and revere that superiority, whether through religion or philosophy, when we begin to work with it instead of against it, our lives will become more fulfilled, our surroundings a million times more pleasant, and we'll take a huge stride forward in our constant search for happiness.

Of course, in these modern times, we *have* to remain realistic, so airy-fairy ideas of 'peace and love, man' simply aren't on. Just like those peasants of old, we too *have* to scratch around earning our living for large parts of our lives. But life is not nearly as hard for most of us as it was, so we do have time to stop and think occasionally. I believe that the garden is the place to do it and that using it as a means of returning to a simpler, more meaningful life should be one of its primary functions.

Apart from anything else we need, from time to time, to get away from the hurly-burly of modern life, just to clear our heads and think. Peace and quiet, disturbed only by birdsong and the gentle hum of insects, together with the colour and perfume of plants and flowers, calm the nerves, rejuvenate the spirit and refresh the soul.

Frankly, they also help you apply yourself even better when the rat-race does catch up with you again on Monday morning!

GIVING NATURE A CHANCE

By now you will probably be thinking that all this peace and quiet, birds, bees and butterflies, colour and perfume which together make up the fabled 'paradise' are very desirable in theory, but where are they going to come from? It might have been easy in Mesopotamia in 4 BC. This, however, is the teeming twentieth century. Not too many of us live deep in the countryside and even if we do, we're surrounded these days by corn prairies and agri-business deserts. Most of the insect life has been sprayed into extinction, the hedges that used to support wild roses, blackberries and a million birds have been ripped out, whole tracts of forest have made way for motorways and hyper-markets and the pollution of the motor car and the factory has tainted even the water we drink and the air we breathe.

I'll agree that's a very understandable reaction. But it ignores a vital fact. Nature is amazingly resilient and, if we work hard to provide the right conditions, all those things we've lost will return – well, almost all.

Even if you live right in the middle of a city, if you plant a tree, you'll attract an insect. If you attract an insect, you'll entice a bird. The bird will want a mate and you're on your way. If you *fill* your garden with as wide a diversity of plants as you can, you'll soon be surrounded by literally millions of creatures.

The arbour at Blacklands House –
a retreat from the world, Victorian-style.

If they've pulled out the hedges, we can plant them again in our own gardens, and if they've driven out the birds, bees and butterflies, we can send them an invitation to live with us instead. And, believe me, they won't decline.

The most destructive and also the most intrusive creature on God's earth, by a long, long way, is the human one. And it's getting away from our fellow human beings that is the most difficult part of the job. Privacy these days is hard to come by but, if your paradise is to mean anything, it's absolutely essential. I've spent a lot of time trying to solve the problem and I think that, in the main, I've succeeded.

The hortus conclusus *or walled garden of medieval times provided a sanctuary, from everyday life.*

There will, of course, be days when the family next door decides to have a barbecue, obliterating the perfume of your roses with the stink of burning fat. Occasionally your neighbour will want to batter your ears with his chainsaw or by shredding his prunings. All you can do then is to lock yourself in the double-glazed conservatory, cotton wool in your ears, and hope it all ends soon. But if that happens four days a year, it's not too much to bear. The rest of the time, when the noise is low-key, you'll be so involved with your garden you won't even notice it.

My own garden is plagued by low-flying Tornado jets and there can be no row more earth-shattering. But amazingly, apart from the odd pilot who fancies himself as a latter-day Cossack, picking up handkerchiefs in his teeth as he flies a few centimetres off the ground, I rarely notice it any more. The birds and insects have become used to it too, so they don't stop singing, and somehow my ear has become attuned to them and oblivious of the air force.

In the gardens designed for this book I have drawn from the past to create a sanctuary that was quite common in medieval times, when chaos reigned and life was fraught with danger. The *hortus conclusus* was a quiet garden enclosed on all sides and symbolizing protection from the outside world. It was intended to produce what was then a rare feeling of security and peace.

Today we still enclose our gardens on all sides, we still value the privacy our boundaries provide and we still have a subconscious feeling of extra security within the bounds of our own 'castle'. The *hortus conclusus* is as valuable today as ever it was.

SATISFYING THE SENSES

A perfect paradise should be balm to the soul and ambrosia to the senses – all five of them. The first, and perhaps the easiest for a gardener to satisfy is that of sight. Naturally and without much effort your eyes will be delighted by the colour and textures of flowers and foliage. In the town garden created for this book I have gone so far as to suggest that you even manage the planting so that certain parts of the garden can suit certain moods.

On summer mornings, before going off to work, you could be invigorated by taking your breakfast in the sunshine, surrounded by a bright mixture of cottage-garden flowers. The evening might see you sitting in your scented arbour, enjoying a drink or a cup of tea in the company of soft, soothing, pastel shades, chosen and planted so that there are no jarring notes: the perfect way to relax and unwind after a day submerged in the rat-race. In winter you could do much the same things, but now in the heated conservatory surrounded by flowering and foliage plants and the warm smell of soil moist after watering.

It's an interesting fact that the colour green – of course, the dominant shade in the garden – has always been seen as the most restful of all. The monastery cloister garth was used by monks for contemplation, prayer and study. It generally consisted of nothing more than an area of grass with no ornament from flowers to distract the attention. Even today every theatre has its green room (originally with green-coloured walls) used by actors to rest, relax and to mug up their lines before they go on. So, if you have the space, include an area of grass where you can simply sit and think, read or study, and also, naturally, fill your garden with the myriad shades of green offered by plants.

In tiny gardens it's not difficult to cram the borders with a tumbling mass of plants. What is harder is to accommodate all those other accoutrements essential to modern gardening but normally offensive to the eye. It's difficult, but by no means impossible, to make even mundane objects like the clothes line and the compost containers attractive. Cover the ugly concrete posts with wire netting and hide them with climbers to turn them into a feature rather than an eyesore. Make the compost containers in the shape of beehives and set them in among the flowers and even they will become things of beauty. With a little ingenuity and craft, every part of the garden can be made beautiful.

Your sense of smell is not difficult to satisfy. Make sure that sitting areas are surrounded by scented plants and that they line the edges of paths where you'll be walking often. You should be able to arrange for sweet perfumes from flowers or foliage to pervade the air at all times of the year. It goes without saying that those plants which have been so highly bred for size and colour that they've lost all trace of their original perfume should be studiously avoided. Some plants have aromatic foliage, so plant them well within picking distance, while others release their perfume when bruised and can be planted in paved areas where your feet will release their magic.

The living arbour in the country garden created for this book is planted with a low hedge of lavender. When I relax on my rustic bench, my nose is almost assaulted by perfume when the plants are in flower, and when they're not I can reach down, pluck a leaf and hold it to my nose for the sweetest of perfumes known and used since Roman times.

In days gone by, before the introduction of those ghastly so-called air-fresheners that we now buy in aerosols, flowers and foliage were brought into the house to mask smells far, far worse than anything we experience. They were also carried as posies, partly in the belief that they would ward off disease, but also to make unwashed clothes, hair and flesh more appealing. Of course, we don't need to go to those extremes today, but we can certainly dispense with the aerosol and go back to grandmother's *pot-pourri* and fresh flowers picked from the garden to bring all the aromas of summer into the house.

The sense of hearing is perhaps the most abused of all these days, with the constant noise of the infernal internal combustion engine everywhere you go, at all times of the day. To drown that out, some bright spark is guaranteed to be playing his or her radio or CD-player at full volume, and when you escape to what you hope will be the peace of the coffee shop, the hotel lift or even the gents your ears are assaulted by the ubiquitous muzac.

All the more reason, when you get home, to crave the peace and quiet of the countryside. And it really is possible to bring that into your garden, even in the town. The sound of passing traffic can be muted very effectively by filling your garden with plants and, though you won't completely drown it, you can at least dilute extraneous noise with the song of birds and the buzzing of insects. All will soothe the savage breast.

In the earliest Islamic gardens, water had great symbolic importance. You can imagine the feeling of cool relief it provided from the arid desert and the fierce eastern sun, but the rivulets and canals of the first *paradeisoi* served also as allegories. They represented the rivers of life running from the central fount of all goodness to the four corners of the earth. Even today the sight of gently moving water is still conducive to thought and philosophy just as it was then.

On another plane the sight and sound of moving water has a truly restful effect and should always be included in your own paradise garden. It also, of course, attracts birds, butterflies and other insects and provides a home for a range of aquatic plants and animals you otherwise couldn't keep. So water forms an important part of both the town and country gardens described in this book.

The sense of touch is perhaps not so obviously easy to satisfy in the garden, but is nonetheless important. Set cool, smooth stones near the water's edge or plant a smooth-barked tree close to the path where you'll stroke it daily as you pass. Above all, feel the texture of soil against your hands as you work. It's very therapeutic.

Of course, a garden is the perfect place to nurture your sense of taste. Even if it's too small for a vegetable plot and there's no room for an orchard, you'll be able to find places to grow a few edible plants among the flowers. They can look very attractive among the borders and will provide the fresh taste of clean, wholesome food you'd forgotten existed.

The combination of formal architecture, water and lush green planting at the Franciscan convent in Dubrovnik creates a timeless tranquillity.

If you have room for only one tree, why not make it an apple or a pear, a peach or a plum? All have delightful blossom in spring followed by large, beautiful fruits in late summer.

A bed of herbs will give you the best of all worlds. They look as lovely as any of the flowers in the borders, many have aromatic leaves that will release their scent into the air if you just brush against them, and others

have soft, furry foliage, delightful to the touch. They'll also attract a million insects and, used in your cooking, they'll transport you straight to the Mediterranean and the flavour of sunshine.

ACHIEVING THE PERFECT BALANCE

Once you've created your garden, unless you're actually sticking your nose into the heart of a rose or salivating over a crisp, freshly picked apple, you're unlikely, after a while anyway, consciously to notice the

Emilia in her fifteenth-century garden – complete with turf seat and roses on the trellis.

atmosphere you've built up. The soothing, calming effect of your garden will comes automatically with no further effort, as your senses naturally react.

However, there are two added extras which complete the picture and make your garden the perfect balance to offset the weight of modern life.

First there's the need to get back into contact with nature. I believe that all of us, even the committed city-dwellers (yes, there are still a few left), see our perfect idyll as bucolic. You may insist that you want to be near the excitement of the 'civilized' pleasures of life – theatres, cinemas, shops and night-clubs – but I'll bet that thoughts of peace still conjure up pictures of the countryside. To have the best of both worlds, it makes sense to build a rural idyll in the middle of the city. The gardens I've suggested in this book will do just that, but they demand a more benign and thoughtful culture than normal modern gardening practices allow.

You won't be able to spray everything out of existence with noxious pesticides and you'll have to get used to a slightly less 'antiseptic' approach: bowling-green lawns with razor-sharp edges and bright red salvias in military rows are not appropriate.

Above all, you need to take the time to *think*. Once you become used to seeing yourself as a small part of the great pattern of nature rather than the controller of it, once you get into the rhythm of the seasons and begin to feel the heartbeat of the natural

world, your life will take on a different meaning and your garden will become a precious sanctuary – a paradise.

Finally gardens should be *used* – and here again we can draw from the past. Large medieval gardens often contained a walled *pleasance*. In it would have been generally square or rectangular beds of flowers, plus a few benches, often turfed with grass, chamomile or sweet-smelling herbs, where ladies and gentlemen, eager no doubt to escape the gloomy, cold and inhospitable interior of the castle, would play board games, read or make music. Such gardens were also the setting for courtship and love-making – and why not, indeed? It beats the back row of the cinema hands down.

Your earthly paradise must be somewhere you can get your hands into the soil. I believe that, to be completely fulfilled, we all have a biological need to use our hands as well as our heads. There's no better place for that than the garden. None of my gardens, therefore, is labour-saving. Heaven forbid! But neither is it arduous. You'll find that you can adjust the design and planting of your own garden to suit your particular lifestyle perfectly.

However, don't underestimate the thera-peutic value of gardening. It's the one area I know where we can all use our nascent creative talents to make a truly satisfying work of art. Every individual, with thought, patience and a large portion of help from nature, has it in them to create their own private paradise: truly a thing of beauty and a joy for ever.

Chapter two

DESIGN

Right from the start, you should allow nature to seep into your bones. Learn from the old country gardeners who, I'm quite sure, never let a thing like design worry them. Most, indeed, had never heard the word and yet they produced wonderful gardens that were a feast for the senses and balm to the soul.

They never worried because they understood nature and the fact that it's ever changing. Just as, in the wild, plants come and go, thrive or disappear because of subtle changes of climate or perhaps competition from neighbouring plants, so we can make similar changes as we discover our plants' preferences.

If that lupin or this lilac would do, or look, better in a new position, there's nothing at all to stop us changing things around. In fact, plants will often do it themselves. Many will spread by underground roots, others will seed themselves around the garden, blown by wind, carried by birds or simply catapulted to a new position. Those that fall on stony ground, or where the light conditions don't suit them, will not succeed, while those that happen to find the right spot will thrive. Undoubtedly the planting plan will change whether you like it or not.

Even the basic layout is unlikely to remain untouched for long. You'll decide that the arbour gets used more in the evening, so facing west is more sensible than facing south after all. When your children are small, you'll probably shun a pond in favour of a sand-pit, but change it to the pond you really wanted when they're old enough not to have to worry about. Your own lifestyle is bound to change too and, as you get older, you may decide to dispense with the barbecue and to make the garden less labour intensive. Above all, you're bound to make mistakes. No one ever gets it right first time – and that's half the fun.

So, while you can't expect to build a brilliant jewel of a garden first time, by a process of learning, changing and adjusting you certainly can over the span of a few years. Remember that whatever you do in the garden that you may later consider to be a mistake, it is *never* completely beyond redemption.

The rill, fed by the lion's head fountain, is almost hidden by the dense planting, but still adds that essential sight and even more essential sound of water to the garden.

NATURAL INSPIRATION

The one thing we all need, even the greatest designers, is some initial inspiration. Once that strikes, there will be no stopping you, because ideas will flow from each other just as soon as you begin work.

Start by thinking about the philosophy of this particular style. You'll be trying to achieve a 'paradise' garden which captures that elusive air of seclusion from the world, where ease and harmony are the keynotes. You want a place where the simple country values prosper, where birds, bees and butter-flies feel at home and where romance lingers on the air.

Your initial inspiration, then, will come exactly as it has to gardeners through the ages, from the natural world itself. Visit the countryside, look especially at country gardens and just let your imagination run free. It doesn't have to be shackled by any rules or preconceptions. If you create a garden that fills your heart with joy, you will have made a work of art as surely as any Degas, Rubens or Picasso. Take your time, be prepared to correct mistakes and approach the job with a relaxed attitude, and nature will throw in her lot with you and help you produce that masterpiece. What's more, you'll enjoy every minute.

REQUIREMENTS

Before you start making any changes, wander around the plot for a day or two, noting especially which way the sun strikes it and where the prevailing wind's coming from. Then simply try to visualize where you would like to sit and relax and what you would like to be looking at as you do so. What would make the best view from the sitting room or kitchen window, and is it necessary to screen out a view or to provide privacy?

In truth most gardens, even some of the very best, were never designed on paper at all. They simply grew and there's no reason why you shouldn't take that approach too. But, just to get a start, it's a good idea to jot down a few ideas, together with a list of your requirements. Then draw out a more-or-less scale drawing of the plot and doodle away during the long winter evenings trying to fit everything in.

Of course, you won't succeed. All the gardeners I know want ten times more in their plot than there's ever room for, so you'll finish up struggling over a list of priorities. This time, you'll just have to face the fact that you can't have the swimming pool *and* the tennis court. When you juggle with your drawing, do make sure that you leave plenty of room for the plants. They are, after all, the very basis of the garden.

You may start out with an existing garden and, just as you couldn't live with someone else's wallpaper, you're bound to want to change it. Begin by giving the garden a full season to show what plants you have and where they are. There's no point in digging up spring bulbs, for example, which you won't be able to see after mid-summer.

If you find you need to shift plants around to fit in with your new design, the best time to do it is when they're dormant or, in the case of evergreens, at least growing slowly. That means late summer and late spring for evergreens and between autumn and spring for deciduous plants.

You can even move large plants if you do so with great care and take a large rootball with them. Really big plants you don't want to risk are best shifted over two seasons. Dig a trench round them about 30cm(1ft) from the main stem and down to the subsoil, cutting the roots as you go. Then refill with soil mixed with garden compost to encourage new, fibrous roots to grow during the year. Moving them in the dormant season the following year then stands a much better chance of success.

I've designed two main gardens for this book, plus a few odd corners to demonstrate other techniques that won't otherwise fit in. I hope that an explanation of the designs will provide the necessary information to help you fashion a country garden of your own. But please – use them as examples only. Your particular Eden *has* to be the product of your own imagination, bearing the stamp of your personality, not mine.

In the town garden, less than one year on, the planting already makes the conservatory far less dominant, and its deep green colour helps it blend in very successfully.

The Town Garden

I confess to being a country lad at heart, so when I built the four walls for the town garden and walked around the bare plot, I felt something like a caged animal. With walls varying in height from 1.8 to 3m (6 to 10ft) the feeling of claustrophobia was intense.

Certainly the walls provide the privacy that I think is vital and they act like a huge storage heater to retain the warmth of the sun, benefiting both plants and humans alike. So they're good to have. But something had to be done to soften the bare brick and to reduce the stark squareness of the plot. I decided on really dense, almost jungle planting. However, the plot is small and it's a great mistake to try to fit too much into a small space or it'll finish up as a bit of a clutter with no real cohesion.

THE CONSERVATORY

I started with the conservatory. Sure, it's a big luxury and it meant going to Skegness instead of St Tropez for my holidays one year. I enjoyed Skegness.

Lots of British gardeners are putting conservatories on the back of their houses these days and it seems to me like a first-class investment. A conservatory adds another room to your house, increasing the value when you eventually sell and providing a perfect, flowery hideaway, out of the gaze of the neighbours, insulated from the noise of the traffic, and a place in which to enjoy the company of plants even in the depths of winter. The only design point to remember here is to ensure that the building is specially made for growing plants. Many of them aren't, but that's all dealt with in chapter 10.

ABOVE The conservatory in the town garden looks enormous in the bare plot, but filled with plants it will make the perfect all-year-round retreat.

BELOW The path from the gate to the conservatory is overgrown to avoid too stark a division.

conservatory

patio

gazebo

pond

rill

lion head fountain

The town garden plan

Naturally the conservatory must blend in style with the house. This garden may be in the town, but I wanted to bring a country feel to it. The red brick walls are soft and mellow, so they're just the job, but the last thing I wanted on them was a white, plastic-looking conservatory, though that might well be perfect in another setting.

COHESION

The building is positioned right opposite the back gate, with a dead-straight path from one to the other. This divides the garden in half and could have the effect of fragmenting it, so it's important to join one half of the plot to the other. One way to do that would have been to curve the path so that the planting made it impossible to see the whole length all at once. But I felt that those solid, square walls were so dominant that they really dictated a formal layout. I therefore decided to make the path straight, but to make it with stepping stones rather than an unbroken ribbon of paving, which allowed planting between the slabs to join one side of the path to the other with vegetation. It means that you have to pick your way carefully down the garden, but it's no bad thing to be forced to slow down a little.

FEATURES

The rill is also designed to carry the eye across the garden. When you sit in the gazebo, you automatically look along the narrow canal up to the lion's head on the wall, which gives a greater feeling of unity. This use of water was inspired partly by the ancient Persian and Moorish gardens and partly by the work of Gertrude Jekyll, the great Victorian/Edwardian designer, who built on a rather

grander scale than most of us have room for. But even though this garden is quite small, the rill fits nicely into the formal design and provides a gentle ripple that's very soothing to the senses. Note the four semi-circular bays designed to take clay pots of irises that are just enough to soften the hard lines.

I sited the gazebo on the west side of the plot looking east, because that suits my lifestyle. If you get up early on summer mornings, there's no greater delight than to breakfast in the gazebo lit by the early sunshine. The birds will be singing their hearts out before the traffic starts to intrude, the bees will have just started work and there's a delicious freshness that makes it the very best part of the day. Just half an hour sets you up for anything the day ahead can throw at you.

If you have no time for that kind of luxury, however, and you simply can't drag yourself out of bed half an hour earlier, you may prefer to sit outside in the evening, relaxing with a gin and tonic instead. In that case the obvious place for the gazebo is against the opposite wall so that you face the evening sun.

I confess to going to town on the gazebo. It is somewhat expensive but did not cost nearly as much as those advertised by large companies in the glossy magazines. Instead of buying from them I went to a local craftsman with a file of pictures (cut from the self-same magazines) of the kind of thing I wanted. After a few quick sketches he reckoned he had the idea and, sure enough, he came up with what I consider to be a masterpiece.

You'll notice that, in the corners created by the arches below the roof, he fitted six wonderful wood carvings. They depict the kind of country symbols that are really the basis of the philosophy of the gardens in this book – a spider in a web, a robin, a country flower or two – and each one cost the price of a dinner for two. I get an enormous pleasure from this kind of country art and we should remember that its survival is, at the end of the day, down to us. Just like the people who complain about the disappearance of the village shop when they do their main shopping at the supermarket, we'll have only ourselves to blame if country craftsmen disappear through lack of patronage.

The slow-moving, rippling rill that runs from the east wall across the garden empties into a pond that encircles the gazebo. If you want to get really high-flown and pretentious, I suppose you could describe it as a symbolic moat, cutting you off from civilization and protecting your privacy. I'm sure that's how a Chelsea Flower Show catalogue would describe it, but of course it's nothing of the sort. It's a delight none the less. On sunny days it reflects the blue of the sky and the plants around it, setting you right in the centre of a four-dimensional arcadia. If you sit there very still and quiet, you'll be able to observe, close at hand, birds as they come down for their early-morning wash and brush-up; butterflies, like flying flowers as they search your plants for pollen; and the glittering, jewelled bodies of dragonflies hunting for places to lay their eggs on the marginal plants round the edges of the pond.

Of course, ponds do cause problems and I would not suggest this feature if you have young children about. They're bound to want to sail their boats on the water, paddle their feet and inevitably fall in. Even very shallow pools can be dangerous for toddlers, so think carefully before you install one. It defeats the object of the garden if you're continually having to worry about your children's safety.

The hole for the pond was made much wider than it seems, lined with a sheet of butyl rubber and then the back area was refilled with soil to form a constantly moist bog garden. That enables me to grow a group of

plants which like to have their feet in permanently wet soil. There's more about how to make the pond and bog garden in chapter 5.

The small patio faces due south, so it should be bathed in sunshine for most of the day. It's the perfect place to sit at weekends in particular, but this area too needs to be softened with massed planting. It was therefore designed in a curved shape to remove the sharp angle of the wall and to

The gazebo, with its delightful finishing touch of country carvings, is deliberately sited to face east and catch the early-morning sun.

Slabs, set on five heaps of mortar, are tamped down with the end of a club hammer, and a straight edge is used to check that they are level.

PLANTING

The curved bed at the back of the patio and the rectangular one in front are planted in cottage-garden style, with a more or less random mixture of different colours. It produces a cheerful effect, but there's one factor here that all the plants have in common. They're all well perfumed to assail the nose and to ensure that they attract millions of insects.

Of course, if it's going to stay, the wildlife that shares your garden will have to be treated with the same hospitality you give your friends. You certainly won't be able to spray with chemical pesticides, so you'll probably be faced with the dreadful problem of half a dozen caterpillar holes in a leaf or two. I know which I'd rather have. Planting details are in chapter 8.

In contrast to the cottage-garden planting around the patio, the remainder is inspired by the wonderful Gertrude Jekyll recreation we visited during the television series. The colours have been carefully blended and co-ordinated with the express intention of providing a restful scene that won't offend the eye or jar the senses.

Next to the pond I used all the deep purples, reds and very intense blues. That could seem a mite sombre, but with plenty of fresh green foliage it has a very soothing effect. I was tempted to add a splash of orange just to brighten it up and, in contrast to the blues , I think it works very well.

That area blends gently into the square on the other side of the path, which lifts the scheme somewhat with brighter reds, pinks

give plenty of planting space behind the paving. Once the planting grows and the climbers begin to cover, the claustrophobia should disappear completely.

I used soft, sandstone-coloured, imitation Yorkstone paving which blends well with the red-brick walls and is restful and soothing to the eye. It's also easy to cut round the curves and not wildly expensive. Of course, if you can afford *real* Yorkstone, so much the better. Here the slabs are laid on a base of 10cm (4in) of concrete, each one set on five heaps of mortar for easy levelling. Each slab is simply butted up to the next, leaving a space between so that water can drain through to the space beneath. The curves are deceptively easy to cut with an angle grinder hired from the local tool-hire shop.

Inspired by the great plantswoman Gertrude Jekyll, the colour scheme here is in soft, relaxing pastel shades with nothing too startlingly bright to jar the senses.

and lighter blues, and then the eye is brought round to the last square which is very much brighter with yellow, scarlet and green.

TREES

Most town gardens are able to take advantage of their neighbours' taller plants which can often be seen over the walls. You can increase the apparent size of your own garden by 'borrowing' them. This is particularly useful in really small gardens and greatly reduces the 'hemmed-in' feeling. If the planting in your own plot is dense enough to hide the walls, your garden could appear to stretch for miles.

Reds, pinks and blues are bright but not gaudy.

Just outside the wall of my town garden are a couple of tall acers which cast a bit of shade but are generally a great delight. To make full use of them to 'enlarge' my own plot, I planted a smaller Japanese maple *(Acer palmatum)* inside the wall to form the third point of a triangle. When the climbers grow up to hide the walls, those two trees will, to all intents and purposes, become mine.

Very often, small gardens are dominated and overshadowed by trees. You can bet your life that they'll all have preservation orders on them, so cutting them down would certainly be illegal and even pruning may be subject to restrictions. It's generally only if trees are dangerous or threaten to undermine the foundations of a house that felling permission is given. Whatever you do, always be certain to contact the local council first or you could be fined.

If you're stuck with your trees, look upon them positively. In fact, they're a great asset and, though you may think at first that they rob the garden of light and nourishment to such an extent that nothing else will grow, this is almost never the case. Whatever the conditions in your garden, there are always plants that will grow there. In fact, as summers seem to get hotter, you may see trees as a great blessing in that they provide welcome shade, filter out noise and pollution and attract more wildlife. Shady woodland gardens have a magic of their own and can provide all the benefits of peace, quiet and seclusion we're looking for (see chapter 4).

DEEP SHADE

Because it faces south and has just a few areas of light shade, most of the garden was fairly easy to plant. There was just one problem area. When the conservatory was built, its position

Old fertilizer sacks make a perfectly adequate liner.

In a very small area like this, it is feasible to alter the nature of the soil.

was already defined by the existing door and, to be affordable it had to be an 'off-the-shelf' job, so I didn't have as much say about the size as I would have liked. So, when it was built, it left a small area between its east end and the wall. It's a tiny, heavily shaded space and the plants have to share it with the outside tap. I decided that the best bet was to alter the soil type to accommodate plants that would thrive in the heavy shade.

I dug out all the soil to a depth of about 45cm (18in) and lined the bottom with a couple of old compost bags. The idea is not to retain water efficiently as you would do for the pond, but simply to retard its progress. The soil then went back in, providing a moist, shady place that should be ideal for ferns.

And if the tap drips, they'll love it.

Once lined with polythene to provide the moist soil that ferns love, this becomes be an ideal spot for them.

The Country Garden

I've called this the country garden because I've tried to give it a really rural feel. I wanted it to seem as if it were in the middle of the woods where I could imagine myself coppicing hazel for thatching pegs or burning charcoal. It certainly doesn't have to be in the country, though, and, indeed, it's designed so that you can achieve this effect even at the back of a modern estate house.

It's just the sort of plot you might get with a small, semi-detached, modern house: big enough to swing a fairly anorexic cat, surrounded on all sides by 1.5m (5ft) fencing, originally in a bilious shade of orange, and overlooked on both sides by similar houses.

How could you possibly turn that into a country retreat?

The first requirement is to pick up the whole garden and transport it to the depths of the country where you can't see a living soul and all you can hear is the bleating of sheep and the song of friendly birds. Wouldn't that be nice! In fact, it's not such a dream as it sounds because, though of course you can't actually take the garden to the countryside, you can certainly bring the countryside to the garden – wherever it happens to be.

BELOW *The country garden, one season on.*

OPPOSITE *The country garden plan.*

gravel storage area

patio

roofing tiles

lawn

arbour

pond

nut tunnel

'wildflower meadow'

FEATURES

Seclusion is an essential, so, however well you may get on with your neighbours, you have to find a way to hide your garden from them. That is often an impossible task, but the plain fact is that you needn't really worry about your neighbours seeing the garden. In fact, by the time you've finished, you're going to be rather proud to show it off. What you want to hide is yourself. The design of this plot, therefore, unlike that of the town garden, starts with the need to provide privacy. The methods are described in detail in the next chapter.

On the west side of the garden is a cross between a tunnel and a nut walk. It's made with hazel and is designed to be about 2.1m (7ft) high. That serves the double purpose of increasing the height of the 1.5m (5ft) fence and also providing a secluded walk to hide you while you progress to the arbour. Here you can sit in the cool shade of hornbeam trees, completely hidden from the world, and read, watch the wildlife that'll soon be visiting your pond or simply reflect on the forgotten joys of the simple life. Just like our medieval ancestors, you'll be surrounded by a flowery mead to delight the eye and concentrate the mind.

The flower-studded 'meadow' could be made in the truly traditional way with turf and wildflowers, but that's neither as straightforward as it may seem nor quite so dramatic. While wildflower meadows are literally awash with flowers in spring, there's nothing like such a display for the rest of the year. So this flowery mead is a more modern concoction, using longer-lasting flowers. Making it and the traditional meadow are explained fully in chapter 6.

The pond was inspired by a country pool I came across on a local nature reserve. In fact, it's in sight of a busy main road, but fortunately it's far enough away to be completely

This wonderfully chunky rustic seat, under an arbour of hornbeam, provides the perfect spot to sit and escape from the world.

quiet. If you sit with your back to the road view, you see nothing but wild countryside. As the sunshine glitters off the gentle ripples, the insects hum gently and the birds chatter, it's easy to let an hour slip by in deep and satisfying reverie. With a bit of butyl-rubber sheeting and a fair amount of elbow grease, it's not at all difficult to reproduce that rural idyll in your own garden wherever you may live. If you provide the water, the wildlife won't be fussy where it is.

Unlike in the town garden I've included an area of grass here, because the house I have in mind is just the sort that many young couples buy as their first. That, of course, is likely to mean that small children will have to be catered for. Certainly the grass could be cut and maintained to standard bowling-green condition if you prefer, but I feel that a slightly more unkempt finish fits the rest of the garden better. So I've left it longer and planted wildflowers in it too (see page 141). That would also obviate the need to buy a lawnmower for this tiny patch. It'll need cutting only twice a year and you could do that easily with shears.

Reclaimed materials, used in an attractive random way, give the garden instant maturity.

PAVING

When I came to plan the patio, I realized that a posh affair like that in the town garden was simply not possible on a tight budget. Instead of buying it new, therefore, I decided on a second-hand, recycled job. A trip to the local reclaim yard and a couple of happy hours rooting around rewarded me with a motley collection of materials. Since they were all odds and ends in tiny quantities, I found no difficulty in acquiring them for a very low price indeed. I think the chap was only too

pleased to see the back of them and probably looked upon me as a bit of a sucker who'd saved him the cost of throwing them away. There were a few paving slabs in different colours and textures, some engineering bricks, cobbles, roofing tiles and even a couple of clay sewer pipes.

If you use a mixture of materials, laying them is not quite so straightforward as laying paving. Start with a concrete base in the usual way, but make it at least 10cm (4in) lower than the required finish level. Bear in mind that you'll be setting thick bricks as well as thinner slabs.

It's as well to start with a couple of paving slabs just to set a guide for your lines and levels. When you lay them, you'll find that you need quite a lot of mortar to make up for the lower concrete base, so it's best to make up at least 5cm (2in) with some dry concrete first. It's made with mixed ballast and cement in the ratio of 8:1, laid just where the slabs are to go and trodden down firmly. Then the slabs can be laid on five heaps of mortar, one at each corner and one in the middle. When you put them down, leave a gap of about 2cm (¾in) between them (it will soon become clear why you need to do this).

With, say, two slabs down, fill in the angle they make with a square of bricks. These are, of course, thicker than the slabs so they can be

TOP LEFT *With materials of varying thicknesses, it is vital to keep checking with a spirit level that all the different elements are level with their neighbours.*

CENTRE LEFT *Fill in some of the larger gaps with mortar, but do leave others into which you can brush gritty compost and then sow alpine seeds.*

BOTTOM LEFT *Use a straight edge to keep checking that the paving is level with the pegs you set out when you started work.*

This mixture of cobbles, rings of sewer pipe, roofing tiles and recycled slabs makes a cheap and very interesting hard surface.

Chip out any dried mortar from the smaller rings of pipe, fill them with gritty compost and plant carpeting alpines like thyme.

laid directly on the concrete base on a thinner bed of mortar.

Then put down perhaps another slab and then a square of cobbles and so on. Cut the sewer pipes into rings about 10cm (4in) deep and set them here and there among the slabs and bricks. Narrow-diameter pipes can be filled later with gritty compost and planted with alpine plants like thymes, while wider diameters can be filled with cobbles set in mortar for a very decorative effect.

The roofing tiles are too thin to lay flat, so these are set on end with a small gap between. To make them go further, I also cut them in half with the angle grinder.

When the whole area was paved, I chose a fine, dry day, to brush in a compost made with equal parts of fine garden soil, sieved garden compost and sharp sand. If you don't have access to these materials, use a soil-based potting compost like John Innes and add an equal amount of sharp sand. You'll find that you have to keep refilling as the compost drifts through the wide spaces between the slabs to fill up the void below, so you'll need a bit of patience. When you can get no more in, buy a few packets of alpine seeds, mix them together and bulk them up with some sharp sand. Then simply brush the mixture around the patio to work the seeds

This creeping alpine, pratia, is ideal for growing in between paving slabs.

into the cracks. Within a few months you'll have transformed the paved area into a beautiful tapestry of colour and texture.

Finally, tucked away in the corner of the patio, is the utility area. It's here that you'll be able to site the dustbin, the compost heap and the coldframe as well as the inevitable junk that we all seem to accumulate. A strong, rose-covered trellis will hide it from view.

PLANTING

The planting here is very much in the country style. As well as the hazel and hornbeam, I've included a few shrubs to form the 'bones' of the borders and to make a permanent background to the herbaceous plantings. Evergreens in particular, like escallonia, holly and viburnum, are all well at home in a country garden and provide good nesting

sites for birds as well as a splash of interest in winter when there's nothing much else. For details of the shrubs to use see chapter 4.

As far as colour schemes go – well, there aren't any. This is traditional cottage-style planting where the main priority is to put plants where they'll thrive. Of course, you need to find out a bit about the plants you want to include, especially whether they prefer sun or shade, heavy or light soil and, naturally, how tall and wide they'll grow. It's far better to research these details before you buy than to buy plants on impulse because they happen to be in flower only to find later that they're too big for your garden or they won't survive in your soil. Armed with this knowledge, put plants where you think they will look good and, if you find later that you were mistaken, simply lift the offending plants and move them somewhere else.

We mustn't forget, of course, that most new gardens of this size are built on a budget, especially if the owners are young first-timers. After you've paid your deposit on your house, bought the carpets and curtains and a new cooker because your old one was gas and now you've only electricity, there's not a lot left for the garden. So most of the plants you put in initially will be clumps your friends and neighbours have dug up for you and those you've raised yourself from seed or cuttings. They may not always be exactly what you want, but grow them anyway. If you later feel that the space would be better occupied by something else, it's the easiest thing in the world to dig up a plant and give it to the young first-time buyer next door.

The only 'style' factor in this garden is that, once again, I wanted my sitting-out area

In just one season, the jumble of perennials and annuals in the country garden creates a mass of colour.

to be perfumed, so the paved area is surrounded in the main by scented plants.

One other idea I have carried over from my cottage gardens and which is explained fully in my book *Geoff Hamilton's Cottage Gardens* is the green fence. Country gardeners would always surround their plots with a hedge, often with roses, honeysuckle or clematis twining through. With no room for such luxury, at least the narrower fence can be made to look a little more like a hedge if you paint it dark green, fix training wires to the posts and grow the same roses, honeysuckle and clematis up it.

GROWING YOUR OWN

Nowhere in either of these plans have I included a vegetable patch or a fruit garden. I feel that the areas are just too small for them. However, that does not mean that I wouldn't recommend growing your own.

While it's important that any rural paradise should delight the eye, soothe the nerves and free the spirit, I strongly believe that we need to occupy our hands too. Over years of practical gardening I've learnt the therapeutic value of getting my hands into the soil and the enormous creative satisfaction which can be derived watching plants grow well because of my own efforts. So I have deliberately avoided making either of my gardens labour-saving. Perish the thought.

If you have the money, of course, it's possible to employ a landscape gardener to lay out your plot and pay a team of gardeners to look after it for you. Certainly you'll enjoy sitting in it, but you should not even consider depriving yourself in such a way. The fact is that you'll miss out on fifty per cent of the joy of gardening and you'll never make the bond with nature that gives you true understanding.

Growing the food you eat, too, cements that bond in the way our ancestors, who of course *had* to grow much of their own food, understood instinctively.

With only a tiny garden, I would first try to get the best of both worlds by renting an allotment locally and using that to grow food crops. But I accept that this is not always possible, especially for busy working people. A very successful alternative is to allow space to grow them among the ornamental plants in the borders. The idea is to leave small spaces, something like 60–90cm (2–3ft) square, near the front of the borders. Then sow or plant the vegetables into those in patches rather than rows.

Most vegetables, like lettuce, carrots, beetroot and onions, look very comely indeed alongside flowers and, because they're grown in small quantities and are hidden away among ornamental plants, they tend to escape the attentions of many pests and diseases completely.

In the small garden, fruit trees are best grown in trained form against the fences, where they take up little space. Shapes like fans or espaliers make a very attractive show, especially in spring when they're covered in superb blossom and in late summer when the bright red, orange, yellow or green fruits are a real sight for sore eyes.

Soft fruit too can be grown, like vegetables, among the flowers. A patch of strawberries, for example, can only enhance the front of the border, with their attractive foliage, white flowers in spring and luscious red fruits in summer. Red, black and white currants become irresistibly beautiful when their brightly coloured berries hang in great strands in mid-summer, while grapes dangling in prolific bunches, perhaps from the roof of your arbour, will transport your imagination to more exotic climes.

GETTING STARTED ON THE GARDEN LAYOUT

In the potager at Barnsley House, the balance of the formal and the informal is just right.

With even only a rough idea of the garden plan drawn on paper, you're now ready to go outside and get started. Armed with a surveyor's tape and a series of canes, the best bet is to mark out the areas with canes and string or to draw them on the ground using a bottle filled with dry sand. When you do, the key word is flexibility. Bear in mind that what you have drawn on paper is a bird's eye view. There's always a tendency, when you're drawing to a much smaller scale, to design pretty shapes. When you get outside on the ground, and you're viewing the garden from an entirely different viewpoint, you may find that it doesn't look quite as good. Often the lines won't appear to be quite so flowingly uniform as they did on paper and, unless you're experienced, you'll almost certainly have put too much in. It doesn't matter a jot.

Remember: the golden rule of landscaping is that, because the aim is to please the eye, if it looks right, it *is* right. So, when you mark out, or even when you start laying your turf or cutting out your borders, don't be afraid to change things. It's never too late.

Chapter three

PRIVACY

From the earliest times human beings have preferred to live in groups. We started by forming primitive communities close together for protection and mutual support; then we began to create much larger towns and cities to facilitate trade and social intercourse; and now we build houses, shops and schools in new towns, estates and villages, partly to protect our last remaining areas of open countryside. Of course there are great advantages in grouping ourselves together, but as the population worldwide has mushroomed most of us are now beginning to feel overcrowded. As a result the most sought-after and jealously guarded possession we have is privacy.

In a hectic, pressurized world we all need, from time to time, our own personal space where we can think our own thoughts, behave as we want to without considering others and just be ourselves. If we want to sit quietly and contemplate life's direction or we feel the need to throw off our clothes and dance like a dervish in the sunshine – why not? And the one place above all where we should be able to find that peace and seclusion is the garden. I don't believe that's being unneighbourly or anti-social. Indeed

the best way to ensure that we get on well with the folk next door is to be able to choose our own times for socializing and to have the option of escape to our own private world when we want to.

During the television series I visited several gardeners who live in terraced houses set cheek-by-jowl with their neighbours. Anne Dexter in Oxford is one who has completely screened not only the houses next door but also all the others around her to make her own leafy oasis. Here she is totally secluded from sight and sound so she can relax and do her own thing. Yet she has been on the friendliest of terms with her neighbours since she moved in over twenty years ago.

Screening

The amount of screening you can do will naturally depend on the space available. If you have room to plant a really good, tall

Just path and plants. Anne Dexter's long, narrow Oxford garden is remarkably private. The dense planting screens all the neighbouring houses so successfully that you really don't know you are overlooked on all sides.

barrier of trees and shrubs, you'll do more than shield yourself from view. Wide areas of planting help to reduce noise and to filter out airborne pollution of all sorts. You have to walk only metres from a busy main road into a wood to feel the change in the atmosphere from choking exhaust fumes to the sweet purity of real fresh air.

In some gardens, though, the air can be a bit *too* fresh. Strong winds, especially if they're salt-laden sea breezes, can make life for more tender plants quite difficult. A barrier that filters the wind rather than stopping it dead, as would a fence or a wall, is the most efficient windbreak of all.

However, if your garden commands a particularly spectacular view, you'll naturally be reluctant to block it with a screen. To get the best of both worlds you'll need to allow for 'windows' here and there to act as viewing points. Planting two upright-growing trees fairly close together is one way. Species like the flowering cherry 'Kanzan' and laburnum both have an upright habit, creating a shape rather like a triangle standing on one of its points. Plant them so that, when fully grown, they'll meet at the top and put in some low-growing shrubs underneath and you'll leave a triangular window that will allow you to see your view. If you plant a formal hedge, you can simply cut out square, rectangular or round windows as the hedge grows.

OPPOSITE ABOVE *An arbour of laurel makes an inviting surround for an otherwise rather stark stone bench.*

OPPOSITE BELOW *Carefully sited hedges can divide large gardens into much more intimate, private 'rooms'.*

RIGHT *A hedge of clipped conifers such as yew forms a dense, green wall. Climbing roses scrambling over it give a more relaxed, country feel.*

HEDGES

If space is slightly more restricted, you might consider a formal hedge that can be clipped to keep it within bounds. Conifers like yew or cypress make excellent, formal hedges which, by regular clipping, can be kept to any height you want. Cypress is known for its speed of growth, but yew is not as slow-growing as is generally believed. Their one snag is that they lack the rural feel that we're after in this kind of garden, so I would prefer to grow something more countrified like hawthorn (*Crataegus monogyna*). It's normally looked upon as a field hedge rather than a garden hedge, but in fact can be clipped closely to make an excellent, dense screen that will

give you the privacy you want. It also makes a very effective, thorny barrier against animals or people, is transformed into a foam of fragrant, white blossom in spring followed by attractive red berries (haws), and can be used as a climbing frame to support wild roses, honeysuckle or clematis. It'll make an excellent home for all kinds of wildlife and virtually guarantees nesting birds too.

Plant young plants 30cm (1ft) apart in well-prepared soil and cut them down to about 10cm (4in) from the ground after planting. Continue to trim the tops a little as

Copper beech, clipped to form a neat hedge, makes a warm foil for the lush green planting in front of it.

they grow to ensure that the fully grown hedge remains thick at the bottom.

Beech and the similar but slightly easier-to-grow hornbeam also make excellent country hedges. Plant them 45cm (18in) apart, but do not trim their tops until they reach the height you want. They have the advantage of keeping their dead leaves during winter, making a very warm, attractive, russet background for the border. Unfortunately they're both perhaps a little slow to shed their old leaves and clothe themselves in fresh green in spring, but it's only a matter of weeks and a small price to pay for all-year-round shelter.

Laurel, with shiny, evergreen leaves, is another excellent choice. Its only

disadvantage is that it really needs cutting with secateurs rather than shears to avoid slashing the large, leathery foliage, but since this is only done once a year, it's not such an arduous task. Plant 60cm (2ft) apart.

If you feel the need to keep out intruders, holly is perfect. It's obtainable in several colours from shiny green to bright yellow, it's evergreen and varieties like 'J. C. van Tol' will ensure winter berries. It is, alas, rather slow-growing and expensive. Plant 90cm (3ft) apart.

Some of the berberis varieties make wonderful hedges with long thorns, excellent for deterring either animal or human intruders. Many of them are evergreen too and produce a fine show of flowers in spring. Most, like the yellow-flowered *Berberis stenophylla*, are grown as informal hedges, taking up a fair amount of room, but it's certainly possible to clip them to shape too if you wish. I've grown the very spiky *B. julianae* into an excellent clipped hedge no more than 60cm (2ft) wide and 90cm (3ft) tall.

Most hedging plants, and certainly the cheaper ones like hawthorn and beech, are best planted in the dormant season between late autumn and early spring. Because they'll be lifted bare-rooted from the field at that time, they'll be very much cheaper than container-grown plants. There will be no risk of their drying out at that time of year either, so they should establish better too.

When you're planting a screen, you'll obviously be anxious to see it form an effective barrier as quickly as possible. Good preparation can make all the difference.

Never plant anything in a hole dug in otherwise uncultivated soil. That turns it into a sump for all the surrounding water and the plant will never thrive. Dig the whole border or as big an area as possible. The strip for a hedge should be at least 90 cm (3ft) wide.

It pays too to improve fertility by working in plenty of organic matter in the form of manure, compost or one of the organic alternatives available at garden centres. If you're planting in the dormant season, supplement this with a handful of bonemeal per plant. If you plant in the late spring or from containers in the growing season, the plants will need the full range of nutrients, so feed them with an organic fertilizer or a slow-release feed. You'll also need to ensure that they never go short of water until they become established.

If your hedge is to act as a windbreak as well as a screen, it may suffer from wind damage itself in the early stages. Conifers, with their very large leaf area, are particularly at risk, so protect them with plastic windbreak netting held on strong posts on the windward side. It need be there only for the first year while the plants become established.

EXTENDED FENCING

Few of us these days have the space for luxuriant planting or even a hedge, but we all have room at least partially to screen our gardens from view. In fact, Anne Dexter's garden is a perfect example.

With a plot no more than about 4.5m (15ft) across, she only has space for a border on each side and a path down the middle, but she has achieved miracles with climbers and shrubs. The first job was to extend the height of the fence with trellis which she supported on new, tall posts set in the ground on her side of the fence. She then planted evergreen wall shrubs like the lovely, grey-tasselled *Garrya elliptica* and several varieties of firethorn (*Pyracantha* hybrids) with their white flowers and red, orange or yellow berries. But Anne confesses to terminal plantaholism, so she was far from content

Make your own trellis panels from inexpensive, pressure-treated roofing laths, and stain them dark green.

Screw your home-made trellis panels to the existing fence posts.

with that. Roses followed, then clematis to climb through them, honeysuckle because she couldn't resist the perfume and, of course, she had to have jasmine. Within a very short time it was quite impossible to see the fence, let alone the neighbours.

I extended the height of my own 1.5m (5ft) fence in a slightly different and somewhat cheaper way. I started by making square trellis panels 45cm (18in) high and 1.9m (6ft 2in) long using 25×30mm (1×1¼in) roofing laths. They're very cheap to buy from the builder's merchant and have the advantage of already being pressure-treated with preservative. The end struts were extended by 60cm (2ft) to allow them to be screwed to the existing posts. If you wanted to extend the height by more than 60cm (2ft), you'd have to increase the thickness of the end struts to 50×50mm (2×2in).

The next job is to wire the fence itself using 12-gauge wire fixed to the posts with large staples. If you want to grow plants that cling with tendrils, or by their leaf-stems like clematis, you'll also need vertical wires of somewhat thinner gauge, twisted round the horizontal ones to form a mesh.

The plants suggested below will all need this kind of training on wires and, when they get tall enough, they can be woven through the trellis at the top of the fence. This has the advantage that your privacy creeps up on your neighbours slowly, causing the minimum offence.

If you already have tall fences or walls, your problem will not be to hide your neighbours but to alleviate the inevitable feeling of claustrophobia that high barriers like these engender. This too is done by planting, starting with climbers, which can be chosen from the list starting on page 49 or from the self-clinging climbers described in chapter 4.

CLIMBERS

Actinidia

Two species are suitable. *Actinidia kolomikta* is grown for its peculiarly variegated leaves. The ends turn cream with a distinct red flush at the very tip, while the top part remains green. It needs sunshine, so a south wall is best, though it may not start to colour until it's a few years old, but it's very well worth the wait. Tie in a framework of shoots and then prune any that become overlong, cutting them back to two or three buds of the main framework in winter.

 A. chinensis (Chinese gooseberry) produces reddish, hairy shoots and large, attractive leaves. It has fragrant, white flowers in late summer and, if it has another plant to pollinate it, could fruit. But don't hold your breath! Prune as above and cut out a few older shoots if the plant gets out of control. This is another candidate for a south wall.

Akebia quinata

A vigorous, semi-evergreen climber with fragrant red/purple flowers in mid-spring. After a hot summer, fruits should appear – up to 10cm (4in) long, purple and shiny, and opening to reveal black seeds in a white pulp. A west wall is ideal.

A climber like Actinidia kolomikta *grown across a window provides privacy without blocking the light.*

Clematis

With dozens of excellent varieties, choice is difficult. It's important to remember, though, that if you want to grow them through roses or other plants, it's essential to choose varieties that won't swamp their host and that will flower from mid-summer onwards. These can then be cut hard back after flowering and they'll repeat the performance the following year. This technique enables you to remove all the old growth from the rose to give it light and air and to allow you to prune.

Late-flowering varieties that are grown on their own should also be pruned hard, but they can be left until late winter when you'll be able to see a strong bud near the base to cut to.

Varieties that flower in early summer should not be pruned in this way or you'll cut

off all next year's blooms. First establish a strong framework of shoots which should be tied in to the position you want them. After flowering the side shoots that come from this framework can be cut back to within two or three buds. Very vigorous varieties like *Clematis montana* are difficult to prune in this way, so I take the easy course and hack at them with shears when they outgrow their space. They're extremely hard to kill!

All new plants should be pruned hard immediately after planting. This results in a strong root system and vigorous growth of several stems from the base. It makes a much better-balanced plant in the long run. Most will flower best facing south or west, but many will produce good results in shadier positions too.

Clematis can add a wonderful splash of colour when grown through evergreen plants , as illustrated here.

Large-flowered Hybrids. There are hundreds of varieties of large-flowered hybrids and new ones coming out every year. Most will grow to about 3m (10ft) but a few, like 'Gypsy Queen' and 'Lady Betty Balfour', will reach 6m (20ft). With these few more vigorous exceptions, all the late-flowering varieties are fine for growing through roses. The most popular is undoubtedly the deep purple 'Jackmanii Superba', but look out too for varieties like 'General Sikorski', which is mid-blue with a red tinge, and the clear red 'Sunset'.

Semi-double and Double Large-flowered Hybrids. These differ a little in the shape of their flowers and in the fact that they really need a spot sheltered from strong winds and cold. The semi-double and double flowers are borne on wood made the previous year, so be careful not to prune them out. Popular varieties include the deep blue 'Beauty of Worcester', the white 'Duchess of Edinburgh' and the purple 'Royalty'.

Grown together, the early and late Dutch honeysuckles provide colour and fragrance all summer long.

Montana Varieties. These are early-flowering and vigorous. Never try to grow them through any other plant except large trees. Even then, they can cause too much congestion. They're ideal for covering spaces quickly, but need a part of the fence to themselves. They flower on wood made the year before, so no pruning is necessary except to shear back unwanted growth as previously suggested. Popular varieties include the pink-flowering 'Rubens' and the creamy white, scented 'Alexander'.

Viticella Varieties. Because they thrive on being pruned back hard in autumn, *Viticella* varieties are among the best for growing through other plants. They produce masses of smaller flowers from mid-summer through to the first frosts. My own favourites are 'Mme Julia Correvon', which has wine-red flowers, and the purple 'Etoile Violette'.

Alpina and Macropetala Varieties. The earliest to flower, *Alpina* and *Macropetala* clematis are therefore very welcome. Growth is not as vigorous as in most others and the flowers are small and nodding, single in *Alpina* and double in *Macropetala* varieties. They're perfectly hardy, but dislike badly drained or cold, wet soil. Good choices are the blue *Alpina* 'Frances Rivis', 'White Columbine' and the red 'Ruby', while among the *Macropetala* varieties look out for the pale blue 'Harry Smith', the dark blue 'Lagoon' and the purple-blue 'Lincolnshire Lady'.

Eccremocarpus scaber
A fast-growing climber that dies back in winter but, in reasonably well-drained soil, will reappear in spring. In colder areas it can be raised annually from seed, which it produces prolifically. The tubular flowers of red, orange and yellow are massed on the plant all summer. Simply cut to the ground and remove the old stems in winter. A south- or west-facing wall is ideal.

Humulus lupulus Hop

The green version is much too vigorous to consider growing in the garden, but the golden variety is easier provided you're prepared to remove suckers with a spade once a year. It's not a difficult job and worth it for the brilliant golden foliage all summer. Grow it on a section of fence on its own. The female flowers, borne in long clusters, are very attractive. It needs full sun and should be cut to the ground in winter. Wait until the new young shoots appear in spring before chopping back those that have intruded where they're not wanted. They can be cooked like asparagus and are quite delicious.

Jasminum Jasmine

All jasmines prefer a sunny, warm spot and well-drained soil. There are three varieties suitable for most gardens.

Jasminum nudiflorum (winter jasmine) is a fine, winter-flowering wall shrub bearing beautiful, yellow flowers on naked stems in winter. Cut back long growths after flowering.

J. officinale (common white jasmine) is much more vigorous and bears deliciously fragrant, white flowers from early summer to early autumn. To contain overvigorous plants, cut back after flowering.

J. stephanense is also vigorous and bears fragrant, pink flowers. Prune as above.

Lonicera Honeysuckle

Several varieties make excellent, long-flowering climbers for fence, house wall or pergola. I've also grown honeysuckle over a metal arch to make a sweet-scented arbour. They're happy in most soils and many varieties will grow well in shade where they're also less prone to attack from aphids. They require little attention other than pruning to keep them within bounds. Most of the popular types, like *Lonicera periclymenum* (woodbine), produce their flowers in clusters at the ends of shoots that were made the year before. They should be pruned after flowering by cutting back to a young, unflowered shoot. Some others flower on the current season's wood and their flowers are produced along the stems. They can be clipped back with shears after flowering or in the winter to keep them in check.

L. americana produces masses of white, scented flowers in early and mid-summer. They fade to pale and finally deep yellow, tinged with purple. It flowers on old wood.

L. henryii is evergreen with yellow flowers stained red in early to mid-summer. It flowers on old wood.

L. japonica is a rampant evergreen with white, very fragrant flowers changing to yellow as they age and produced from early summer onwards. The variety 'Halliana' is most often offered at nurseries. It flowers on the current season's growths.

L. periclymenum is a British native, producing creamy white flowers tinged purple on the outside and darkening with age. This is the most sweetly scented of all. The variety 'Belgica' (early Dutch honey-suckle) bears blooms which are reddish purple outside and flowers from late spring to early summer and then again later in the season. 'Serotina' (late Dutch honeysuckle) has similar flowers from mid-summer to mid-autumn. All flower on old wood.

L. sempervirens (trumpet honeysuckle) is semi-evergreen and carries long, orange/scarlet flowers with yellow inside. It's very hardy and seems untroubled by aphids. It flowers on old wood.

L. tellmanniana opens from red buds to rich, coppery yellow flowers in early to mid-summer. It's especially good on a north fence and does best in a shady spot. It too flowers on old wood.

Rosa Rose

My own favourite combination is roses and clematis. The roses provide the first flush of colour and the clematis follow in mid- to late summer, often while the roses are still flowering. But of course, if you choose carefully, roses grown on their own can give a fine show of colour right through the summer.

For fences in small gardens, it's recommended in the main to opt for the less vigorous climbing rather than the rambling roses which generally flower only once and can be somewhat rampant.

Though it's hard to bring yourself to do it, it's best to cut newly planted roses back hard, to within 8–10cm (3–4in), cutting back to a good, strong bud. When the new shoots grow, they should be tied in to wires to form a regular fan shape and the lower shoots pulled down as far as possible. This encourages further shoots all the way down the stem and these too should be tied in until the fence or wall is covered. Any that aren't needed to fill a space or don't fit into the fan shape should be cut back to two to three buds.

Pruning climbing roses consists of shortening side shoots to two to three buds immediately after flowering. Most varieties prefer sun, but some perform well even on north-facing walls.

Rosa 'Blush Noisette' bears small, semi-double, scented flowers in large clusters. They start pink and fade to white and repeat regularly throughout the season.

R. 'Céline Forestier' produces beautiful, cabbage blooms of pale yellow, deepening towards the centre with an attractive perfume. It flowers throughout the summer. This rose needs a south-facing position.

R. 'Compassion' is an excellent modern climber with well-shaped, hybrid-tea flowers of salmon pink tinted with apricot and a sweet fragrance throughout the summer.

R. 'Gloire de Dijon', a favourite with cottage gardeners, produces large, superbly scented flowers of buff yellow with a hint of pink and gold. It flowers early and continues well.

R. 'Golden Showers' is one of the best for a north-facing position. Throughout summer it produces absolutely masses of golden-yellow, semi-double flowers with a pleasant fragrance.

R. 'Guinée' flowers once with just a few blooms later, but is worth including as the best of the deep crimson, very well-scented roses.

R. 'Iceberg', in its climbing version, produces sprays of pure white flowers throughout summer.

Roses and clematis, like the late-summer-flowering, wine-red Clematis viticella 'Mme Julia Correvon' here, are the perfect combination for covering fences or walls.

Palest pink rose 'New Dawn' is grown here with the brighter pink 'Bantry Bay'.

R. 'Kathleen Harrop' is a sport of 'Zéphirine Drouhin' with soft pink, very fragrant flowers all summer. It's good on a north fence.

R. 'Lady Hillingdon' is a superb tea rose with rich apricot-yellow, scented flowers, red stems and bronze foliage.

R. 'Lady Sylvia' is available in a climbing version with deep pink flowers suffused with apricot, a fine fragrance and a repeat-flowering habit – an excellent rose.

R. 'Leaping Salmon', a fine, new, repeat-flowering climber with deep salmon-pink flowers, has a strong perfume.

R. 'Mme Alfred Carrière' bears large, well-scented, white blooms throughout summer, but is perhaps a trifle vigorous.

R. 'New Dawn', a modern climber with clusters of silvery pink flowers deepening towards the centre and a fine, fruity perfume, is a perpetual flowerer, which makes it a must.

R. 'Ophelia', available as a climber, has long, pale pink buds of superb shape and a strong fragrance. It produces masses of blooms and repeats well.

R. 'Zéphirine Drouhin', the well-known thornless rose, producing a profusion of deep, rose-pink flowers all summer, is excellent for a north-facing position.

Solanum Potato vine

Though they're generally reckoned to grow only in mild gardens, I've grown both the following species in my own garden in the chilly East Midlands of England. It's best to give them a sunny, south-facing fence if you can, but even facing east both have survived and flourished.

Solanum crispum is a vigorous shrub bearing masses of potato-like flowers of purple-blue with bright yellow stamens. The variety 'Glasnevin' flowers from mid-summer to the first frosts.

S. jasminoïdes bears similar flowers but lighter blue with yellow stamens. It blooms from mid-summer to the first hard frosts. The variety 'Album' has superb, fresh white flowers.

Vitis Grape vine

A superb foliage plant for covering fences, it can smother other plants, so it's best grown on its own or perhaps with late-flowering clematis growing through it. Some varieties produce small bunches of grapes which can be used for wine or grape juice. The flowers are insignificant. Prune by cutting back long shoots to a framework in late autumn just as the leaves have fallen. Vines do well in all positions.

Vitis 'Brant' is a popular variety producing many small bunches of red grapes. Its main attraction is its beautiful foliage, which turns deep crimson in autumn.

V. coignetiae is one of the most spectacular vines, with huge, green leaves reddish beneath and turning crimson and scarlet in autumn. It produces its best colours on poor soils and with restricted roots. (See also page 245 for fruiting varieties.)

Wisteria

A well-known climber producing masses of attractively shaped leaves and great tassels of blue or white flowers, this needs a south-facing

position to flower best and you should always ask for a grafted plant to ensure that it blooms early in its life. Prune by shortening branches to 8cm (3in) in late summer and again in late winter, cutting back to 2.5cm (1in).

Wisteria floribunda (Japanese wisteria) is one of the loveliest, but will take longer to flower. The form 'Multijuga' produces huge, fragrant tassels of lilac tinged with purple, up to 90cm (3ft) long.

W. sinensis is the most commonly grown and produces fragrant mauve-purple flowers. The variety 'Alba' is white, 'Black Dragon' has double blooms of dark purple and 'Plena' bears double lilac flowers.

Wisteria sinensis 'Alba' is magnificent grown over a pergola.

A Green Tunnel

Another way to provide privacy is to screen your daily walk down the garden by enclosing yourself in a living tunnel and for this we can draw on past experience. It's only quite recently that we have become obsessed with browning our bodies. From Tudor to Victorian times, people with what we would now regard as a healthy suntan were considered unworthy to mix in polite society. You got the tan by working outside with your hands and no gentleman ever did that. As for gentlewomen – well, heaven forbid! So, in order to keep the sun from their milky white skins, rough old gardeners like you and me planted leafy tunnels and arbours to protect them. It's a sobering thought that, for a completely different reason – to prevent damage to the skin by the sun's rays – we may have to resurrect the fashion today.

The nut tunnel in my country garden has the fourfold value that it grows somewhat higher than the fence, helping to screen the whole garden, it shields anyone using it from view, it looks wonderful and, if you choose the varieties carefully and can beat the squirrels to it, it'll produce a fine crop of nuts. It's really quite easy to make, though you'll have to search out the materials.

The first job is to make the path underneath and I decided to do it in the cheapest way I know. Start by setting out 75×25mm (3×1in) pressure-treated boards to form the edging. Nail these to pegs made from the same timber, making sure that they're level. Then level the soil, treading it down hard with your heels, and cover it with a layer of pea shingle. You'll find that the gravel tends to work down into the path surface and to find its way into the borders, so you'll have to top it up from time to time, but it's very cheap.

Next bang in some 50×50mm (2×2in) posts 60cm (2ft) long on the outside of the path at 1.8m (6ft) intervals and screw the boards to them to make them really firm. They'll be used to support the hazel arches.

Now make the training arches for the young hazel trees – again, I looked for the cheapest way to do it. You could use one of the many metal-tubing tunnels that are widely advertised in gardening magazines, but they look a bit too municipal for the setting and they cost much more than my method. To train my growing hazel, I used freshly cut hazel.

If you live in a town, you may find hazel or willow withies, as the long shoots are called, hard to come by, but certainly not impossible. The best bet is to ask your local garden centre. They often have a supply of bean poles or pea sticks delivered, and you can bet your life that the same woodsman who supplies these would be able to get you some hazel. Alternatively you'll have to travel to the country and look for woodsmen or even woodyards in the telephone directory. If all else fails, you'll find advertisements for willow and hazel fencing hurdles in every gardening magazine. Most suppliers of these will be able to provide you with withies, but the carriage will make them more expensive. The best time to enquire is late winter, because they cut them in early spring.

You'll need withies about 3m (10ft) long and freshly cut. Set to work as soon as they arrive because it's essential to use them while they're still supple. After about a fortnight, they tend to get too stiff to bend easily.

You may feel, incidentally, that the wanton destruction of woodland by removing hazel or willow withies is nothing short of ecological vandalism. In fact, quite the reverse is the case. Both types of woodland were, in the past, coppiced especially to produce the withies which were used to make thatching pegs, sheep hurdles, fencing, baskets and so on. Coppicing consists of pruning back long growths to a low point on the main trunk of the tree every few years, resulting in the periodic opening-up of forest glades. The admission of more sunshine creates perfect conditions for a different type of undergrowth to grow, attracting a much wider range of insects and birds. In the coppiced woodland I visited during the filming of the television series I discovered huge tracts of bluebells, wood anemones, ferns, herb robert and even orchids where virtually nothing had grown in the dense shade prior to the coppicing. They had just been sitting there in the soil, waiting.

Coppicing fell into disuse as thatching became rarer and country crafts obsolete, but it's now enjoying a renaissance. There's a new demand for wattle hurdles for fencing, and hazel and willow are being used more and more to make arbours, furniture and even garden sculpture. The country crafts are being kept alive and new habitats are being created for wildlife. So go ahead and make your tunnel, knowing that you're actually doing a bit of good for the countryside and the people who work there. In fact there's no reason why you shouldn't practise the art of coppicing in your own back garden, however small it is.

Make the template for the arches by banging pegs into the ground. Naturally you'll need to measure carefully to see that you make the arches just a little wider than the path and about 2.4m (8ft) tall. That will allow for a 2.1m- (7ft-) tall tunnel with 30cm (1ft) in the ground.

To form an arch bend two withies round the template and wire the tops together at about 15cm (6in) intervals. Continue in this way with pairs of withies until you have the number of arches you need for the tunnel.

To make a template for the hazel arches, mark out the shape on the grass, hammer in stout pegs and bend the withies round them.

To create arches about 2.4m (8ft) tall, join two 3m (10ft) withies together at the top, fixing them with loops of wire about 15cm (6in) apart.

Push each arch into the ground, then nail it to a short wooden post, using another hammer to hold the post steady as you work.

Wiring on horizontal struts between the arches will help pull the tunnel into shape.

To form the tunnel push the arches into the ground next to the short posts banged in earlier. It's often not easy to push them in fully because, of course, you can't bang them in, so you may have to make a hole first with a crowbar or a wooden post.

Step back and view the tunnel, making sure it's as uniform a curve as you can manage, but don't worry too much at this stage if it's not perfect. Then drill the bottoms of the withies to prevent them splitting and nail them to the short wooden posts with two nails.

When all the arches are in, the tunnel will look somewhat higgledy-piggledy. However, this can be corrected when you wire on the horizontal struts. Ideally sort out withies at least 3.5m (12ft) long to span three arches, though this is not absolutely necessary. Start by wiring on the top rail, stepping back regularly to check visually that the curves are uniform. Then wire on the side rails and you should be able to get a fairly even result. It will still, of course, be more rustic-looking than a metal arch, but that simply adds to the charm. Bear in mind, too, that the dead hazel is only there to train the living trees, so it won't actually be a permanent feature. In three or four years, when the trees have grown enough and have set in shape, the arches can be removed.

If you use willow withies, you'll find that most will root. To stop them growing into trees and overtaking the nuts, you'll have to remove all the leaves and young shoots as they form, just rubbing them off with your fingers.

You'll have to search out the nut trees for the tunnel, because not all garden centres will stock them. Specialist fruit nurseries are the best bet and you'll need single-stemmed trees as tall as possible. They're very fast-growing, so you should be able to buy one- or two-year-old plants up to about 1.8m (6ft) or more in height at a reasonable price.

Plant single-stemmed nut trees on both sides of each arch and firm them in gently with your foot.

Tie the stems to the arch and if they already meet in the middle prune off the growing tips to encourage bushy growth. Tie in any suitable side branches to the horizontal struts.

If you want your tunnel to bear fruit, choose good fruiting varieties and make sure that you have a pollinator, because no varieties are self-fertile. 'Kentish Cob' is the traditional variety planted in the Kent nut orchards, but there are several newer ones, mostly from the USA, which produce good crops of excellent quality. 'Butler' is a very heavy cropper and bears large nuts with an excellent, strong flavour. 'Ennis' has even larger nuts with a fine flavour, but it is a rather light cropper and tends to be biennial. 'Gunslehert' is one of the best, reliably producing very heavy crops of medium to large nuts of very good flavour.

After planting, tie the stems in to the arch and prune them by cutting back the leading shoot once the two opposite each other meet at the top. There may be a few side branches at this stage and, if they're in the right position, they can be trained in to the horizontals. If they're not, prune them hard back too.

In commercial nut orchards the trees are grown on a stool system with shoots arising from the base of the plant. This is the natural habit of the plant and is encouraged by regular pruning. However, it's the last thing that's wanted for a nut tunnel, so remove any shoots arising from the base while they're still young, preferably by pulling them off.

The finishing touch is to plant the base of the walk with *Alchemilla mollis* (lady's mantle). It's a marvellous plant that will do well in sun or shade and is happy in most soils. Its attractive foliage catches drops of water which in sun will shine like diamonds, and in early summer it'll be awash with greenish yellow, starry flowers. Be warned, however, that it's best to cut off the flowers when they start to turn brown since it's a prolific seeder and could become a nuisance.

A VINE WALK

Vines were brought to the British Isles by the Romans as early as the third century. They must have been somewhat disappointed with the crops and the varieties that would succeed in a climate that was rather more harsh than they were used to. Nonetheless cultivation continued and developed until, by the fifteenth century, England was a major wine-growing country.

Vines were also used widely as shade plants to grow up pergolas, arbours and tunnels. Indeed they were the major climbers in use right up to the eighteenth century, so growing them in modern gardens would create an interesting link with the past.

For the vine walk a more permanent metal structure is the best support. These can easily be obtained from garden centres and by mail order. They're very simple to erect. The arches are generally set at 75cm (30in) apart, which is an ideal spacing for the vines.

If you simply want a decorative and shading effect, choose a vine variety like *Vitis* 'Brant' or *V. coignetiae* (both described on pages 54–5). However, most gardeners, I'm sure, would prefer to grow a crop of grapes too. Vines are really very decorative plants, bearing fine summer foliage with attractive tints in the autumn, and they can be used for wine and grape juice and in good summers will be sweet enough to eat. It's probably best to take local advice on varieties, but the following are my own general recommendations.

V. 'Seyval Blanc' is fairly trouble free, makes a good shade plant and quite acceptable wine; 'Strawberry Grape' is a North American variety with a strawberry colour when ripe and is good for eating and wine-making; 'Triomphe d'Alsace', a very strong grower, produces black grapes to make red wine; 'Chardonnay' is an excellent white wine grape for cooler areas in particular; 'Madeleine Angevine 7972' has pale green fruit and is good for wine and dessert; 'Pinot Blanc' is another excellent white grape for cool conditions and makes superb wine; and 'Siegerrebe' produces heavy crops of golden-yellow grapes good for both wine and dessert.

After planting, the plants should be cut back to about 30cm (1ft) from the ground.

Subsequently two or three shoots should be allowed to grow in the first year to cover the space. Side shoots should be tied in where they're needed and, after leaf fall, cut back to about 15cm (6in). You have to make something of a compromise between sufficient shade and privacy in the tunnel and a good crop of fruit, but generally it's best to pinch out the tips of side shoots when they've made five leaves.

AN APPLE WALK

The same ready-made metal structure that formed the vine walk can be used to support apples, which make a fine show of blossom in spring and produce heavy crops of fruit in late summer. Again, the 75cm (30in) spacing of the tunnel arches is ideal.

Choose varieties that will give a good continuity of harvesting and will pollinate each other. There are many that are suitable, but my own choice for warmer areas would be: 'Discovery'; 'Fiesta'; 'James Grieve'; 'Jupiter'; 'Kent' and 'Spartan'. For cooler places it's best to stick to late flowerers to avoid frosts. Here I would go for 'Ashmead's Kernel'; 'Merton Charm'; 'Orleans Reinette'; 'Suntan' and 'Tydeman's Late Orange'. For cooking my choice would be 'Bramley's Seedling'; 'Grenadier'; 'Howgate Wonder' or 'Lane's Prince Albert'.

Buy one-year-old trees and reduce the main stem by a third after planting. Tie in the trees to the arches with soft string as they grow.

An apple walk adds welcome structure to the garden even in winter.

All the pruning thereafter is done in late summer. Look first at shoots that have grown directly from the main stem in that year and reduce them to 8cm (3in). Then look for side shoots that have come from these shortened ones and prune them to 2.5cm (1in). It really is a very easy method of cultivation and will provide spring colour, large crops of apples, shade and privacy too.

ALLEES

In Italy, in the fiteenth and sixteenth centuries, the fashion for shaded walks was at its height. Then tunnels and walks, or allees as they were known, were made with species like lime and laburnum. You can still see many fine examples in larger gardens today and, indeed,

if you choose the right species, you could grow a somewhat condensed version in your own garden. Hazels, for example, don't have to be trained into a tunnel, but can instead be grown on horizontal wires to form an open-topped nut walk.

Lime was generally pleached – the trees were pruned into a two-dimensional shape to form a very formal, colonnaded avenue. It's perhaps too vigorous to be recommended for most small gardens today, but laburnum could certainly work well. The best way to grow this is as a tunnel, made just like the nut tunnel (page 56) except for the training. Laburnum has an upright habit of growth, so spread out the young shoots in a fan shape and tie them in over the framework. Subsequent pruning is aimed at providing a succession of young shoots by completely cutting out a proportion of older ones. If you have young children, however, bear in mind that the seeds of laburnum are poisonous.

Another alternative to the nut tunnel is to make a similar construction but with willow. Because you don't have to use rooted trees, it can be done very cheaply. Local councils often have willows that are coppiced every year, so it's worthwhile asking for the offcuts. When freshly cut stems are pushed into the ground, most will root. I have been surprised at the size of cuttings that successfully produce roots having seen them in Holland planted at about 2.5cm (1in) diameter. Plant the cuttings rather closer than those of hazel at about 23–30cm (9in–1ft) apart. Other than that, do much the same as suggested for hazel. It's also worth taking the precaution of planting half a dozen extra cuttings in a corner just in case some fail to take.

The world-famous laburnum walk at Barnsley House is underplanted with alliums.

ARBOURS

The art of gardening in the Western world has, over the centuries, been greatly influenced by the ancient gardens of countries further to the east. Persia, Greece, Italy and Moorish Spain have all provided inspiration for British gardeners, even though our climate, our geography and our national character have little in common. The relatively watery sunshine in Britain, for example, doesn't compare with the scorching noonday heat of Middle Eastern countries, yet we have enthusiastically adopted sub-tropical ways to cope with it.

The cool, plant-covered arbour was originally designed to protect its occupant from fierce Mediterranean sunshine without interrupting the view of the garden and landscape beyond. Yet, through centuries of usage, it has become traditional in the cooler West too. What could be more 'English' than a rose- or honeysuckle-covered arbour?

Apart from sunshine we have other meteorological phenomena to worry about, and with more justification. Nurseryman and botanist John Rea perfectly summed up the usefulness of an arbour in an English garden in his description of the need for a summer-house in 1665. He felt that it should be 'finished with seats about and a table in the middle which serveth for not only delight and entertainment, to sit in and behold the beauties of the flowers but for many other necessary purposes. For writing the names, both in planting and taking up, of all flowers, for shelter in case of a sudden shower of rain and divers other purposes…'

Victorian gardeners took up summer-houses enthusiastically and invented a modification which they called the gazebo (supposedly rather pseudo Latin for 'I gaze'). Many were made of elaborate 'rustic-work',

To make a living arbour with hornbeam, plant young trees and attach them securely to a stout stake with a plastic tree tie.

When all the trees are in, pull the tops together in the centre and tie them with a plastic rose tie, trying to get the curves as even as you can.

using branches selected for their twisted shapes, and with elaborately thatched roofs. Others were fashioned from wire bent and welded together to make sometimes quite fantastic structures designed to be covered with roses in particular.

By the Edwardian era, garden structures had become more restrained and classical in appearance. The structure I've used in the town garden is based on just such a design with a high, curved roof topped by a decorative ball. It serves as a quiet place to sit and contemplate the garden or, indeed, to note down the names of plants as they're planted or lifted in the way John Rea describes, but it's also a very decorative piece

of garden architecture. The smaller the garden, the more important it becomes for everything in it to be beautiful.

Leafy, living arbours are once again becoming fashionable, especially in country gardens, though there's no reason at all why they should not also grace a town garden designed on more rustic lines. The craft has been practised for generations, with some more eccentric Victorian gardeners, in particular, making elaborate and unusual designs. One dog-lover is reputed to have made his favourite hound a leafy dog kennel, while another capped them all with a bizarre willow cathedral. Recently several young designers and sculptors have rediscovered

Pull together any side shoots that are long enough to start forming the dome of the arbour. Cut back outward-facing shoots to 8cm (3in).

A simple rustic floor is made by levelling the soil, treading it down hard and spreading a layer of chipped bark which will suppress weed growth.

the art of construction using living or recently cut material and this more naturalistic approach is much to be welcomed.

My own arbour was made in the simplest way possible and was inspired by a desire to emulate the soft, dappled shade of the woodland I love so much, without shading the whole garden. It's a method that has been used since Roman times when gardens often contained an arbour made with clipped yew or beech. It needs a little patience because it takes time to become fully covered.

Several types of tree could be used, the only proviso being that they should be amenable to clipping to create the bushy growth that's required to provide really

dense shade. Beech is perfect because, though not evergreen, it retains its dead leaves during the winter. It is difficult for my own garden in that it doesn't do well in badly drained soil, so I used the slightly easier-to-grow hornbeam. This looks much the same with perhaps not quite the russet hue of beech in winter, but it'll grow just about anywhere. Evergreen cotoneaster like *Cotoneaster frigidus* or *C. watereri* would also do very well, or you could use a deciduous species like willow which has very attractive yellow or reddish bark in winter.

Start by improving the soil for planting in the normal way, using manure or compost on light soil plus grit on heavy land. Then mark out a circle to the required size. Mine was 2.4m (8ft) in diameter.

Mark where the trees are to be planted, allowing for a slightly wider space where the entrance will be. Generally they'd need to be about 60cm (2ft) apart. Plant the trees upright and stake them with stout stakes and a single plastic tree tie about 90cm (3ft) up the trunk.

To create the roof, simply pull the tops of the trees into the middle and tie them together. I used plastic rose ties for this job, because you need something wide and flexible that won't cut into the bark. It's a fiddly task to get the curves more or less right, but don't worry too much about it. Once the side shoots grow and you start clipping, you'll be able to shape the dome perfectly.

If there are any long side shoots, pull them together and tie them to start making the shape of the dome. Then simply trim back to 8cm (3in) any shoots that are facing directly away from the arbour, stand back and wait for it to grow. I shall eventually trim mine to create a series of arches, leaving the bottoms of the trunks bare to give an uninterrupted view of the garden.

The floor is simply levelled, trodden down firmly and covered with chipped bark. To finish it off and define the circular shape, I planted a low hedge of sweet-smelling lavender. With 30cm (1ft) between them, quite a few plants are needed, but to reduce the cost you can grow them quite quickly from seed. Sow them on the top of a pot of moist coir compost, ideally in late winter or early spring, though any time up to mid-autumn will do. Cover with a thin layer of vermiculite and then place a piece of clear plastic over the top. If it's early in the year, they'll require the gentle heat of the kitchen windowsill. Once they're through, give them as much light as possible until they're 5cm (2in) high. Then transfer them to individual pots and put them outside in a coldframe to grow on. They'll be ready to plant out by early summer and some varieties could be in flower the same season. If, like mine, your soil's very heavy, you'll need to prepare for planting even more thoroughly than you did for the trees, so work in extra gravel to improve the drainage as much as possible. The heavier the soil, the more gravel you'll need.

You might prefer to make the hedge with perhaps rosemary, cotton lavender or one of the shrubby thymes like 'Silver Posie'. Whichever you choose, bear in mind that they'll need regular clipping in early spring. If you neglect them, the plants will become straggly and woody in the centre very quickly and then they're difficult, if not impossible, to rejuvenate.

ALTERNATIVE ARBOURS

There are other ways to make living arbours, perhaps requiring more skill but certainly not beyond the capabilities of gardeners with a little manual dexterity and patience.

During the television series I visited Claire Wilkes, a young sculptor who specializes in using living materials. Her arbour was made with cuttings of different species of willow. She used coloured varieties like the orange-red *Salix rubens* 'Basfordiana', *S. purpurea* (purple osier), *S. alba* 'Britzensis' (scarlet willow) and *S. vitellina* (golden willow).

It's important to buy the cuttings freshly cut in winter and to do the job then. When the weather's cold and wet, they'll last some time without drying out, but it's always best to bury the ends of the cuttings temporarily if the job will take a long time.

The simplest of structures is soon covered with climbing plants to create a delightful secluded spot.

Push the cuttings into holes, ideally made with a soil auger, though if you can't find somewhere to hire one, a pointed stake will do. They need to go in about 30cm (1ft) deep and 15–23cm (6–9in) apart.

If you're going to have a seat in the arbour, tackle that first. To make it strong enough to support one or two people right from the start, set a few logs on a gravel base and weave the cuttings over those. Once they've grown and thickened up, they'll become self-supporting. Put the cuttings for the seat in a more or less straight line at the front of the seat and curved backwards over the logs. Then weave thinner willow withies through them as if you were making a basket. These lateral shoots are not actually alive, but eventually the cuttings will start to shoot and then the living shoots can also be woven into the seat.

It has to be said that a fair amount of skill and practice is needed to get this job right. A good amateur basket-maker would be able to manage, but if you think it's beyond you, simply make the arbour and make or buy a wooden seat to put in it. Weaving the arbour is easier.

For the arbour itself start by marking out a circle and pushing in four long cuttings at equal distances around it. Bring these together at the top and tie them. Then the art is to push in other cuttings to weave in and out in a series of arches to make a dome shape rather like an igloo. No more tying is required, because the weaving should hold the structure together very firmly. Try to get the shape uniform as you work and, when you've finished, weave in any small shoots that are poking out away from the structure or cut them off.

In spring the whole arbour will start to shoot and then the fun starts. The shoots can be woven into the structure to form quite a dense wall. Eventually, of course, some will have to be trimmed off and, if the job is done assiduously at least once a year, the size of the original cuttings will be restricted and the arbour should last for many years.

A LEAFY BOWER

This excellent alternative to a fully-fledged arbour is, in essence, simply a seat covered with a structure which will carry climbing plants. It could have a back or it could be sited against a wall, fence or hedge. The easiest way to make one is to buy a tubular-metal frame designed for the job. Make holes for the legs with a crowbar and sink them into the ground. A wire or plastic clip-on mesh is often provided for climbers to scramble over.

You could use many of the same climbing plants suggested for adorning fences (see page 49), or you could train a laburnum over the bower with roses and clematis on the back to supplement the spring display of flowers.

If you want to make your own bower, simply sink four 2.4m (8ft) posts into the ground or, better still, put them into metal sockets either driven or concreted in. It's quite easy to make an apex roof or, even simpler, a flat one and then to fill in the structure with wooden trellis to carry the plants. With a bench placed inside it makes a delightful, fragrant place to sit and dream.

CLOCKWISE FROM TOP LEFT

In winter, freshly harvested willow cuttings are pushed into the soil and then woven together to form the frame-work of the arbour. Claire Wilkes makes it look easy.

Various warm, natural shades of willow like the scarlet Salix alba *'Britzensis' and the golden* S. vitellina *are woven together to create an attractive, curving seat.*

By spring the cuttings have burst into growth which can be woven into the structure to form a living wall.

Chapter four

A WOODLAND GLADE

Some people become seriously uncomfortable in small, enclosed places. Thankfully, few of us are afflicted, but there are also lesser degrees of claustrophobia. Walking deep into a cave or a tunnel often gives quite rational people a feeling of unease and we all know folk who would rather use the stairs than the lift in a hotel or store. In the same way small gardens enclosed by high, sombre walls, while hardly causing claustrophobia, can sometimes produce a closed-in feeling, which becomes overpowering and somewhat depressing – quite the reverse of their required function.

Yet walking into a woodland clearing, though we are still surrounded and walled in on all sides by plants, produces in most of us a very pleasant feeling of peace without pressure and solitude without loneliness. There's an airiness about plants, a lack of physical density that makes even an impenetrable barrier far less threatening. Add to that the constant noise from leaves rustling in the wind and the sound of insects, birds and small mammals going about their daily business and, far from being threatened, you feel you're among friends.

In the town garden my solution to the high, brick walls that frowned on me from between 1.8m (6ft) and 3.3m (11ft) high was to turn them into a friendly woodland glade. The idea was to replace the solidity of the high walls with the much more open confinement of leaves, branches and flowers. So the walls were first covered with climbing plants and then planted at their base, in an informal way, with wall shrubs. This left the central part of the garden – the 'glade' – to be planted in the normal way with smaller shrubs and herbaceous plants.

Of course, it's important to ensure when you plant that you don't completely obscure the sun. There will still be space for quite tall trees and shrubs to hide the walls, provided they're sited so that they don't cast too much shade. Be even more vigilant about the area where you plan to sit since you'll almost certainly want this to be in full sunshine. Before you plant, make sure that you know exactly where the sun rises and sets and where it's likely to be during those precious hours when you are able to relax in the garden.

The wonderfully open, airy quality of the silver birches in this woodland area gives a pleasing sensation of enclosure, not confinement; of solitude, not loneliness.

It may seem something of a contradiction, but there's no doubt that the smallness and squareness of any garden can be relieved by really dense planting. If you can't actually see the boundaries, you get the impression that the garden goes on forever. The first job is to plant around the base of the wall to hide the brickwork.

PLANTING

The strip of soil underneath walls generally presents a problem. Most, except for the one that faces the prevailing wind, are likely to be very dry. This is particularly true of house walls where the overhanging eaves efficiently prevent every drop of rain reaching the soil.

It's therefore important to prepare the planting site very well. Work in lots of water-retaining material like well-rotted manure, spent mushroom compost (except where you want to grow acid-loving plants), garden compost or one of the alternatives you can buy from the garden centre.

When you plant, it's best to position the plants at least 30cm (1ft) away from the wall so that the young roots can quickly get into moister soil. Mulch with more organic matter after planting and pay particular attention to watering afterwards. It may be a year or even more before the plants have put out enough roots away from the wall to be able to flourish without your help, so you'll have to make a long-term commitment.

SELF-CLINGING CLIMBERS

If you provide training wires on the walls, you can use any of the climbing plants recommended in chapter 3 for covering fences. Just bear in mind that you should choose plants suitable for the aspect of the particular wall you wish to cover. While south- and west-facing walls are easy, those with a north or easterly aspect require rather tougher characters. In fact, because a brick or stone wall will absorb heat during the day and release it at night, rather like a large storage heater, you should be able to grow slightly more tender plants than you would on a fence.

Self-clinging climbers, of course, require less outlay in fixings and no labour in training except perhaps trimming with shears from time to time if they get overexuberant.

The wedding cake shrub, Viburnum plicatum 'Mariesii' looks wonderful in the dappled shade of a woodland setting.

Many gardeners worry about damage to walls caused by self-clingers and also about damp creeping inside the house. Generally these fears are unfounded, except in one particular instance. If you decide to grow a strong climber like ivy or Virginia creeper against an old wall built with lime mortar, and then you change your mind and remove it, you can damage the mortar by pulling it out with the roots of the climber. I did this in my own garden when I decided that it was a shame to cover lovely old sandstone walls with ivy. It had been growing there for many years before I took over the garden, so it had developed some strong stems. When pulled away, they dragged great chunks of mortar with them and the wall had to be repointed in places. However, I found that, by cutting off the stems at ground level and leaving the tops to die off first, damage was reduced to a minimum. The mortar used for building newer, generally post-1930s houses is much stronger and will rarely be damaged.

It's possible to buy very big climbing plants in garden centres these days. They're generally in an extra-large container and trained up a wooden trellis where they look highly attractive and, despite the high cost, very desirable, especially if you're in a hurry to hide the wall. Frankly I can see no point in them whatever. Self-clinging climbers will attach themselves to walls or fences only with new growths. The small, clinging roots on old wood will have dried off and become inoperative long ago so, to get any value from them, you'll have to fix trellis or training wires to the walls – and that defeats the object completely. It's much better to buy vigorous, young plants which will attach themselves fairly quickly.

However, you still have to be patient. Most self-clingers are painfully slow to get established. All you can do is plant them and

The walls of the malt house at East Lambrook Manor, covered with the bright gold ivy 'Buttercup'.

point them at the wall. Then you'll just have to wait until a young shoot finds something to fix to and that could take a whole season. But once it does get a grip, it'll go away like an express train.

Of course, if your wall is old and attractive, you may feel reluctant to hide it completely. Mellow red brick or honey-coloured sandstone is a marvellous feature in its own right and rarely needs covering. If that's the case, consider partial cover, leaving areas where the wall is allowed to show through here and there. The illusion of increased space will be just as effective.

Euonymus fortunei
Best-known as ground-cover plants, some varieties of this variegated shrub have a trailing habit and will also cling to walls

where they'll slowly reach up to 3m (10ft). All are suitable for north- or east-facing positions. 'Emerald 'n' Gold' has green leaves with a bright gold margin becoming cream and tinted red in winter. 'Silver Queen' has green leaves with a creamy white margin.

Hedera Ivy

There's a wide range of ivies in many leaf colours that are suitable for even cold, north-facing walls. Most are vigorous and fast-growing and will cover large areas. They have the one disadvantage that, as well as climbing the walls, they'll also spread fast across the borders, rooting in as they go. At least annual attention is required, but they generally pull out quite easily. Naturally this makes them very simple indeed to propagate.

Hedera colchica (Persian ivy) has the largest, most dramatic leaves of all. One of the best is the variety 'Dentata Variegata', which has large, bright green foliage shading to grey and with creamy yellow margins which become whiter as they mature. Look out too for 'Sulphur Heart', also sold as 'Paddy's Pride'. In this the centres of the leaves are splashed yellow with the occasional pure yellow leaf.

Hedera helix (common ivy), a British native, is very adaptable. It's hardy on any wall and makes a good home for insects and birds. There are numerous varieties to choose from, so a trip to the nursery is recommended. They include 'Buttercup' with golden-yellow leaves; the green, bronze and purple 'Chicago'; 'Glacier' with silvery grey leaves margined white; 'Goldheart' with a conspicuous splash of yellow in the leaf centres; 'Harald' with grey-green leaves edged cream; 'Parsley Crested' which has green leaves curiously crimped and twisted; and 'Tricolor' which has dainty, grey-green leaves edged white with a red rim in winter.

Climbing hydrangea with its large, flat heads of creamy white flowers is an excellent climber for shade, while below it the foliage of rodgersia and thalictrum makes an interesting contrast in size and shape.

Hedera hibernica (Irish ivy) is closely related and generally represented by the variety 'Deltoidea' which has larger leaves than common ivy, green in colour becoming tinged with bronze in winter.

Hydrangea petiolaris Climbing hydrangea

This is a splendid climber which seems happy in almost any soil and any position. Even on a cold north wall it's as tough as nails, growing vigorously and flowering its heart out. The flowers, borne in early summer, are large and greenish white with several white florets at the margins. But it's a plant that requires patience because, while it becomes very vigorous eventually, it will remain firmly in the doldrums until it fixes to the wall – and there's nothing you can do about it.

Parthenocissus quinquefolia **Virginia creeper**

A well-known self-clinging climber with attractive, green foliage, turning brilliant scarlet and orange in autumn. It's suitable for any wall and is happy in most soils. It's often mistaken for *Parthenocissus tricuspidata* (Boston ivy), which is very similar but has larger leaves that turn more crimson in autumn. Also closely related is my own favourite of the family, *P. henryana,* which has the same habit and leaf shape but is distinguished by the summer leaves which are conspicuously veined with white. The veining is especially prominent when the plant is grown in shade.

The glorious autumnal bonfire colours of Parthenocissus quinquefolia.

Pileostegia viburnoïdes

A close relative of the climbing hydrangea, this has the great advantage of being evergreen. It flowers in late summer and autumn, producing large, creamy white flowers, and it's suitable for any wall.

Schizophragma

Another hydrangea relative, suitable for any wall. In garden centres it's usually represented by *Schizophragma hydrangeoïdes,* which produces large heads of flowers in mid-summer. It's a superb climber, but something of a slow starter, needing encouragement in its early stages. Water it, mulch it, feed it annually in spring and speak to it nicely. Look out too for *S. integrifolium,* which is more vigorous and produces bigger heads of flowers, sometimes as large as 30cm (1ft) across.

Trachelospermum

If you live in a warm area and have a south-facing wall, this is a plant not to be missed. In colder areas it's one for the conservatory. The hardiest species is *Trachelospermum asiaticum*, which has dense, glossy, evergreen foliage and in late summer produces sweetly scented, jasmine-like flowers, white with a buff centre later turning yellow. Slightly slower-growing is *T. jasminoïdes*, which has larger, very fragrant, white flowers that become cream with age. The variety 'Japonicum' is worth looking out for since it's more vigorous and will cover a larger area. 'Variegatum' has leaves marked and margined with cream, with a slight red tinge in winter.

WALL SHRUBS

Another very effective way to cover walls is simply to plant shrubs in front of them. There are several that are particularly well suited. A few, like the well-known *Pyracantha* (firethorn) will need to be trained on wires, but many others have a stiff enough habit to stand alone, even though they'll grow taller in the shelter of the wall than they would free-standing. Others, like the evergreen ceanothus, may need the occasional tie and this is best achieved using wall nails which can normally be hammered straight into the mortar, though on modern walls with harder mortar you may have to drill first. Then a loop of flexible plastic tape or tarred string to the plant unobtrusively does the job.

Camellia

Though the flowers look exotic, many camellias are perfectly hardy and will do well against a north wall even in colder areas. The flowers will drop if early-morning sun catches them after a freezing night, so in cold areas a north-facing site is often preferable. They will, however, flower better with more sunshine, so a south or west wall is a better choice if the plants can be shaded from the early sunshine. But if they're allowed to dry out at any time of the year, the buds could drop, so in a south-facing position particular care must be taken to ensure that they never go dry. They're also acid-lovers and will not thrive in limy soils.

There are more than 200 species and literally thousands of varieties, so a trip to the nursery is called for. *Camellia japonica* (common camellia) is one of the best for this situation. Plants against walls will comfortably reach 4.5–6m (15–20ft) and look superb in spring and early summer when they're covered in large, exotic blooms in colours ranging from white through pink to deep crimson.

C. williamsii is even more free-flowering and deserves the very best spot you can find. The flowers are exquisitely beautiful and produced over a long period from late autumn to late spring depending on variety.

Carpenteria californica

A plant for a south-facing wall but well worth pride of place. Alas, it could be too tender for colder areas, standing only about 5 degrees of frost, but if cut to the ground, it'll normally regrow. In mid-summer it produces masses of large, saucer-shaped, white flowers with yellow centres. Remove a third of the older wood each spring. It can be grown free-standing, but does best when fan-trained on wires.

Ceanothus Californian lilac

The evergreen forms, like 'A. T. Johnson', 'Cascade', 'Delight', 'Puget Blue' and *Ceanothus thyrsiflorus*, produce masses of superb blue flowers in spring and often again in late summer to early autumn. Others, like 'Autumnal Blue' and 'Burkwoodii', also produce blue flowers but in summer and autumn. Look out too for the white form, *C. thyrsiflorus* 'Millerton Point', which flowers in spring and summer. Train the plants as fans or espaliers and prune new shoots by a third after flowering.

There are also several worthy deciduous types, the most popular of which is 'Gloire de Versailles', with powder-blue flowers in summer. Also recommended are the deeper blue 'Henri Desfossé', the pale pink 'Marie Simon' and the darker pink 'Perle Rose'. Again, train the plants in a fan or espalier shape and prune hard in spring, cutting all last year's shoots back to about 10cm (4in).

Chaenomeles Flowering quince

The varieties of *Chaenomeles speciosa* and *C. superba*, though small shrubs if grown free-standing, will reach 2.4–3m (8–10ft) when trained against a wall. Ideally they should be trained on wires into a fan or espalier shape and pruned back in spring just before flowering, when all the previous season's growth should be cut back to two buds, care being taken not to remove the flower buds. The flowers, which are borne in early to mid-spring, are similar to apple blossom and available in colours ranging from the white tinged with pink of 'Apple Blossom' to the deep crimson of 'Rowallane'.

Choisya ternata Mexican orange blossom

This glossy-leaved evergreen has foliage attractive enough to earn its place even without flowers. But in late spring or early summer it's unfailingly covered in white flowers that smell strongly of orange blossom. The plant is equally at home in sun or quite dense shade, but on a north wall could be touched by frost. In very severe winters the

Camellia japonica *'Pink Perfection'*.

stems could be cut to the ground, but would normally regrow. *Choisya* does not need to be trained, but is best protected by planting close to a wall. Pruning consists of cutting the whole plant to ground level every three or four years or removing one stem in three annually. Both methods will rejuvenate the plant, keep the leaves glossy and the shape more compact. Look out too for the variety 'Sundance', which has golden foliage but is slightly more tender and needs light shade.

Cytisus battandieri Pineapple broom

Though a relative of the common broom, this plant is really nothing like it. It makes a tall shrub with superb, silvery foliage, becoming grey as it ages. In early to mid-summer it produces large, yellow, pineapple-scented flowers. The plant needs no pruning, but if it gets too big, cut back young wood after flowering. It's best trained into a fan shape on wires; but, given plenty of space, will grow free-standing too. It prefers a south wall.

Fatshedera lizei **Aralia ivy**
A fine foliage shrub that will quickly fill a large space, this is grown for its very attractive, ivy-like leaves, though it does also produce clusters of green flowers. It can be trained on wires or grown free-standing. It's best grown in light to deep shade, but needs some protection from north winds. No pruning is required, but old stems can be removed to allow light to younger growths.

Fremontodendron californicum **Fremontia**
A spectacular plant for a south- or west-facing wall. It's fast-growing and produces flowers almost continuously from spring to late autumn. And what flowers they are – large, yellow saucers with a big bunch of golden stamens in the middle. Pruning consists of cutting back two-thirds of the current season's growth in mid-summer. It's best trained in a fan shape on wires.

Garrya elliptica **Silk tassel bush**
One of the great sights of winter, this is an ideal shrub for a north wall, though it produces more catkins in sunshine so it can be grown anywhere. The glossy, dark green leaves are the perfect foil for long, silver-grey catkins. Male plants have longer catkins and the variety 'James Roof' is considered the best of all. It can be grown free-standing or attached here and there to the wall. No pruning is required.

Itea ilicifolia
This spectacular shrub deserves a sheltered wall where it will be protected from cold north or east winds which will scorch its evergreen leaves. A south-facing wall is best, though it will take some shade, so a western aspect is also successful. In late summer it produces extra-long, fragrant, silken tassels of greenish white. The foliage is rather holly-like, dark, shiny, green on top and silvery underneath. It's best trained like a fan on wires where it will eventually develop a very attractive, weeping habit. No pruning is required.

Phygelius **Cape figwort**
Phygelius aequalis and *P. capensis* are often grown as free-standing shrubs. These late-summer-flowering, deciduous plants adapt well to growing on a south or west wall where they attain about 2.1m (7ft). Their flowers are long, tubular and very prolific in yellow, orange or red depending on variety. Grow them on wires and trim them lightly in spring.

Piptanthus nepalensis **Evergreen laburnum**
An attractive evergreen for any wall, trained on wires or simply planted near it. In spring the plant produces yellow flowers very much like those of laburnum and some good autumn leaf colour too. Free-standing it'll reach about 3m (10ft) and a little higher on a wall. Older shrubs should have some stems shortened each year after flowering to encourage new growth.

Pyracantha **Firethorn**
A well-known shrub ideal for growing on any wall, though in cold districts it prefers to be sheltered from east or north winds. It will grow very well in quite deep shade, but won't produce quite such compact growth or so many flowers and berries. It's noted for its fine, glossy, evergreen foliage and white flowers in spring, followed by brilliant clusters of berries in red, yellow, orange and white depending on variety. They're at their best in late summer or early autumn and last well into winter.

The plant is best grown on wires in a fan or espalier shape. First make the main structure of the plant, tying in the branches where they're needed and cutting side shoots back to three or four buds. Once the shape is established there are two recommended methods of maintaining it. If you don't want too much work, simply clip back the plant with shears in early spring. For the best show of berries, cut back new shoots in mid-summer to two or three buds to expose the berries and encourage new flower buds.

Ribes Flowering currant

Ribes speciosum and *R. laurifolium*, two rather different forms of flowering currant, richly deserve a place on a south wall, though the latter will also do very well facing west. *R. speciosum* is called the fuchsia-flowered currant for its masses of pendulous, red flowers from mid to late spring. It's best fan-trained on wires and no pruning is necessary, though long shoots can be cut back after flowering. *R. laurifolium* is an interesting evergreen bearing dull, grey-green leaves with lighter grey undersides. Its hanging clusters of yellowish green flowers are produced in winter when there's not much else of interest in flower. It's best trained on wires and no pruning is necessary.

Teucrium fruticans Wall germander

A delightful shrub that benefits greatly from a south-facing wall, where it'll grow to about 2.4m (8ft), this has soft grey, evergreen foliage and a succession of light blue flowers throughout the summer. It dislikes a wet soil, so you may have to improve drainage on heavy ground. It pays to shorten the previous season's growth by about three-quarters in mid-spring to encourage new shoots and flowers. It needs wires to train it as a fan or it can be anchored here and there with wall nails.

TREES

The plants on the walls will eventually hide the brickwork, but they'll retain a rather regimented, square look. What's needed now is an informal area in front of the walls, planted with taller trees and shrubs, grading down to smaller shrubs and herbaceous perennials near the front to turn the garden into a glade. Of course you must be careful not to overdo it, especially if the garden's small, or you'll simply create too much shade. Set aside several days to find out exactly where the sun strikes your plot so that you don't plant trees that will block it out completely. What you're after is a sunny, open area surrounded by taller plants.

You'll find glades like this in every woodland, and very pleasant places they are too. Notice that, while the plants under the trees are often limited, a sunnier space will support a much wider range of flowering species. Despite the fact that with careful choice of plants you'll be able to achieve a much more varied and attractive planting beneath the trees, there's no doubt that lack of light and dryness at the roots are considerable limitations.

You may need only a couple of trees, and indeed in my own town garden I felt I had room for just one and a small one at that. The rest of the softening effect was done with taller shrubs.

Before choosing trees, find out about their eventual height and their habit too. Naturally a spreading one will cast more shade than a species with an upright habit. Many new gardeners are put off when they read of the eventual heights of trees. Something that'll grow to 9m (30ft) sounds absolutely enormous but would in fact be classed as a small tree. First, bear in mind that a tree could take twenty years to reach its final height and

that, in reality, anything below 12m (40ft) is certainly no giant. If you still feel worried, tie a few long canes together to reach 9m (30ft) – four 2.4m (8ft) canes will do it – sit in what will be your glade and get someone to hold up the canes when the sun is in a position where you think it might be blocked out. I think you'll soon stop worrying. My list is limited to trees that would be out of place only in the tiniest of gardens.

Autumn is the best time to plant most trees. Once they've lost their leaves, they put on a spurt of root growth and, with the soil still warm from summer, they soon get established. It's worth searching out a nursery which grows the trees in the field. They'll generally be bigger and stronger and you should also be able to buy them slightly cheaper too. If you do buy them bare-rooted rather than in a container, remember to keep the roots out of the sun and wind. The tiny root hairs that are responsible for absorbing water and nutrients are very easily damaged if they dry out at all, so keep them covered until the very last moment before you plant.

Make the hole big enough to take the full spread of roots and just deep enough so that the tree will be growing at exactly the same depth it grew on the nursery.

Bang in a short stake before planting, putting it on the windward side of the tree so that it will blow away from the stake rather than towards it. The stake should be long enough to reach a third of the way up the trunk to allow some swaying in the wind. This tends to strengthen both the stem and the root system.

Very few native woodland plants have bright flowers and similarly, in a garden setting, pale colours like the white and pink of these roses shows up best in shade.

There's generally no need to improve the soil you dug out unless it's really very heavy and sticky. Then do so with a barrowload of compost or manure (not peat, which does more harm than good by surrounding roots with wet, cold, inert material).

Plant the tree in the hole and refill with a little compost. Then grab the trunk and shake it up and down to settle soil around the finer roots. Refill completely and firm gently with your boot. Tie the tree to the stake with a proper plastic tree tie and mulch around the bottom with a good thick layer of manure or compost or with a piece of black polythene. This prevents competition from weeds and helps retain moisture.

The one and only limitation with buying bare-rooted is that the job will have to be done in the dormant season. For deciduous trees that means from late autumn to early spring; for evergreens, which have no dormant season, the best times are early autumn and early spring. If you simply can't wait until then, you'll have to plant container-grown trees.

The technique is the same as for bare-rooted trees but with two important differences. Once you've soaked the plant, take it out of its pot and check to see whether the roots are running round the bottom of the rootball. If they are, they must be gently teased out; and that's sometimes easier said than done. If they're choked together, forming a dense mat, you must untangle them a little, even if that means breaking some of them. If you don't, the roots have a habit of continuing to spiral, making a bad anchorage: it's possible that the tree could grow quite large and then fall over.

If the tree has been in a very large pot, preventing you getting it close enough to the stake, put the stake in the hole at an angle, with the point facing the prevailing wind.

The Japanese maple, Acer japonicum, *has brilliant autumn colour.*

Acer Maple

An easy tree for most soils and situations, grown for its foliage and occasionally its bark colour. Some acers can grow very tall, so be careful with your selection.

Acer griseum (paperbark maple) is a very slow-growing tree in its later stages and therefore, though it can reach 15m (50ft) eventually, it's ideal for most small gardens. The main feature is the cinnamon-coloured, peeling bark, so make sure you don't hide it with too much planting in front. The attractive green leaves turn bright red in autumn.

A. japonicum (fullmoon maple) makes a small tree with soft, downy, green leaves which turn brilliant red, orange or yellow in autumn. The red flowers with yellow anthers are borne on drooping stalks when the leaves are young and bronze. The leaves of the variety 'Aconitifolium' are deeply cut and delicately attractive. It grows to 10m (33ft).

A. negundo 'Flamingo' (a variety of the box elder) has green leaves with soft pink margins that change to white with age. It's really best grown as a shrub, when it can be pruned hard in winter to improve the leaf colour. It can grow to 20m (65ft), but may be kept small by pruning.

A. palmatum (Japanese maple) is available in several forms that make superb foliage plants. Generally sold as large shrubs, they can sometimes be obtained as small trees. Alternatively they can be carefully pruned to produce a short trunk and can be easily kept down to about 6m (20ft). Different leaf colours are obtainable, excellent throughout the year and among the most striking in autumn. They're best on neutral to acid soils, though they will tolerate some lime. What they won't stand is scorching sunshine and cold winds, so plant them in a sheltered and slightly shaded place.

A. pensylvanicum is an excellent small tree with fine yellow autumn colour. The main attraction possibly is the bark, which is striped with white and especially noticeable in winter. The form 'Erythrocladum', whose young shoots are bright pink with white striations, is especially attractive. Unfortunately it doesn't do well on chalky soil. It grows to 8m (26ft).

Amelanchier lamarckii Snowy mespilus

A tree with so much to offer, this is almost obligatory for a small garden. In early spring the new leaves are fresh bronze, forming the perfect background to clouds of delicate, white flowers. Later the leaves will become green and in autumn they turn brilliant red-orange in sunshine and yellow in shade. The small, purple berries are not dramatic, but are edible. It grows to about 10m (33ft). It's said to require an acid soil, but I've grown it very successfully in slightly limy land for many years.

Aralia elata Japanese angelica tree
Generally a large, Oriental-looking shrub, this can be grown as a tree reaching about 10m (33ft). The very attractive leaves consist of many toothed leaflets which colour well in autumn. The flowers are borne in large, greenish white clusters in autumn. The stems are often spiny and the plant has a suckering habit which, if you want to grow it as a single-stemmed tree, needs to be controlled. The habit of the tree is quite open, so it won't cast a lot of shade.

Arbutus Strawberry tree
The best-known and most widely available of the genus is *Arbutus unedo,* an evergreen with white flowers followed by red, straw-berry-like fruits, but this is by no means the best. Harder to find, but worth searching out, is *A. andrachnoïdes*, which not only has similar flowers and fruits but also superb, mahogany, peeling bark. It's slow-growing to about 6m (20ft) and is tolerant of soils with some lime.

Betula utilis Himalayan birch
I include this big tree without reservation or apology because, though it'll eventually reach 25m (80ft), it takes a long time getting there. In any case it has such an open habit that its shade is not a problem. It's one of the best silver birches for bark colour provided you get a white-barked selection, so look for the variety generally sold as 'Jaquemontii'. The male form has long, drooping, yellow catkins absolutely filled to the brim with pollen.

Catalpa bignonioïdes Indian bean tree
Grown for its large leaves, this South American tree is best in the form 'Aurea', which sports superb, soft, golden foliage. It'll grow to 15m (50ft), but is much better when kept small by pruning back hard every spring once it has reached the required height: the colour and size of the leaves are much improved. Left to grow, it will eventually produce lovely, foxglove-like flowers, but if you want them, you'll have to allow it to reach full size.

Cercidiphyllum japonicum Katsura tree
One of my own favourites, this lovely tree will eventually grow to about 30m (100ft), but is very slow and can be kept in check by pruning. Don't be without it. It's grown for its leaves, which in spring are silken bronze. During the summer they become blue-green and in autumn they turn yellow with pink and purple overtones. At the same time they give out a strong smell of burnt toffee – delicious.

Cercis siliquastrum Judas tree
A small, spreading tree or large shrub with attractive, rounded foliage. In late spring the older wood and sometimes even the trunk become covered in superb, rosy pink, pea-like flowers followed by purple pods. It does best in full sun and will eventually reach 10m (33ft).

Cornus Dogwood/cornel
One of the most striking trees in my own garden is *Cornus controversa* 'Variegata'. Its branches are layered like a wedding cake and the leaves are green with an attractive yellow variegation. It's much slower-growing than the type, so it's eminently suitable for a small garden.

Another, generally kept as a shrub, though eventually it could become a small tree, is 'Eddie's White Wonder'. It's grown for its large, white flowers (actually bracts), which appear in summer. As a bonus the leaves turn vivid red-orange in autumn. A similar species is *C. florida,* but look out especially for the pink form 'Cherokee Chief'. They'll both grow to about 12m (40ft).

C. kousa 'Chinensis' makes a slightly bigger tree, reaching about 15m (50ft), again with white bracts and deeper bronze autumn foliage. It's not too keen on chalky soils.

Cotoneaster frigidus

The true species is rarely seen. What is generally offered is one of several hybrids of *Cotoneaster watereri,* but no matter – they're all superb trees for our purposes. They grow to about 10m (33ft) and have the enormous advantage of being evergreen. In spring their clusters of white flowers are perhaps somewhat disappointing, but these are more than made up for by brilliant scarlet berries in autumn. And the birds seem to leave them alone until the last minute, so they'll last well into the new year. They'll thrive almost anywhere.

Crataegus Flowering thorn

An important group of trees if you want to attract wildlife into the garden. They provide homes for insects, nesting sites and nourishment for birds and, not so happily, food for caterpillars. Those described here will reach a height of 6–10m (20–33ft) and form a spreading, rounded head. They're very hardy and will grow almost anywhere.

Crataegus laevigata is one of the most commonly offered. There are several hybrids, with the red, double-flowered variety 'Paul's Scarlet' heading the list. Look out too for 'Plena' with double white blooms and 'Rosea Flore Pleno' with double pink flowers.

C. prunifolia is another excellent, small tree bearing lovely, white flowers with red

anthers. The large berries start greenish purple and become red, and the leaves in autumn turn a fiery orange-yellow.

Cydonia oblonga Common quince

The fruiting quince has been grown in Europe for centuries to produce fruit for cooking and wine-making. It forms a small tree about 5m (17ft) high with dark green leaves, grey and downy beneath. The flowers, pale pink or white and borne in late spring, are followed by large, yellow, edible fruits. The variety 'Vranja' is most commonly grown for fruiting. It's very hardy and will do well in most soils.

Ficus carica Fig

Because it's frequently grown as a wall plant, the common fig is often overlooked as a very attractive foliage tree for milder districts. There is also, of course, the bonus of fruit. The large, glossy, deeply divided leaves are highly decorative, and free-standing trees will often bear quite good crops. Give it a sheltered position and it should perform well. It'll grow to about 10m (33ft).

Gleditsia triacanthos 'Sunburst' Honey locust

A popular small tree grown for its superb, bright golden foliage becoming green in late summer. It survives in just about any soil that's not badly drained and can reach 15m (50ft).

Hoheria Mountain ribbonwood

A large shrub or small tree with glossy leaves and fragrant, white flowers, this is not generally recommended for cold areas unless in a protected site. The hybrid 'Glory of Amlwch' bears large, pure white flowers and retains its leaves in mild winters. *Hoheria sexstylosa* is a superb tree with large, white, scented flowers in clusters. They grow to 8m (26ft).

Laburnum watereri 'Vossii' **Golden rain tree**
A well-known small tree bearing long tassels
of brilliant yellow, scented flowers in late
spring. It should be remembered that all parts
of the tree, and especially the seeds, are
poisonous. It grows in most soils and
positions to about 7m (23ft).

Magnolia

Generally looked upon as large shrubs, some
make very big trees in the wild and in the
garden, and even small species can be grown
on a central stem if you want to plant underneath. Most nurseries offer them as shrubs, so
if you wish to do this you'll need to prune
away some of the lower branches as they
grow, to form a trunk.

If your garden's small, avoid the huge
species like *Magnolia campbellii*, which grows
to 30m (100ft) and choose smaller (and if
your soil's chalky), lime-tolerant species and
varieties like the fragrant, white-flowered
M. loebneri 'Merrill', the pink *M. loebneri*
'Leonard Messel', the hybrid 'Maryland'
with large, white, lemon-scented blooms, or
the superb *M. sinensis* which bears
pendulous, perfumed, white flowers with a
central boss of red stamens. These grow to
about 10m (33ft).

Malus **Apple**

Malus domestica (the cultivated apple) should
always be considered as an ornamental as
well as a productive tree, especially for small
gardens. Because it can be bought on a range
of rootstocks which control its eventual size,
it can be more or less tailored to the height
you require. It grows in any fertile soil and is
entirely hardy, though if you want fruit (and
of course you do), it should have a position
sheltered from the coldest winds. In colder
areas it's also wise to choose late-flowering
varieties in an attempt to avoid frost damage.

The exquisite pure white flowers of
Magnolia sinensis.

Bear in mind too that you need at least two
varieties for effective pollination to produce a
full crop of fruit. As you know, they produce
wonderful pink-and-white blossom in spring
followed by large, green, red or yellow edible
fruits.

Most of the ornamental crab apples are
not really edible. If you want to make crab-
apple jelly, go for the variety 'John Downie',
whose pink buds open to white flowers
which are followed by oval, orange fruits
flushed red. There are dozens of other
varieties to choose from, bearing flowers of
pink and white, pink, red or pure white and
different fruits in a range of colours through
yellow, orange and red or combinations of
these. All are small and suitable for most soils
and situations.

Mespilus germanica Medlar

Another ancient tree in Europe, grown not only for its large, brown, edible fruits but also for its architectural habit, large, white flowers and long, green leaves. The fruit, which should be picked when over-ripe, makes a fine jelly.

The tree grows to about 6m (20ft) in most soils and situations. The best variety to look for is 'Nottingham'.

Morus nigra Black mulberry

The mulberry has been cultivated in Europe for centuries and forms a fine, architectural, small tree up to about 10m (33ft). Eventually the branches take on an interesting, gnarled look which, together with the reddish bark and heart-shaped leaves, make it a real asset. It also produces delicious fruit.

The mulberry performs best in a rich soil with ample manuring. The white mulberry is quite a bit bigger, but has a weeping form, *Morus alba* 'Pendula', which is well worth consideration.

Prunus cerasifera Cherry plum

A very decorative, small tree, growing to about 8m (26ft). In early spring the branches are wreathed in white flowers, or pink ones in the variety 'Rosea'. The leaves, which appear later, are green, but in the varieties 'Nigra' and 'Pissardii' they are a deep reddish purple. All are very hardy and will grow in any type of soil.

Prunus dulcis Almond

A fine ornamental tree which will also produce nuts in warm years, this bears single pink flowers in early to mid-spring. It's unfortunately subject to peach-leaf curl, so would need spraying with copper fungicide. It grows to about 8m (26ft) in most soils and situations.

Prunus hybrids Flowering cherry

By far the largest and best-known group and with good reason. There are dozens of good varieties which should not exceed 10m (33ft). 'Kanzan' is by far the most popular, with masses of double pink blossoms on steeply ascending branches, though it is not, in my opinion, the best. Look out especially for 'Accolade', one of the earliest to produce double pink flowers even on young trees. 'Shirofugen' has pink buds opening to white, double flowers that turn pink again before they fall. One of the best of all is 'Tai Haku' which bears the largest single white flowers set against bronze foliage, and one of my own favourites is 'Pink Shell', with masses of delicate pink flowers against fresh green leaves in spring.

Prunus persica Peach

Though the best crops come from wall-grown trees, in warmer areas peaches will also produce quite good crops if grown free-standing. They're excellent ornamental trees too, with masses of pale pink, single flowers and of course orange-yellow fruits in summer. Unfortunately they suffer badly from peach-leaf curl, so are best avoided if you don't want to spray. They grow to about 8m (26ft).

Prunus subhirtella 'Autumnalis' Spring cherry

One of the most valuable autumn- and winter-flowering trees. In fact it produces its white flowers on and off right through until mid-spring. The semi-double flowers are white, tinged with pink, and hang in pendulous clusters. The variety 'Autumnalis Rosea' has deeper pink flowers. Trees will reach about 6m (20ft) and will grow in most soils and situations. There's also a weeping form, 'Pendula Rosea', which has single pink flowers.

Pyrus salicifolia 'Pendula'
Willow-leaved pear

A weeping habit and silvery grey foliage make this a highly attractive tree. It bears creamy white flowers in spring and tiny, insignificant pears later. It grows to about 10m (33ft) and is very tolerant of soil and situation.

Rhus typhina **Stag's horn sumach**

A large shrub or small tree grown for its lovely, deeply dissected foliage borne on brown stems covered in velvety hairs. In summer it bears large clusters of green flowers and brown fruits resembling cones. In autumn the leaves light up the garden with brilliant orange. It can grow in time to about 6m (20ft). Unfortunately it has a suckering habit, easy to control in the borders but difficult if shoots come up in the lawn.

The stag's horn sumach, Rhus typhina.

Robinia pseudoacacia 'Frisia'

A really dramatic, small tree with superb, golden-yellow foliage from spring to autumn. It grows in most soils and is at its very best planted so that the sun shines through the leaves. It doesn't transplant well, so it's best bought container-grown. It also suffers from die-back of branches, so you may have to prune back dead wood to healthy growth in spring, but it's very well worth the extra trouble. The tree can reach about 15m (50ft).

Sorbus **Rowan/mountain ash**

This genus contains some highly attractive, native trees and their varieties, and they are excellent wildlife attractors. Their berries provide a rich food source for birds in winter. Most will grow to about 15m (50ft).

Sorbus aria 'Lutescens' is a fine spring tree in particular. The leaves have a silky, silver down on the upper surface, becoming greener with age.

S. aucuparia is the well-known rowan, which produces white flowers in spring followed by clusters of brilliant red berries. Look out for the varieties 'Edulis' with much larger, edible berries and 'Sheerwater Seedling' with orange fruits.

S. cashmiriana is a smaller tree than most, growing to 8m (26ft) with soft pink flowers in late spring followed by glistening, pure white berries.

S. insignis is a superb tree with white flowers and pink fruits which last until the early spring. It has the added advantage of fiery autumn leaf colour too.

'Joseph Rock' also has fine autumn foliage colour which sets off the yellow berries to perfection.

S. thibetica 'John Mitchell', sometimes sold as *S. mitchellii*, is well worth a place for its huge, green leaves with brilliant silver undersides.

S. vilmorinii is a fine, small tree with superb autumn leaf colour and berries which start red and gradually turn to pink and then white as winter progresses.

SHRUBS

The remainder of the permanent planting consists of shrubs and herbaceous perennials. The trees and shrubs form the main framework of the garden and create a lasting backdrop to the generally more showy but shorter-lived perennials and annuals. They'll also provide the main interest in winter when the rest have died back, so you should start by including some evergreens which have all-year-round colour and interest.

When choosing shrubs and herbaceous plants, it's important to remember that in summer the trees will cast considerable shade. Where the shade falls, sun-lovers will naturally not thrive, so you'll need to select plants that prefer shady condiitions. There are lots of them.

EVERGREEN SHRUBS

Planting evergreen shrubs is much the same as described for trees except that, naturally, no stake is necessary and the timing is slightly different. Deciduous trees are planted after leaf fall because at that time they need little water and also put on a natural spurt of root growth. Evergreens lose their leaves much more gradually, right through the year, so they don't have a dormant season.

The best time to move them is when the soil is warm but growth has slowed. Late summer and early autumn are ideal for the hardiest plants that will have no problems in a cold winter. But any plant in the least suspect is best left until late spring, letting the nurseryman take the risk of winter losses. The soil will have started to warm up, the plants will be starting to grow vigorously again and the danger of frosts hard enough to damage them will have passed.

You will, however, have to be diligent with watering. At that time of year, prolonged dry spells are not uncommon and, without an established root system, new plants will depend entirely on you for their survival. Many of the evergreens have quite shallow, fibrous root systems, so it's even more important to mulch well, not only to conserve moisture but also to prevent frost damage to roots.

Many attractive shrubs like Viburnum opulus *(snowball tree) thrive in the dappled shade cast by native woodland trees.*

Of course, there are hundreds of shrubs to choose from and I couldn't possibly mention them all here. The very best way to improve your knowledge of them, and to fill your garden with the choicest, is to make frequent visits to other gardens, particularly the bigger ones open to the public. Take a camera and notebook with you and a good supply of cash too, because many of them also sell small versions of those plants you'll see in the gardens.

My own list consists of those I think would fit best into a more natural design and those that I feel I couldn't live without. I have also excluded plants that will grow only in acid soils. If you want to grow rhododendrons, azaleas, pieris, skimmias and the like, make sure you do a soil test first or you're doomed to disappointment. Bear in mind, too, that many of the plants listed under 'Trees' (page 79) can also be grown as large shrubs.

Berberis darwinii *has bright golden-orange flowers in spring.*

Arbutus Strawberry tree
See page 83.

Artemisia Lad's love
Silver-foliage shrub that revels in a hot, sunny spot and must have excellent drainage, this will survive on heavy land only if the soil is raised and drained by the incorporation of quantities of coarse grit. It's well worth per-severing with for its finely cut, silver leaves. Look out for the varieties 'Lambrook Silver' and 'Powis Castle'. In cold winters they may die back and it's best to prune them hard back in spring to encourage brighter young leaves. They'll grow to about 60cm–1.2m (2–4ft).

Aucuba japonica Spotted laurel
Every dull, dreary Victorian front garden grew one of these, so they became much despised. However, new varieties are much

brighter and they're enjoying a deserved comeback. The glossy, green leaves of newer varieties are spotted and splashed with bright gold. They'll grow in sun or very dense shade in most soils to about 2.1–3m (7–10ft). Among the best varieties are the boldly marked 'Picturata' and 'Mr Goldstrike'.

Berberis Barberry
A really valuable group of both evergreen and deciduous (see page 98) shrubs, they'll grow almost anywhere, are as hardy as nails and never fail to flower. All have prickles or sometimes quite vicious spikes.

Berberis candidula forms a low, mounded bush with shiny, green leaves that are blue underneath. It produces masses of bright yellow flowers in late spring followed by purple berries.

B. darwinii has attractive, arching branches covered in orange flowers in late spring. It'll grow to about 2.1m (7ft), but can be kept smaller by pruning after flowering.

B. julianae grows to about 2.4m (8ft) and bears yellow flowers. It makes an excellent, impenetrable hedge but is too thorny for places where you might come into frequent contact.

B. lologensis is one of the best hybrids with glossy, green foliage and large, apricot flowers. It grows to about 2.4m (8ft). The varieties 'Apricot Queen' and 'Gertrude Hardijzer' are especially recommended.

B. stenophylla is one of the best-known species with arching branches covered in small, yellow flowers in late spring. It grows to about 2.4m (8ft) and is often used for informal hedging. The variety 'Claret Cascade' is lower-growing, to about 1.2m (4ft), and spreading as wide. It has orange flowers stained purple and the new shoots and leaves have a purplish-red hue. 'Cream Showers' grows to about 1.8m (6ft) and has cream flowers.

Brachyglottis 'Sunshine' Senecio

An attractive, grey-leaved shrub, still often sold as *Senecio greyii,* this grows to about 90cm (3ft) and bears masses of bright yellow, daisy flowers over a long period in summer. It must have a sunny, well-drained situation and should be lightly pruned in spring to keep it compact. If plants get straggly, cut them hard back in spring.

Camellia

See page 76. Some camellias are slightly tender and it's best in colder areas to stick with varieties of *Camellia japonica* and *C. williamsii*. Heights vary considerably according to variety, so check these carefully when buying plants for the open border. Most you'll be offered at the garden centre will grow fairly slowly to about 3m (10ft), but if they're happy some will become very large. They vary in flower colour from white, like the excellent single variety *C. japonica* 'Alba Simplex', with a striking central cluster of yellow stamens, through pink like the best-known of all, *C. williamsii* 'Donation', to brilliant red like *C. japonica* 'Grand Prix'.

Ceanothus Californian lilac

These superb flowering shrubs are often recommended for growing on walls (see page 76), but there are two in particular that are highly recommended for the open border. 'Blue Mound', as the name suggests, produces a mound of glossy, evergreen foliage about 75cm (30in) high and covered with light blue flowers in spring and often again in autumn. *Ceanothus thyrsiflorus repens* is quite different in habit, making a vigorously spreading mound about 90cm (3ft) high and twice as wide. It's covered in deep blue, bottlebrush flowers in spring and early summer.

Choisya ternata Mexican orange blossom

See page 77. A new hybrid ,'Aztec Pearl', has pink buds opening to white flowers and is definitely worthwhile.

Cistus Sun rose

A small shrub, growing generally to about 90cm (3ft), with greyish foliage and a succession of lovely, often attractively marked, single flowers. It must have full sunshine and well-drained soil, but does well on chalky land. It doesn't transplant well, so buy it pot-grown and avoid replanting them later. It also tends to be rather short-lived and will not regrow from old wood, but don't let that put you off.

Among the many varieties, the following are especially worth checking out at a nursery: *Cistus purpureus* has crimson flowers with a maroon blotch contrasting with yellow stamens; *C. aguilari* 'Maculatus' bears superb white flowers with blotches of crimson and central rings of yellow and orange; *C.* 'Silver Pink' produces large clusters of silver-pink flowers and is very hardy; and *C. hybridus*, still often sold as *C. × corbariensis* for its flowers of pure white that open from crimson buds, is one of the hardiest of all.

Coronilla valentina

A small shrub growing to about 1.5m (5ft) and producing superb, yellow, pea-like, scented flowers from mid-spring, this needs full sun and good drainage. In late winter cut back old or damaged shoots to ground level.

Cotoneaster

A large and valuable group of shrubs which will grow almost anywhere and are well suited to this type of garden. They have smallish leaves, sometimes deciduous and sometimes evergreen. In colder districts in cold years, some of the evergreens may lose their leaves; however, they will soon replace them in spring. They produce white spring flowers, but their most noticeable asset is their prolific berries in late summer and autumn. They grow well in sun or shade, so the prostrate types are often used for ground cover. However some, like the popular *Cotoneaster dammeri*, will root as they spread and can become quite a nuisance: not recommended for small gardens.

C. franchetii has a spreading habit and grows to about 2.4m (8ft) in height. It bears brilliant red berries.

C. lacteus has darker red berries and is distinguished by its attractive foliage, green above and silvery beneath.

C. microphyllus is a much smaller, rounded shrub growing to about 60cm (2ft) and again produces red berries.

C. salicifolius reaches about 3m (10ft) in height with slender, arching branches and copious, bright red berries.

Cytisus Broom

Few shrubs will give the sheer mass of colour afforded by brooms. They grow in most soils and prefer full sun. They're relatively short-lived and can become untidy, so prune them with shears after flowering, but avoid cutting into old wood.

Cytisus kewensis has a low, spreading habit, growing to about 30cm (1ft). It has creamy white flowers in early summer, while its variety 'Niki' has yellow flowers.

C. praecox (Warminster broom) is a superb shrub, especially for small gardens. It reaches about 1.5m (5ft) and has creamy yellow flowers. Look out too for the varieties 'Albus', which bears white blooms; 'Allgold', yellow; 'Hollandia', cream and cerise; and 'Zeelandia', pink and white.

Elaeagnus Oleaster

A bright shrub with green foliage generously variegated with golden yellow, it prefers sun but will grow in most soils. It reaches about 1.8m (6ft) in height. *Elaeagnus ebbingei* 'Gilt Edge' is margined yellow, while 'Limelight' has a yellow centre.

E. pungens 'Maculata', the most widely planted, has leaves splashed and blotched with gold, while 'Goldrim' has yellow margins. All varieties can be kept bushier if shoots are pruned by a third in late winter.

The wooden carving looks just right in this natural woodland setting, with native plants like foxgloves to balance the artifice.

Escallonia

Often used for hedging, this attractive evergreen will grow in most soils that are well drained. It prefers sun and is excellent near the sea. It grows to about 1.5m (5ft). It produces plenty of colourful, tubular flowers in several colours from white to crimson, so choose from the nursery. 'Apple Blossom' is pink and very free-flowering; 'C. F. Ball' is crimson; 'Donard Brilliance' is free-flowering and red; 'Donard Seedling' is pink and white; and 'Slieve Donard' is shell-pink.

Fatshedera lizei Aralia ivy
See page 78.

Fatsia japonica

Related and rather similar to *Fatshedera lizei*, with large, palm-like, glossy, green leaves. It grows to about 4m (13ft), but can be kept smaller by pruning in spring. Cut straggly stems hard back to the base to encourage young growth. It needs a spot sheltered from cold winds but has the great advantage that it thrives in quite deep shade.

Garrya eliptica Silk tassel bush
See page 78.

Hebe

A superb, free-flowering evergreen, many varities of which are tender. Choose carefully and give them a sunny, sheltered spot. They do grow out well from old wood, so damage can be cut away in spring.

Hebe albicans 'Red Edge' is a fine new introduction. It makes a compact bush about 45cm (18in) tall and 60cm (2ft) across. The blue-green leaves are attractively margined red and there's the bonus of white flowers in summer.

H. 'Amy' has purplish foliage and blue flowers; 'Autumn Glory' is an old favourite with purple foliage and flowers; 'Baby Marie' bears masses of pale pink and white flowers over a very long period; 'Great Orme' has pink flowers; 'Nicola's Blush' is pale pink fading to white; and 'Primley Gem', sometimes sold as 'Margery Fish', produces violet-blue flowers over a long period.

Ilex Holly

There's a very wide range of varieties, most of which make ideal evergreen shrubs for this type of garden. They also provide food and homes for butterflies, other insects and birds too. Most hollies require a male and a female variety to effect pollination, but there are a few self-fertile varieties. They're very tolerant of soil and situation. They'll grow to about 20m (65ft), but can easily be pruned to keep them to a size suitable for small gardens and, indeed, they can be clipped to make formal topiary specimens. They're also excellent hedging plants.

Ilex altaclerensis has several excellent varieties. 'Golden King' is, believe it or not, a female form, producing lots of red berries provided it's pollinated. As with all variegated holly, keep an eye open for green shoots and cut them off straight away. 'Belgica Aurea', sometimes sold as 'Silver Sentinel', has grey leaves edged with cream or yellow plus orange fruits, while 'Lawsoniana' bears green leaves with a central yellow splash.

I. aquifolium is a European native, so almost obligatory for British gardens. Apart from the normal green, there are several variegated varieties. 'Argentea Marginata' has silver edges to the leaves; 'Silver Queen' (yes, it's a male!) produces grey-green leaves edged with cream; and 'Handsworth New Silver' has purple shoots and white-edged leaves. 'J. C. van Tol' bears shining, green leaves and is self-fertile, so always produces good crops of berries.

I. meserveae is known as the blue holly for its blue-green leaves on purplish shoots. 'Blue Prince' and Blue Princess' are the hardiest varieties and both produce red berries. It would pay to visit a nursery when choosing.

Lavandula Lavender

A well-known and indispensable plant for this type of garden – indeed, for any garden. It bears attractive, grey, aromatic foliage and plentiful blue or white flowers over a long period in summer. It must have a sunny spot and well-drained soil; on heavy land, to avoid problems, dig in a large quantity of coarse grit and good garden compost before planting. Even with these precautions the plant will be shorter-lived on heavy soil, so take cuttings every few years to renew it. It's also essential to cut back last year's growth in early spring each year to keep the plant compact. If you want a lavender hedge, as I did for the country garden, you can reduce costs by growing the plants from seed sown in gentle heat in late winter or early spring. Unchecked, they'll grow to about 75cm (30in).

Lavandula angustifolia is the common lavender, sometimes called Old English lavender, though it isn't English at all. There are several good varieties. 'Hidcote' is one of the best-known compact ones, with violet flowers. 'Munstead' is also compact and has bluer flowers, while 'Grappenhall' bears flowers of the true lavender colour and is more robust. 'Lady' is an excellent variety to raise from seed since it seems to come very uniform this way. 'Alba' bears white flowers, while those of 'Hidcote Pink' and 'Loddon Pink' are, as you would expect, pink.

L. stoechas pedunculata (French lavender) bears quite different flowers, still with the lavender colour but curiously shaped with 'ears' of purple bracts arising from the top of the flower. It's not quite as hardy as the others.

French lavender (Lavendula stoechas) *has curious twisted ears on its flowers.*

Ligustrum ovalifolium Privet

This is a well-known plant for hedging, but the variegated forms make excellent shrubs too. They'll grow absolutely anywhere in almost any soil. They reach about 3m (10ft), but are easily controlled by pruning and can even be shaped into topiary. In this form they were great favourites of country cottage gardeners who fashioned them into a whole range of interesting and sometimes eccentric shapes.

The plain green variety is unexciting and also very competitive, but the variety 'Aureum' is green with a yellow splash while 'Argenteum' is variegated creamy white.

The hybrid 'Vicaryi' has attractive golden foliage which turns purple in winter. It's best pruned back in spring to encourage better-coloured new growth.

Mahonia

An interesting range of evergreens, some with superb architectural foliage and all with good, mostly winter flowers.

Mahonia aquifolium (Oregon grape) is not the most decorative of the range, but is superb for growing in dry, shady places under trees or in sunshine. It has glossy, green foliage and bright yellow flowers in spring. The somewhat more compact variety 'Apollo' bears larger flowers, and 'Atropurpurea' has purple winter foliage.

Varieties of *M. media* grow to about 3m (10ft) and have fine, deeply cut foliage and large spikes of scented, yellow flowers in winter. They do best in light shade with some protection from cold winds. The varieties 'Charity' and 'Winter Sun' are both good.

Phlomis fruticosa Jerusalem sage

A woolly, grey-leaved shrub growing to about 90cm (3ft) and producing whorls of bright yellow flowers in summer. It needs a warm, sunny position and a well-drained soil.

Phormium New Zealand flax

Anywhere a touch of the exotic is needed, this is the plant to provide it. It needs sunshine and a well-drained soil, and different forms vary in hardiness, though many are suitable for all but the coldest gardens. It's best to buy from a local nursery or garden centre. All varieties form a clump of spiky, striped foliage and some will, on older plants in a good summer, produce great spikes of exotic flowers.

Varieties of *Phormium tenax* are among the hardiest and grow to about 1.5m (5ft). Look out for 'Purpureum' with glossy, bronze leaves, 'Radiance' with creamy yellow stripes and 'Sundowner' with stripes of grey, red and pink.

There are several good hybrids and new ones coming along all the time. They're slightly smaller at about 60cm–1.2m (2–4ft).

'Maori Chief' has leaves of red, maroon and bronze; 'Dazzler' is striped maroon and carmine; and 'Cream Delight' has a central band of creamy yellow.

Photinia fraseri 'Red Robin'

Grown mainly for its superb, glossy, green leaves and particularly for its bright red, young foliage in spring which lasts right through the summer. It prefers good garden soil and a sunny or lightly shaded spot and reaches about 3m (10ft) in height. However, it can be controlled by pruning, which should be done in early spring to encourage strong, new, young growth which will have the best colour.

Santolina chamaecyparissus Cotton lavender

Filigree silver or green foliage topped by small, yellow, button flowers make this an attractive shrub for a sunny, well-drained spot. It grows to about 60cm (2ft), but tends to become straggly after a few years. Cutting back hard to remove all old growth each spring will keep it compact and slightly shorter. It makes an excellent dwarf hedge too.

Santolina virens is an interesting variation with bright green foliage contrasting well with the yellow flowers.

Sarcococca Sweet box

This genus of small, mainly suckering shrubs, which do well in even quite deep shade, have little to offer in summer but in winter are covered in small, highly scented, white or pale pink flowers.

Sarcococca hookeriana digyna produces its fragrant, pink flowers from mid-winter to early spring. You may need to control it by cutting out suckers with a spade. It grows to about 1.2m (4ft). *S. humilis* grows to only 45cm (18in) and bears fragrant, white flowers, while *S. ruscifolia chinensis* is similar but more vigorous, reaching about 90cm (3ft).

Viburnum

Several species of this large genus are evergreen and well suited to this type of garden. Most will grow in any good garden soil and ask only protection from cold winds. Prune in spring only if it's necessary to shape the bush and prevent it from becoming overcrowded.

Viburnum burkwoodii is a superb, medium-sized shrub, growing to about 1.8m (6ft). The foliage is shining green with a greyish brown, felted reverse and it bears fragrant clusters of white flowers opening from pink buds from early to late spring. The varieties 'Fulbrook' and 'Park Farm Hybrid' produce slightly larger flowers a little later.

Hardy cyclamen thrive in a woodland setting.

V. davidii forms a compact, rounded bush about 75cm (30in) tall. Its leaves are shiny, green and corrugated. The white flowers are rather dull, but if you plant a few bushes, you'll be rewarded with prolific, metallic-blue berries in autumn. It's possible to buy male and female plants to ensure pollination. They do best in light shade.

V. tinus is a fine evergreen with attractive, green foliage and masses of white flowers opening from pink buds. It grows to about 2.4m (8ft), but can be restricted in size by quite hard pruning in mid- to late spring. It prefers sun, yet will grow in light shade. Look for the improved variety 'Eve Price' which is slightly smaller and has fragrant, white flowers opening from red buds over a very long period from late autumn to mid-spring.

DECIDUOUS SHRUBS

Evergreens are, of course, invaluable to add sparkle and interest to the winter garden, but if you grew them exclusively, you'd be missing a lot. Some shrubs that lose their leaves have very attractive bark colour in winter or fine architectural shapes that look as interesting without leaves as they do with them. Others pay their way with extra flower or superb foliage in the spring and summer months.

As in the selection of evergreens, I have had to restrict myself to the relatively few plants that you really shouldn't be without, so don't take it as the final, definitive list

Again, I have excluded acid-lovers like the lovely Japanese maples. I believe that the essence of a garden built for relaxation and the refreshment of the spirit is to make life easy by working with nature. While it would certainly be possible to grow acid-lovers on limy soil by raising the beds and using acid compost or by growing in containers and watering with rainwater, it simply defeats the object of the garden. In any case there are always good alternatives to the acid-lovers which will give you no such troubles. If, on the other hand, you're blessed with acid soil, your horizons are virtually limitless. You'd be well advised to cock a snook at us lesser mortals and grow the woodland rhododendrons, pieris, acers, azaleas and the rest. Who could blame you?

Aesculus parviflora Buckeye

A fairly large, suckering shrub that, if growing well, may need controlling by having suckers cut out with a spade. In sun or light shade and in moisture-retentive soil, it'll form a thicket of stems bearing heavily scented, white flowers with conspicuous, red anthers in summer. Under ideal conditions it'll grow to about 3m (10ft).

Arbutus Strawberry tree
See page 83.

Berberis Barberry

A large and varied genus of prickly, berried, both deciduous and evergreen (see page 90) shrubs, all of which are very accommodating in terms of soil and situation. They're also very hardy, so make a good first line of defence against wind, and all provide homes and food for wildlife.

Berberis carminea varieties are grown for their autumn leaf colour and highly coloured fruits. They'll do well in sun or part-shade in any garden soil, suckering to produce thorny thickets. You may find you need to control them by digging out suckers. The variety 'Barbarossa' produces brilliant red fruit and grows to 1.8m (6ft); 'Buccaneer' is a little shorter and has bright carmine berries; and 'Pirate King' is the same height and bears bright orange fruits.

B. media 'Red Jewel' is a smaller shrub reaching about 1.2m (4ft). It bears clusters of single, yellow flowers in spring, and in autumn the almost-spineless leaves turn rich, metallic purple and bronze.

B. ottawensis 'Superba' is one not to miss. A fine, deciduous shrub growing to about 1.8m (6ft), with rounded leaves of bronze-purple, it bears yellow flowers in spring followed by rather sparse red berries.

B. thunbergii bears yellow flowers followed by dark purple berries and grows to about 2.4m (8ft). It has several varied and valuable varieties. 'Atropurpurea' reaches 1.8m (6ft) and has purple-red leaves, with the best colour coming from plants in sunshine. It has good autumn leaf colour too. Its smaller counterpart, 'Atropurpurea Nana', makes a rounded bush about 45cm (18in) tall. A bright golden form, 'Aurea', needs sunshine and shelter from cold winds. 'Red Chief' and 'Red

Pillar' grow to about 1.5m (5ft) and have red stems and leaves. 'Golden Ring' bears reddish purple leaves with a distinct gold ring and grows to 1.8m (6ft). 'Rose Glow' is slightly shorter and has possibly been infected with a virus to give it variegations of cream and pink. Since the best colour comes from new growth, prune hard in spring.

B. wilsoniae, with bluish green leaves, grows to about 1.5m (5ft). Its large clusters of coral-pink fruit contrast well with the autumn foliage.

Buddleia Butterfly bush

A medium to large shrub, renowned for its ability to attract butterflies.

Buddleia alternifolia is a large shrub with a somewhat weeping habit, becoming covered in fragrant, lilac flowers in summer. It grows to about 3m (10ft). After flowering, prune the current season's growth by about a third.

B. davidii is well known, making a tall shrub which can be reduced by pruning to about 2.4m (8ft). The long, conical flowers are fragrant and very attractive to insects. There are several colours, depending on variety, from 'White Profusion', through 'Nanho Blue' to the lilac-pink 'Fascinating' and the deep purple 'Black Knight'. All should be pruned back to two or three buds in late winter.

B. weyeriana bears quite unusual, scented, orange flowers. Look out for the variety 'Sungold'. It grows to 2.4m (8ft) and should be lightly pruned in spring.

Caryopteris clandonensis Blue spiraea

A lovely, aromatic shrub for a well-drained soil and a sunny spot. Prune back hard in spring to about 15cm (6in) of the ground to produce new growth and more blooms. It'll bear bright blue flowers over a long period in late summer and grow to about 75cm (30in). The variety 'Heavenly Blue' is certainly the best.

Ceanothus Californian lilac

The evergreen varieties of this superb shrub are listed on page 91, but there are a few French varieties worth growing if you have a sunny, sheltered spot. 'Gloire de Versailles' is the best known with powder-blue flowers, while 'Topaz' is indigo-blue and 'Marie Simon' bears pink flowers. All grow to about 1.8m (6ft) and should be pruned hard in late spring.

Ceratostigma willmottianum Hardy plumbago

An upright shrub needing sun and well-drained soil, this grows to about 90cm (3ft) and bears bright blue flowers in late summer and autumn when the foliage also colours well. Prune it hard to the ground in late spring.

Cestrum parqui Willow-leaved jessamine

A slightly tender shrub worth growing for its spikes of night-scented, yellow flowers. It grows to about 1.2m (4ft) in a well-drained, warm spot. Frost may cut it down, but it generally recovers to flower again from early to mid-summer. Cut it back hard in early spring.

Chaenomeles Flowering quince

See page 77.

Cornus Dogwood/cornel

A large group, some grown for their foliage, some for flowers and others for winter bark colour.

Cornus alba (red-barked dogwood) has many good varieties. They form thickets of stems about 1.2m (4ft) high if pruned each spring to produce the best bark colour. They'll grow in most soils, preferring a sunny spot. 'Aurea' has leaves suffused with soft yellow; the foliage of 'Elegantissima' is splashed with creamy white against maroon stems ; 'Kesselringii' is grown for its dark

purple, winter stems; 'Sibirica' has coral-red bark and good autumn leaf colour; while 'Sibirica Variegata' has deep red stems and leaves with creamy margins. 'Spaethii' bears outstanding gold-variegated leaves.

C. alternifolia 'Argentea' is a fine, silver-variegated shrub which grows with layered, tiered branches. It will reach about 3m (10ft) high.

C. mas (cornelian cherry) is a valuable late-winter-flowering shrub suitable for most soils in sun or part-shade. It grows to about 1.8m (6ft) and is covered in small, yellow flowers on naked twigs followed by bright red, edible fruits and good autumn foliage colour. The variety 'Variegata' has leaves margined with white.

C. sanguinea 'Winter Beauty' bears green leaves that turn yellow in autumn, but is grown for its superb winter bark colour of orange-yellow and red. It grows to about 1.5m (5ft) and should be pruned hard in late spring.

C. stolonifera 'Flaviramea' is often grown with the *C. alba* varieties for the contrast of its bright yellow bark. The variety 'White Gold' has leaves margined with white.

See also the flowering varieties on page 83.

Cotinus coggygria **Smoke bush**

A superb, large shrub that grows to about 3m (10ft), though it can be pruned to keep it smaller. Cutting back hard in spring will also enlarge the size of the attractive leaves, but there will be none of the fluffy, beige-pink flowers that float over the plant in late summer, giving it its common name. The species has light green leaves, turning yellow or red in autumn. The variety 'Royal Purple' is the most common red-leaved one, but look

---

Deutzia magnifica 'Pride of Rochester' *has particularly large white flowers.*

out too for 'Velvet Cloak' which bears very dark, almost black leaves and for 'Grace' which has very large, reddish purple foliage and is, I think, the best of the lot.

Cotoneaster

A large and very useful group which will grow in most soils and situations. See also the evergreens on page 92.

Cotoneaster adpressus is a low-growing, spreading shrub that reaches 30cm (1ft), with white spring flowers followed by bright red berries and scarlet autumn foliage.

C. bullatus is one of the best. It grows to about 2.4m (8ft), with white flowers on arching branches and corrugated leaves which turn red in autumn together with bright red berries.

C. 'Cornubia', which is semi-evergreen, is grown for its masses of bright red autumn berries.

C. 'Exburiensis' grows to 3m (10ft) and bears white flowers in spring followed in autumn by pendulous clusters of pale yellow berries becoming tinged with pink.

C. horizontalis is well known for its herringbone-patterned branches covered in red berries in autumn. It can be used as ground cover or can be induced to grow up close against a wall where it'll reach about 1.5m (5ft).

C. 'Hybridus Pendulus' is generally seen grafted on to a tall stem and grown as a small tree. Its glossy, green leaves and red berries in autumn make it very effective.

Daphne

This group includes some of the best perfumed shrubs around, though some are quite a challenge to grow and most are short-lived. All benefit from a retentive soil, so dig in manure or compost when planting and mulch regularly. I would include two that have proved fairly trouble-free. *Daphne burkwoodii* 'Albert Burkwood' has deliciously scented, pink flowers in clusters all along its branches from spring to early summer and again in autumn. The variety 'Somerset' has slightly paler flowers. They grow to 1.2m (4ft).

D. mezereum (mezereon) is well known for its superb perfume from deep, purple-pink flowers in late winter. The variety 'Alba' has white flowers, while 'Rubra' is reddish-purple. They grow to 90cm (3ft).

Deutzia

An easy, uncomplaining shrub that will always reward you with masses of flowers, this likes a fertile soil in sun or part-shade. Prune after flowering, removing a third of the older wood to encourage new shoots from the base.

Deutzia elegantissima bears clusters of pink flowers in summer. Look out for the variety 'Rosealind' with deeper pink, scented flowers. It grows to about 1.2m (4ft).

There are several excellent hybrids, the most popular being the very free-flowering 'Montrose', which has clear pink, starry flowers with yellow anthers. 'Magicien' has red buds opening to deep pink flowers, while 'Pink Pompon' bears double pink flowers that fade to white. They grow to about 1.8m (6ft).

D. scabra is a vigorous species, also with some well worthwhile varieties. 'Candidissima' produces double, white flowers; 'Pride of Rochester' is also double, pink outside and white inside, while 'Flore Pleno' is much the same but slightly darker. They'll grow to 2.4m (8ft).

A lower-growing, new variety, 'Nikko', is excellent where space is restricted. It has a spreading habit to about 60cm (2ft) and is covered in clusters of white flowers over a long period in the late spring and early summer.

Exochorda Bridal wreath

In spring, when this shrub is covered in the purest white flowers, it's nothing short of breathtaking. The commonest and the best for smaller gardens is *Exochorda macrantha* 'The Bride', which grows to about 1.5m (5ft) and has a slightly weeping habit. *E. giraldii* grows a bit taller and has larger flowers borne on pinkish stems. These shrubs can tend to become untidy, so prune them to tidy them up. Since they flower on wood they made the year before, this is best done just after flowering.

Forsythia

A common plant, but with very good reason. It's easy to grow and it never fails to be wreathed in bright yellow flowers in early spring when there's not much else about. It grows in almost any soil and prefers sun. Reaching about 2.4m (8ft) if given the chance, it should be pruned soon after flowering: remove a third of the old shoots and generally tidy up the plant. 'Lynwood' is the most popular variety with large, bright flowers, 'Beatrix Farrand' and 'Karl Sax' have somewhat deeper yellow flowers, while 'Spectabilis' is an older variety with perhaps the most prolific flowering. For the smaller garden, look for 'Golden Nugget' which is very free-flowering and grows to only 1.5m (5ft) in height.

Forsythia suspensa is rather a lax plant and so tends to become untidy, but it's absolutely covered in flower in spring, so is well worth growing. It reaches 1.8m (6ft).

Fuchsia

The hardy cousins of the pot-plant fuchsias have all their merits and no disadvantages. They prefer a sunny spot and retentive, well-drained soil. In winter they're likely to be cut to the ground, but in most areas will recover to shoot again in spring. In the coldest parts it's worth covering the plants with a mulch of compost, straw or bracken. The hardy varieties grow to about 90cm–1.2m (3–4ft) and should be pruned in early spring, when the old shoots need cutting right down to ground level.

There are many good varieties, so a trip to the nursery is best. Look out for *Fuchsia magellanica* 'Aurea' with yellow leaves and red flowers; 'Pumila' with crimson and purple flowers; and 'Versicolor' with leaves flushed pink and cream.

There are several good hybrids too. 'Mrs Popple' is very hardy with crimson and purple blooms; 'Tom Thumb' is also crimson and purple and a little smaller; 'Alice Hoffman' is red and white; and 'Chillerton Beauty' is pink and purple.

Genista

Closely related to broom, this late-spring- and summer-flowering shrub loves a sunny, well-drained spot and is very soil-tolerant.

Genista aetnensis (Mount Etna broom) grows to about 3m (10ft) and makes a spectacular show of brilliant yellow flowers in late summer.

G. hispanica (Spanish broom) makes rounded hummocks about 60cm (2ft) high and is also covered in yellow flowers, but in late spring. It has the disadvantage of being extremely prickly.

G. pilosa is a British native and has a quite different habit, spreading to cover a wide area with yellow in early summer. Though it grows only about 23cm (9in) high, it can spread as much as 1.5m (5ft). The varieties 'Lemon Spreader' and 'Vancouver Gold' are worth searching out.

G. lydia is another spreader, but this time with more arching branches, and grows to about 60cm (2ft). It flowers in the early summer.

Hamamelis Witch hazel

One of the best taller-growing shrubs for fragrant, winter flowers. Most species and varieties will reach about 2.4m (8ft) and will be successful in any good garden soil that's not too chalky. Dig in lots of organic matter before planting and mulch regularly. If it's necessary, prune after flowering.

Hamamelis intermedia includes a group of highly coloured hybrids which really need careful planting to show off the flowers to their best effect. Look out for the yellow 'Arnold Promise', the copper-orange 'Jelena' and the yellow 'Westerstede'.

The best variety by far of *H. mollis*, and indeed the best and most popular of them all, is the yellow 'Pallida'.

Hydrangea

This is a large and diverse genus containing many different habits and colours. For the type of garden we're interested in here, I feel that the common mop-head varieties look somehow too overbred and artificial, so I would not include them. There are, however, others which should definitely not be missed. Some thrive in sun, but most prefer dappled shade and are therefore ideal for planting at the outer edge of the spread of trees. All will reward you for a moist soil, so dig in organic matter at planting and mulch.

Hydrangea arborescens will grow happily in quite deep shade, but flowers better in some – even full – sunshine. It flowers on the current season's growth, so prune hard in spring. The best and most compact variety is 'Annabelle' which is covered in huge, white flowers up to 30cm (1ft) across in late summer and autumn.

H. macrophylla is the species that contains the mop-head types which I have excluded. However, it also boasts the superb lacecaps, which bear a central cluster of florets surrounded by a circle of much more eye-catching ones. These like dappled shade and they flower on wood they made the previous season, so the spring pruning consists of cutting back growths that have flowered to new wood and, on older plants, removing a small proportion of old wood right to the ground to encourage new. They reach a height of about 1.5m (5ft).

'Blue Wave' is one of the best and most popular varieties; it has blue flowers surrounded by a ring of pink florets if grown on limy soil, blue if grown on acid soil. 'Geoffrey Chadbund' is brick-red in lime or purple on acid soil; 'Lanarth White' is one of the best with pink or blue flowers surrounded by pure white florets; 'Maculata' is unusual in that it's grown for its fine,

The brick red flowers of Hydrangea
'Geoffrey Chadbund'.

yellow-variegated leaves (the white flowers are unprepossessing); 'Mariesii' is pink or blue; and 'Tricolour' has attractive foliage variegated green, grey and pale yellow, with plentifully produced, white flowers. 'White Wave' bears pink or blue flowers surrounded by creamy white florets; it's slightly smaller and flowers better in sunshine.

H. paniculata varieties form large shrubs to about 3m (10ft), but can be pruned to size as required. They flower in summer. Pruning increases the flower size, though it is perhaps best done every two or three years to produce a more shapely bush. In early spring cut back last year's growths to about two buds. The flower heads are large, upright and conical. 'Grandiflora' is a superb variety with large heads of white fading to soft pink; 'Kyushu' is a popular variety with glossy leaves and creamy white flowers; 'Pink Diamond' has very large, white flower heads turning pink.

H. serrata is a much smaller shrub, growing to about 90cm (3ft) and well worth garden space. The flat flower heads consist of a central flower cluster of white or blue with a circle of white, pink or blue florets which often turn crimson in autumn. Grow them like *H. macrophylla* varieties. 'Belle Deckle' has blue or pink florets; 'Bluebird' is larger with dark blue central flowers surrounded by lighter blue or reddish purple ray florets; 'Grayswood' is one of the best, with blue flowers surrounded by white florets changing to pink and then crimson; 'Preziosa' makes rounded heads of pink flowers deepening to crimson-purple in autumn.

Hypericum
Invaluable, easy-to-grow shrubs with large, bright yellow flowers, followed by coloured berries. They're happy in full sun or part-shade and in most soils. You can reduce them in size and tidy them up by cutting back shoots by

about a third in the autumn or early spring and rejuvenate the plants by cutting them close to the ground every three years or so. Unfortunately some – especially *Hypericum calycinum* and *H. inodorum* – are increasingly subject to rust.

H. androsaemum (tutsan hypericum) has smallish, yellow flowers with prominent stamens followed by maroon fruits sometimes turning black. It grows to about 90cm (3ft). Two varieties, 'Dart's Golden Penny' and 'Hysan', are free-flowering and worth looking out for.

H. calycinum (rose of Sharon) is a low-growing ground-coverer, spreading by means of vigorous, underground runners. It can become a nuisance and should be grown only on banks or under trees where it can be easily controlled. Surrounding a bed with grass, for example, is an effective way to keep it in check. The variety 'Hidcote' is one of the most popular. It makes a vigorous bush about 1.5m (5ft) tall, covered with large flowers all summer. It bears no fruit.

H. inodorum has two especially good varieties: 'Elstead', which produces spectacular red berries in autumn, and 'Albury Purple', which has purple young leaves. Both, alas, are prone to rust, but I have had some success in controlling this by cutting them down to the ground each autumn.

Kolkwitzia amabilis **Beauty bush**

Very easy to grow in almost any soil in sun or part-shade, this produces clouds of lovely, pale pink trumpets with yellow throats over a long period in the early summer. It grows to 2.4m (8ft) in height. Prune congested bushes by removing up to a third of the older wood down to the base immediately after flowering. The variety 'Pink Cloud' has deeper pink flowers.

Lavatera thuringiaca **Tree mallow**

This medium-sized shrub is invaluable for most gardens. The well-known cottage-garden variety 'Rosea' is traditionally known and still sometimes sold as *Lavatera olbia*; it bears large, saucer-shaped, deep pink flowers all summer and autumn. There are better varieties now, including the popular 'Barnsley' which has white flowers with red centres fading to pink; it grows to about 3m (10ft). 'Burgundy Wine' is a little shorter and bears wine red flowers; 'Candy Floss' is pale pink; 'Ice Cool' is white with a pale green flush; 'Pink Frills' is semi-double and grows to only about 1.2m (4ft). Plants will often get hit by hard frost, which can cut them to the ground, but they'll usually shoot again, often not until summer. In spring prune back quite hard to leave only about 30cm (1ft) of the main stems and cut away any damaged wood. During the season, any shoots that revert should be removed.

Leycesteria formosa
Himalayan honeysuckle/nutmeg tree

An easy shrub for all soils that are not too dry and happy in sun or part-shade. Plant with plenty of organic matter and mulch regularly. The hollow stems are green and grow to about 1.8m (6ft). In late summer they bear white flowers on the ends of pendulous clusters of wine-red bracts. They can be pruned hard to the ground in spring to rejuvenate the plant and produce fresh, green shoots. Alternatively, for a taller bush, prune out a third of the older stems.

Magnolia
See page 85.

Nandina domestica 'Firepower'
Sacred bamboo

This is, in fact, not a bamboo, but is well worth

growing for its yellow-green leaves which turn red or purple in autumn. In very hot summers it produces plumes of white flowers followed by red fruits. It needs a sheltered position in full sun and grows to about 45cm (18in).

Perovskia atriplicifolia 'Blue Spire' Russian sage

A valuable shrub for a sunny, well-drained spot, this grows to about 1.5m (5ft). It has attractive, grey foliage, almost white stems and in late summer and autumn is covered in blue, lavender-like flowers. Prune to 15cm (6in) from the ground in spring.

Philadelphus Mock orange

A popular and widely grown shrub invaluable for its saucer-shaped, scented, white flowers in summer. It's easy to grow in most soils in sunshine, but it'll handsomely repay a bit of coddling. Plant with plenty of organic matter, mulch regularly and feed with an organic fertilizer in spring. Prune after flowering by removing a third of the older wood to the base.

'Avalanche' is a fine hybrid growing to about 1.5m (5ft) with masses of small, single, highly scented, white flowers weighing down the branches in summer. 'Beauclerk' is slightly taller with larger flowers, white with a ring of red at the base and highly fragrant. 'Belle Etoile' grows to about 1.8m (6ft) and bears carmine-centred flowers. 'Manteau d'Hermine' grows to 1.2m (4ft) and has double flowers. 'Virginal' grows to about 2.4m (8ft) and produces large, strongly scented, double, white flowers.

The species *Philadelphus coronarius* 'Aureus' is very different in that it's grown for its brilliant golden foliage, while the variety 'Variegatus' has white-edged leaves and white flowers. Both grow to 2.4m (8ft).

Physocarpus opulifolius 'Dart's Gold'

Grown for its bright yellow foliage, this small shrub is best pruned to within 30cm (1ft) of the ground in spring to encourage better leaf colour. It reaches about 1.5m (5ft). To retain the white, pink-flushed flowers, remove only a third of the shoots. It grows well in sunshine or part-shade and responds well to an annual mulch.

Potentilla Shrubby cinquefoil

A very hardy and easy-to-grow shrub for any soil, flowering especially well on poor land. Most varieties like full sunshine but reds and pinks tend to fade if not given some shade at the hottest part of the day. Prune by removing about a third of the oldest wood and, if the plant needs rejuvenating, it can be cut hard back in spring.

Potentilla fruticosa *'Tilford Cream' flowers all summer.*

Hybrids of *Potentilla davurica* and *P. fruticosa* are many and varied. Unless stated otherwise, those listed here grow to about 90cm–1.2m (3–4ft) and flower all summer. 'Abbotswood' is an especially reliable flowerer, producing masses of pure white flowers; 'Beesii' has yellow flowers and lovely silvery foliage and reaches about 45cm (18in); 'Dart's Golddigger' bears large, yellow flowers; 'Daydawn' is pink with cream overtones and fares best in shade; 'Elizabeth' is one of the best, with masses of rich yellow flowers; 'Goldfinger' grows to about 90cm (3ft) and has blue-green foliage and masses of yellow flowers; 'Katherine Dykes' grows to 1.8m (6ft) and bears light primrose-yellow flowers; 'Red Ace', which achieves a height of about 60cm (2ft), has orange-red flowers with cream backs and needs shade to prevent it fading to yellow; 'Tangerine' produces coppery yellow flowers and also is best in shade.

Ribes Flowering currant

Well-known and popular, early-spring-flowering shrubs, these bear tassels of flowers in varying colours, often on bare stems or just as the leaves begin to unfurl. They're easily grown in most soils in sun or part-shade. Prune annually, removing a third of the older wood and shortening weak stems.

Ribes odoratum grows to about 1.8m (6ft) and bears clear yellow flowers with a pronounced scent of cloves.

R. sanguineum is the popular flowering currant, with flowers varying from white to deep red and sometimes followed by black berries. There are several named varieties worth searching out. 'Albescens' has white flowers flushed pink; 'Brocklebankii' bears yellow leaves and pink flowers, is somewhat smaller and slower-growing and tends to burn in full

sun; 'King Edward VII' produces crimson flowers; 'Pulborough Scarlet' is deep red; 'Tydeman's White' is the best white-flowered variety.

See page 79 for varieties suitable for growing as wall shrubs.

Rosa Rose

See pages 53, 165, 174, 81 and 93.

Rubus Bramble

This is a very large family, but there are only two which interest us. Some of them can be very invasive, and therefore great care must be taken. They produce long, arching stems which root into the ground where they touch, so they can soon spread alarmingly and are not easy to get rid of.

Rubus cockburnianus 'Golden Vale' forms an arching clump about 1.8m (6ft) tall. The stems are purple and in winter become covered in an eye-catching white bloom. The leaves in summer are a beautiful, fresh yellow. Prune it hard in spring to encourage fresh, new growth.

R. thibetanus 'Silver Fern' grows to about 1.2m (4ft) with purplish stems covered in a white bloom. The attractive leaves are coarse-toothed and ferny, silvery above and white beneath. In winter the white stems are outstanding. Again, prune hard in late spring.

Salix Willow

Another large genus with many huge trees much too big for most gardens. However, some of these can be used if they are pruned back hard every year to encourage them to produce a thicket of young growth. Those with attractive bark are invaluable for winter colour and especially useful where the soil lies wet. Other species are naturally small and need little or no pruning.

Salix alba has two superb varieties for winter bark. 'Britzensis' has brilliant orange-scarlet bark, while 'Vitellina' is bright yellow. They must be pollarded back to a stump every year, when they'll produce much the best bark colour on shoots up to 2.4m (8ft).

S. daphnoïdes is also grown for its bark colour which is purple-violet overlaid with a striking, white bloom. Again, prune every year or at least every other year.

S. gracilistyla 'Melanostachys' has violet stems and the deepest red, almost black catkins. Prune it annually after flowering.

S. hastata 'Wehrhahnii' is a small shrub growing to 1.5m (5ft), with purplish stems that contrast with silvery catkins later turning yellow.

S. helvetica is a small shrub that reaches 60cm (2ft) to form an attractive dome of silver-grey leaves which are white beneath. It bears silver catkins in spring.

S. lanata is a low, spreading bush up to 1.2m (4ft) with rounded, silver-grey leaves and yellow, woolly catkins in spring.

Spiraea

A diverse range of flowering and foliage shrubs that are happy in most soils but repay the addition of organic matter before and after planting. They will tolerate either sun or light shade. Those grown mainly for their foliage will produce stronger colours if they're pruned hard to the ground in early spring every two or three years.

Spiraea arguta (bridal wreath) is a shrub that doesn't have much to commend it after its spring flowering, but it's well worth growing none the less. Its arching branches are wreathed with brilliant white flowers over a long period at a time when fresh colour is particularly welcome. It grows to 1.8m (6ft). Prune after flowering, removing a third of the older wood completely.

Syringa vulgaris
'Souvenir de Louis Späth'.

S. betulifolia is a dwarf shrub that forms mounds of reddish stems. The foliage is fresh green, turning red in autumn. The flat heads of white flowers appear in early summer. It grows to about 90cm (3ft). Prune hard in early spring.

S. billardii 'Triumphans' is a suckering shrub bearing attractive, conical heads of red flowers in summer. It grows to about 1.8m (6ft) and can become invasive, though it's easily controlled with a spade. Again, it can be pruned to the ground in early spring every few years.

S. japonica (Japanese spiraea) is certainly the most popular and most useful of the spiraeas. Confusingly, it used to be classed as *S. bumalda*. Those varieties that are primarily grown for their foliage colour can be pruned hard to the ground in early spring just before growth begins. 'Anthony Waterer' has green leaves, though is occasionally variegated with cream or pink. Its flat heads of rosy flowers last for a long time in summer. It grows to 1.2m (4ft). 'Dart's Red' is similar, but has deeper red flowers. 'Golden Princess' is an improvement on the popular 'Goldflame', growing to 90cm (3ft) and with bronze young shoots and clear yellow leaves and pink flowers, while 'Little Princess' reaches 60cm (2ft) and bears green leaves and pink flowers.

S. nipponica 'Snowmound' grows to about 1.8m (6ft) and has arching branches covered in masses of white flowers in late spring and early summer. Prune out a third of the older wood after flowering.

S. prunifolia 'Plena' produces lots of tight, double flowers like tiny, white roses along its branches over a long period in summer, followed by rich red autumn leaf colour. It too grows to about 1.8m (6ft). Prune out a third of the older wood after flowering.

Syringa Lilac

Lilac has been grown in gardens for generations and is still among our most popular shrubs. It thrives in chalky soils, so makes an excellent alternative to the showy rhododendrons, and its large flowers bear an exquisite perfume like none other. The one disadvantage with *Syringa vulgaris* (common lilac) is that it can sucker, so it's worthwhile searching out plants that have been micropropagated and do not have this problem. Lilac prefers full sun and benefits from regular mulching and an annual feed.

S. hyacinthiflora flowers in spring and grows to about 2.4m (8ft). The variety 'Esther Stanley' is one of the best, with red buds opening to slightly scented, pink flowers.

S. josiflexa 'Bellicent' is a tall, upright-growing plant bearing huge, conical clusters of rose-pink flowers. It grows to about 3m (10ft), but its upright habit makes it still a fine plant for a small garden.

S. meyeri 'Palibin' is often sold as a 'dwarf' lilac, though it will actually grow to 2.4m (8ft). Still, it's a suitable plant for small gardens. It flowers in spring and continues for a very long period during summer, producing large clusters of lilac-pink blooms.

S. prestoniae hybrids have been bred in Canada and make large, very hardy shrubs with abundant, fragrant flowers in early to mid-summer. 'Audrey' has deep pink flowers; 'Elinor' is purple in bud, opening to pale lavender; 'Isabella' is lilac-pink and 'Royalty' a deeper purple-pink. They grow to 3m (10ft).

S. vulgaris (common lilac) is widely grown. It makes a tall, bushy shrub, but expect to wait two to three years after planting for it to reach its full flowering potential. After flowering it's best to dead-head the plants, cutting back to a plump bud. To restrict growth, some branches can be cut back half-way immediately after flowering.

There are several attractive hybrids in a wide variety of colours. 'Charles Joly' has deep purple, double flowers; 'Congo' bears smallish flowers of lilac-red; 'Firmament' is lilac-blue and early-flowering; 'Katherine Havemeyer' bears deep lavender, double flowers fading to pink; 'Madame Lemoine' is a double white with cream buds; 'Masséna' is deep red-purple; 'Maud Notcutt' is pure white; 'Mrs Edward Harding' has double, red flowers shaded pink and is very prolific in flower. 'Président Grévy' is another double with huge, lilac-blue flowers; 'Primrose' is pale yellow with fairly small, only slightly scented flowers; 'Sensation' is purplish red edged with white (though inclined to revert); 'Souvenir de Louis Späth' is a superb wine-red.

Tamarix Tamarisk

A large shrub with a loose, somewhat untidy habit that thrives by the sea or, given sun and a retentive soil, inland.

Tamarix ramosissima, which used to be called *T. pentandra*, grows to about 3m (10ft) with reddish branches and is covered in tiny, pink flowers in late summer. Look out for the variety 'Rubra', which is the darkest pink and best. Prune in early spring, cutting back the previous year's growth to two buds.

T. tetandra flowers in spring when the arching branches are covered in pale pink flowers. Prune immediately after flowering.

Viburnum

A very large genus containing some of the most beautiful of flowering shrubs (for evergreen forms see page 97). Few are fussy about soil or situation but, as always, they'll repay good preparation, annual mulching and/or feeding. Little pruning is required, but plants may need shaping and should be thinned if they get overcrowded immediately after flowering.

Viburnum bodnantense is valued for its scented, winter flowers but has little to offer later. The most popular variety is 'Dawn', with deep pink buds opening to paler pink flowers along bare branches from autumn to spring. It grows to about 2.4m (8ft).

I've left out the fine species *V. carlesii* and *V. carlcephalum* since I believe they're inferior to the splendid *V. juddii* . It grows to about 1.5m (5ft) and in mid-spring produces many large clusters of superbly scented, pink-tinted white flowers. It has a better constitution than the other two and is less prone to greenfly attack.

V. opulus (guelder rose) is a European native often found growing wild in hedgerows. It reaches about 1.8m (6ft) and in early summer produces flat, white flowers rather like those of a lacecap hydrangea. These are followed in autumn by large clusters of shining, red fruits. The variety 'Aureum' has yellow leaves, but requires a slightly shaded spot to escape scorch.

'Compactum' grows to only about 1.2m (4ft) and is very free-flowering. 'Xanthocarpum' produces eye-catching, amber berries in autumn which become translucent as they age. *V. opulus* 'Roseum', which used to be 'Sterile' (snowball tree), produces lots of round, greenish white flower heads which mature to pure white. It does not fruit.

V. plicatum is a spreading shrub that needs space because much of its beauty lies in its growth habit. It produces layers of branches that give a tiered effect and when, in early summer, these are covered with large, white, lacecap flowers held upwards above the branches, it's a sight to be seen. The variety 'Lanarth' is a strong grower, but not as horizontally branched as 'Mariesii'. They'll grow to about 1.8m (6ft). The variety 'Rowallane' is slightly less vigorous and produces good crops of red fruits.

V. sargentii is a large, spreading shrub with lacecap-like flowers. Most are too spreading for smaller gardens; however, a newish variety, 'Onondaga', is ideal. It has an upright habit of growth to about 1.8m (6ft) and spreads to about half that. It has bronze shoots and deep maroon-purple leaves, and the red flower buds are surrounded by white florets.

Weigela

A very easily grown shrub preferring a sunny spot, but quite unfussy about soil. It produces tubular flowers in great profusion in summer and some forms have excellent coloured foliage too. Prune flowering types after they have bloomed by cutting out about a third of the older wood. Those grown primarily for their foliage can be cut hard back in spring to rejuvenate the plant and produce much better foliage colour, though the flowers will be lost.

Weigela florida grows to about 1.5m (5ft) with green leaves and red-pink flowers, paler inside. The variety 'Foliis Purpureis' has purple-flushed leaves and pink flowers; 'Tango' bears red flowers and purple foliage. 'Florida Variegata' is one of the best foliage shrubs with green leaves edged creamy yellow; the flowers are pink, but it's worth losing at least some of them to encourage new growth by pruning.

There are several excellent hybrids in a variety of flower colours. 'Abel Carrière' has red buds opening to pink and is very prolific; 'Bristol Ruby' bears brilliant red flowers; 'Eva Rathke' produces bright crimson flowers with yellow anthers; 'Evita' is smaller and spreading with red flowers; 'Looymansii Aurea' has pink flowers well set off by golden foliage and does best in shade; 'Mont Blanc' is the best of the whites; 'Newport Red' is like 'Eva Rathke' but with bigger red flowers. 'Olympiade', sold also as 'Rubidor' and 'Rubigold', bears golden leaves and red flowers; you should plant it in the shade to avoid scorch.

HERBACEOUS PERENNIALS

In the town garden I made for the television series I planted the herbaceous perennials in colour-themed borders, so I have listed these according to their colours in chapter 7.

Naturalized bluebells thrive under the trees.

Chapter five

WATER GARDENS

The earliest gardens dedicated to pleasure came from the East. There's evidence of ornamental gardening in Babylonia as long ago as the third millennium BC and later in Egypt and Assyria. In Greece in the fourth century BC there were flower gardens dedicated to the gods and these influenced gardening in Rome which, in turn, was to have a profound and longlasting effect on European garden design. In Spain the main influence came from Islam, when Arab armies conquered the southern and north-eastern territories. Evidence of the conquerors' art can still be seen today, notably in the breathtaking gardens of the Alhambra and Generalife at Granada.

What all these gardens had in common was that they existed in hot countries where water and shade were highly valued. Every garden was shaded by trees and had pools, canals or fountains to cool the air and to provide the relaxing sound of gently moving water. In fact the canals sometimes served in a practical capacity too. They were made of stone and often had holes in the sides to allow water to seep out into irrigation channels or directly on to the soil to water the borders.

In England medieval monasteries used water widely – first to raise fish for the kitchens, but also for its qualities of peace and tranquillity, conducive to reflection and contemplation. Indeed gardens universally were then considered special, almost holy places where the proximity of nature would direct the mind to higher things.

Of course, that quality remains to this day. Sit beside a country dew-pond, on banks shaded by trees and studded with wildflowers, watching a bird ripple the surface while washing the dust from its feathers. Listen as insects buzz around the surface and dragonflies flit from plant to plant, searching for a place to lay their eggs, and you'll very soon feel your tensions slip away. Alas, country ponds are now few and far between and access is often denied. All the more reason, then, to transport that idyllic country dew-pond to your own garden or even to travel further abroad and bring back the canals and fountains of the Alhambra to install in your own back yard. Certainly you'll have to reduce the scale and minimize the grandeur to suit a somewhat more

The still surface of the pool reflects the ever-changing patterns of the clouds, and the broad stone surround invites you to sit and let your tensions slip away.

humble setting. But your water feature will have exactly the same effect on your senses as it did on those of its Moorish designers all those years ago.

DESIGN

By the time you start to think about a water feature, you'll have long ago decided on the kind of garden you want to achieve. It's important to make it fit the overall design and never to allow it to become overwhelming. In the country garden, for example, a magnificent stone basin with fountains playing, underwater lighting and taped music by the Coldstream Guards would be a fraction over the top. It might be just the job for Buckingham Palace, but not for Bourton-on-the-Water. Our country dew-pond would fit this particular bill, and even then it should not dominate the garden.

You'll also have to decide whether or not you want moving water. The constant tinkle of running water irritates some people, who probably associate it with rain. Eastern gardeners, on the other hand, used to long periods of scorching drought, would have found the self-same sound delightful and optimistic. We all have our own preferences.

In the country garden, my aim is to create a tranquil, contemplative atmosphere and I would therefore rather keep the surface of the water still and limpid, with the sky reflected in its surface. You, on the other hand, might prefer to bubble a little water on the top from time to time, so you may wish to allow yourself that option by installing a pump, even though you won't use it all the time.

In the town garden slightly more formality is called for. Because the squareness of the plot and the high brick walls allow for a little of the Alhambra inspiration to be used, I fashioned a small, formal canal fed from a traditional lion's head. Even so, the 'moat' surrounding the gazebo is something of a hybrid between the formal and the informal.

You may feel that you don't want to go to the extreme of making a full-blown water feature yet still want an aquatic element, if only for its very effective, wildlife-attracting qualities. In that case the pond can be quite small, but then you'll have to take another factor into consideration. Small areas of water heat up quickly, providing perfect conditions for the growth of slimy, green algae. There's no pleasure in that. It's therefore vital to keep the water cool by choosing a shaded site for the pond, making it deeper than it is wide and sinking it in the ground.

I suppose the ultimate water feature for a country garden is a stream. It evokes memories of childhood adventures in most of us and it provides a movement and interest in the garden which enchant and soothe the imagination. Unlike that of the formal canal, the emphasis here must be on natural informality. If it even hints at being man-made, this sort of feature becomes kitsch and vulgar. It must wind lazily with the natural contours of the land, plants must spill over its sides and there should never be even a hint of visible concrete or plastic. Heaven forbid!

Finally, before you turn a spade of soil in your new plot, think carefully about whether or not you want moving water. If you do, you'll have to dig trenches for the electricity supply and, in the case of a stream or waterfall, for the pipes that carry the water from the pond to the entry point of the water. Get that disruption over first and you'll save yourself a lot of bother.

Surrounded by dense planting, the country pond looks so natural that it is hard to believe that, less than a year before, it was merely a hole in bare ground.

A Country Pond

The inspiration for the pond in my country garden came from a lovely, peaceful dew-pond in the countryside near where I live. It's shaded mainly by hawthorn trees, which are abundantly blessed with pure white blossom in spring and later sprinkle the surface of the water with confetti. Reeds and bulrushes rise from the water near the wildflower-studded banks, and birds, insects and small mammals fill the air with their chatter as they congregate to drink. It's touched by magic and, if you believe that the little people still inhabit the countryside, this is where you'll find them. Above all, the pond is modest and unpretentious, so I too have avoided complicated designs: no fashionable kidney-shapes, no towering rock banks and certainly no fountains here. The shape is a rough circle simply surrounded by the grasses and flowers of my flowery mead. But more of that later.

CONSTRUCTION

Building a small pond is simplicity itself provided you take the trouble to lay it out carefully in the first place. I won't bore you with details of how to mark out a rough circle, but I will take the liberty of reminding you that water *always* lies level. And that means that, to avoid acres of ugly plastic liner or soil showing above the water at one side, the top of the pool has to be level too.

Start by marking out the shape with a few pegs and digging out about 10cm (4in) of soil. Then bang in pegs all round the edge, levelling them with a spirit level as you go. If you mark a line on the pegs 5cm (2in) below the top, it's quite easy to level the soil to the line.

Then come in about 15cm (6in) from the pegs and start digging. The hole should be about 90cm (3ft) deep in the middle, rising slowly on at least one side so that animals that stumble in will have no trouble getting out again and birds can drink and wash at the water's edge.

An informal 'country' pond.

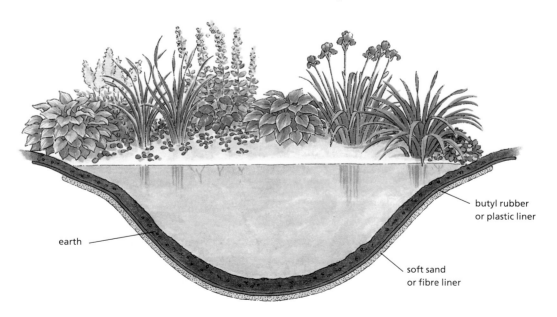

earth

butyl rubber
or plastic liner

soft sand
or fibre liner

The next step is to line the hole, either with an 8cm (3in) layer of soft sand or, better still, with a special fibre liner available from the aquatic supplier. Fold it and tuck it as neatly as you can. Then cover it with a liner made of butyl rubber or plastic. With this particular method none of the liner will be exposed to sunlight, so you could use a cheaper plastic liner or even something like a farmer's silage sheet. Really, any thick plastic will do.

A word here about ordering the liner. To avoid leaks it needs to be in one piece. To work out the size, measure the diameter of the pond at its widest point and add twice its depth.

The liner should now be covered with soil, though naturally you'll need to protect it from sharp stones cutting it from above as well as below. Another fibre liner is the ultimate answer but wildly expensive, so I prefer to use elbow grease instead and sieve the soil that goes back in. You'll need a layer about 10–15cm (4–6in) deep.

Once you start filling with water, you'll find at first that a little soil at the top slips downwards, so you'll almost certainly need to go round the edges topping up. Don't worry too much, because once the plants get a hold everything stays as steady as a rock.

TOP LEFT *Water always lies level, so it will be very obvious if the top of your pool isn't. It's well worth taking the trouble to make sure it's absolutely spot-on.*

CENTRE LEFT *To protect the butyl rubber or plastic liner from sharp stones in the soil, use a layer of sand or a special fibre underliner like this.*

BELOW LEFT *Cover the liner with soil, carefully sieved to remove any sharp stones which could cut it and cause leaks.*

When you've filled the pond with water you'll be utterly dismayed. It'll look as muddy as an elephants' watering hole in the Serengeti. Don't despair: it'll take a couple of days to clear, but clear it will.

Finally go round the edge cutting off the excess liner to leave about 15cm (6in) overlap to cover with soil and you're ready to plant (see page 125).

A Town Garden Pond

The pond in the town garden was made in much the same way as the country pond but involved a bit more construction. I wanted the water to lap against the gazebo to give the illusion of actually sitting in the middle of the pond, so I had first to make a solid foundation. If you're handy, it's not difficult, though you may prefer to call in a builder who'd make mincemeat of it in a couple of days.

CONSTRUCTION

First dig the hole and then install a concrete foundation and build a concrete-block wall on it. Since the whole thing is to be hidden by the pond, you don't need to be a master bricklayer to make a satisfactory job of it. Fill the back of the wall with hardcore and concrete to make the base for the gazebo.

Lay the fibre and plastic liners for the pond in the normal way (see page 117), cover with soil and fill with water. I also wanted to make a bog garden to enable me to grow a quite different range of plants that like to have their feet in water, so at one end of the pond nearest the wall I put in a lot more soil. It made a bank rising right out of the water and coming about 1.2m (4ft) from the wall. Because the soil slopes up out of the water, I was able to plant bog plants that required a variety of conditions. Some marginal plants, like water irises, needed to go in about 15cm (6in) below the water level, while others, like

OPPOSITE *The town garden pond one year on is surrounded by lush planting.*

BELOW *The town garden pond is connected to the iris rill and partially surrounds the gazebo.*

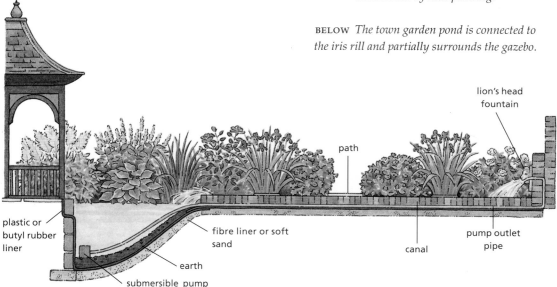

plastic or butyl rubber liner

fibre liner or soft sand

earth

submersible pump

path

lion's head fountain

pump outlet pipe

canal

primulas and filipendulas, needed to be out of the water but in very moist soil. I had the best of all worlds to play with.

An alternative way to build a bog garden next to the pond is to dig out another hole about 90cm (3ft) deep, putting the soil to one side. Then line the bottom and sides with polythene. The cheapest method is to use old plastic bags that once held perhaps compost or fertilizer – even dustbin bags will do. The idea here is not to prevent water loss completely but only to restrict the drainage.

Refill with 15cm (6in) layers of the soil you dug out interspersed with layers of manure or compost. This will naturally bring the level to considerably higher than it was before, but try to get all the soil back in to allow for subsequent settlement. You'll have perfect conditions for planting moisture-loving plants, though in very dry weather you'll need to put the hosepipe on the area to keep it to the required dampness.

When I had built the pond, I was still far from finished. With my Moorish turban planted firmly on my head, I had a yen to make a formal canal to feed the pond, creating a gentle tinkle of water at the same time.

The water would be fed into the canal through a traditional lion's head. You can buy them made for the job with a hole for the water pipe in the mouth. The head can be set straight into the wall and the pipe to feed the water cut into the brickwork. That's quite a job, though, and it's much easier to buy a few bricks to match those of your wall and to build a hollow pier to take the lion's head. Then you can install the pipework as you build. The plastic pipe needs to be long enough to go from the deepest point of the pond to the outlet in the lion's mouth.

The base of the canal is made with a 10cm (4in) strip of concrete laid dead level. Note the semi-circular bulges at intervals, designed to take pots of irises. When the base has hardened, lay a strip of liner material on it so that it overlaps the edges about 25cm (10in) each side. There's no need for the fibre protection sheet this time, because the weight of water will be negligible, but it's not a bad idea to put down a piece of cheap builder's plastic just in case. The bricks for the sides are set on top of the liner so that it can later be brought up behind them and held in place by soil, making a perfectly watertight job.

The bricks are laid on end, rather than flat in the normal way. You could, of course, lay two courses flat instead, but that would make it very difficult to form the semi-circles and would involve some pretty fancy brick cutting. I like the look of them this way too.

Naturally it's important to ensure that water remains in the canal even when the pump is switched off so the base must be set dead level. When you come to lay the brickwork walls at the sides, set one course across the end where the water empties into the pond and it will remain at that level.

Unless you want to spend a fortune buying a vast area of plastic liner, the strip for the canal will not be part of the liner used for the pond, so you'll need to be careful to lay it so that a leak doesn't occur between the two. That's simply a case of ensuring that the liner for the pond finishes above the water level and that for the canal lies on top of it. Then no leakage can occur, as the illustration shows clearly.

Finally put a layer of gravel in the bottom of the canal and you're ready to fit the pump. These days there's an excellent selection of submersible pumps that are simply put into the water. They're so much easier to install that I would consider no other. The cable for it runs over the top of the liner where it's very quickly hidden by plants.

When you buy the pump, you'll need to know how far it will have to move the water,

A bypass valve fitted to the pump enables you to control the flow of water to create precisely the effect you want.

Electricity in the garden is potentially dangerous, especially when combined with water, so always use the correct waterproof fittings.

the diameter of the pipe and, critically, the difference in height between where the pump sucks it out and where it's delivered from the lion's head. The supplier will also ask you how much water you wish to deliver per hour and he knows as well as we do that it's an impossible question to answer. I certainly haven't the vaguest idea, so tell him that you need only a trickle but ensure that the pump is if anything on the big side and that it comes equipped with a bypass valve – a plastic gismo with a tap that fits on the pump. When you open it, you let a certain amount of water back into the pond, effectively allowing you to control the flow exactly as you want it.

The pump is fixed to the pipe with a jubilee clip and the electricity cable runs to a convenient socket. Here extra care is called for. Electricity in the garden is dangerous and when it goes under water it's doubly so. Unless you're very competent, get an electrician to do the job for you.

The cable for the supply to the socket will almost always come from the house. It must go into a conduit, which would normally be a piece of alkathene pipe. The socket and the plug to connect it to the pump must be waterproof and, ideally, set in a little box to keep them dry. And, like the supply cable, if the cable from the pump runs underground where you're likely to dig, that must go into some alkathene pipe too. It may all seem like a lot of trouble, but remember that the main reason for this garden is the pursuit of tranquillity, relaxation and the reduction of stress. It's best to have peace of mind.

Once the pump's installed and working, you'll almost certainly find that your lion's head spits out a jet of water several metres long, swamping the canal and the surrounding borders . Simply open the bypass valve and set the flow to a trickle.

The final touch comes from the irises (see page 128). They should be potted into attractive terracotta pots in soil-based compost and set in the bottom of the canal to flower their hearts out. Remove them in winter and stand them on the patio lest they become too waterlogged and rot.

A Barrel Pond

If your garden doesn't have room for a pond, try to find a corner for a small water feature of some sort. All insects, birds and mammals need a drink from time to time and a source of water will be a sure-fire attraction to them. Even a bird bath will have them queueing up in summer.

You can make a very attractive pond with a cut-off wooden beer barrel from the garden centre. Plug the hole in the bottom with a suitably sized piece of dowel just driven in with no glue or bitumen around it. When it gets wet, it will swell to fill the hole. The barrel itself will probably have shrunk enough to leak water in quantity too. If you can, submerge it, but if you have no container big enough, you'll have to keep filling it with water until it swells enough to seal the joints.

Sink the barrel in the ground to guard against future drying out and level it all ways with a spirit level. Put a little soil in the bottom, fill with water, plant it up and the job's done.

Just take one precaution against animal casualties. Pot up a marginal plant (see page 126) in an attractive terracotta pot and set it on a brick in the pond so that the top of the pot is just below water level. This will provide a step for animals that might fall into or voluntarily enter the water and have difficulty getting up the steep sides.

ABOVE *You can grow attractive pond plants even in a half-barrel.*

BELOW *Note the way the liner overlaps when making a stream.*

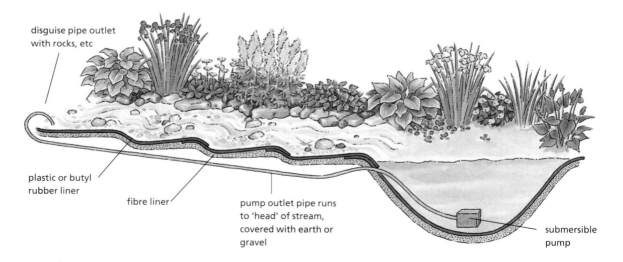

disguise pipe outlet with rocks, etc

plastic or butyl rubber liner

fibre liner

pump outlet pipe runs to 'head' of stream, covered with earth or gravel

submersible pump

A Stream

Y ou drink a lot of tea making a stream.
Every time you start a new section, it's
worth stopping and thinking carefully before
you continue, because you need to be extra
careful about levels.

Naturally you'll want a very informal
design, so make the pond first in the way
decribed for the dew-pond in the country
garden (see page 116).

TOP LEFT *When you're building a stream, it's essential*
to get the levels right.

LEFT *Dig out the stream so that, starting at the pond,*
each level is a little higher than the one before, but
sloping slightly backwards so that water will stay in the
stream even when the pump is switched off.

BELOW *Making the stream meander not only looks*
more natural, but also enables you to pack a lot of
stream into a very small space.

Then mark out the shape of the stream which, as I've already suggested, looks best if it's allowed to meander a little. Now have a cup of tea and think carefully about the levels. If the stream meanders, you'll need to line it in sections to save the cost of a huge liner to cover it all. At the planning stage work out how many sections you need to minimize the amount of liner you have to buy. Each section must step upwards slightly, away from the pond.

Your first step is already fixed for you by the edge of the pond. From there you may consider that the bottom of the stream should slope gently upwards to create a flow, but in fact precisely the reverse is the case. If the water is going to stay in the stream when the pump is switched off, as it must, the bottom needs to slope *downwards* from the edge of the pond.

Overlap the liner generously to avoid leaks.

The front edge of the second section should be something like 8cm (3in) above the level of the edge of the pond, though this could vary depending on the slope of the land. The bottom of the second and all subsequent sections should also slope backwards. Section three starts 8cm (3in) above the front edge of section two and so on.

When you're sure your levelling is accurate, line the first section of the stream with the protective fibre and the rubber or plastic liner. To make it waterproof the liner should come over the pond liner and over the front edge of section two. So, when that section is lined, the section-two liner will come over the top of the section-one liner. Then it can't leak. The illustration should make it clear.

With all sections lined, cut off the excess at the edges, just as you did for the pond, and cover with soil. Then line the bottom of the stream with pebbles and larger stones. Include a few quite big, rounded ones which come above the surface of the water, creating swirling eddies to add interest.

The submersible pump is fitted as for the one in the town garden (see page 120), with the outlet at the head of the stream. The best way to disguise it is to use a small pile of larger pebbles. Plants will eventually conceal it completely.

It won't have escaped your notice that, unless you're very accurate with your levelling, the stream could extract a lot of water from the pond when you first switch on the pump. Since there's always a bit of evaporation, the stream will, in any case, always need a certain amount of topping-up before it starts to flow and that has to come from the pond. If your levels are not accurate, more water will be required and that could lower the level of the pond too much. It's easy to see why great care is needed at the levelling stage.

Planting

There are hundreds of aquatic plants to choose from, so a trip to a specialist is called for. Alternatively there are some excellent mail-order nurseries which will send them through the post, so ask for a catalogue.

The one thing to avoid (and I've made this mistake myself) is the temptation to grow rampant native plants. Believe me, if you fill your bog garden with bulrushes, you'll soon lose all your other, choicer plants to their rampaging habit. Cultivated and foreign species will attract their share of wildlife in just the same way.

Planting marginal plants is the simplest thing in the world. Just roll up your sleeves and push the roots into the mud. With taller plants it's often best to cut them back a little to prevent them falling over. The nurseryman's catalogue will tell you how much water should be over the roots of each plant and you should follow this instruction carefully.

Waterlilies and other deep-water aquatics are best potted into special plastic baskets. Line the basket with sacking and use heavy garden soil to cover the roots of the plant. Prune away any large leaves, and particularly any that are damaged, and then cover the top of the basket with gravel to prevent the soil floating out.

If you can't reach to put the basket into the place you want it, run a couple of strings through the holes in the plastic and, with the help of a friend holding the other end of the string, lower it into the water. The strings can be removed afterwards.

Naturally it's pretty difficult to label aquatic plants, so, if you want a record of what you've got, you'll have to make a plan and mark them in.

DEEP-WATER AQUATICS

Deep-water aquatic plants are those that grow below water in depths ranging from 15cm (6in) to 1.8m (6ft). Suggested planting depths are given in the following list.

Aponogeton distachyus **Water hawthorn**
Strap-like leaves lie on the surface and white flowers with black centres are produced in spring and autumn. Plant 15–45cm (6–18in) deep.

Nymphaea **Waterlily**
By far the most desirable and popular aquatic plants for still-water pools, they all produce rounded, floating leaves that will serve to shade the water and reduce the incidence of green algae. The flowers are always superb and available in many different colours, and some varieties are fragrant. There are forms to suit any size of pool, so when choosing it's important to know the depth of water in which they're to grow. Those marked 'small' need 15–23cm (6–9in) of water; those marked 'medium' need 45–75cm (18–30in); and those marked 'large' need 60cm–1.8m (2–6ft).

Nymphaea alba is a very vigorous native, suitable only for large pools. The flowers are white with a yellow centre. Large.

'Attraction' has garnet-red flowers up to 20cm (8in) across. Large.

'Charles de Meurville' bears wine-purple flowers streaked with white and is very vigorous. Large.

'Conqueror' is a free-flowering variety with red flowers marked with white. Medium.

'Escarboucle' is the best crimson, very free-flowering and fragrant too. Large.

'Froebelii' is very free-flowering, producing lovely, blood-red flowers. Medium.

'Gladstoneana' has huge, pure white flowers, and is very vigorous. Large.

'Gonnère' produces pure white, globular, double flowers: one of the best. Medium.

'Graziella' has rounded flowers of orange-red fading with age. Medium.

'Hermine' bears star-shaped, white flowers and grows well in shade. Medium.

'James Brydon' has double flowers of dark pink and reddish leaves. It does well in shade. Medium.

N. laydekeri varieties are excellent for small pools. The flowers vary from pink to magenta-crimson depending on variety. Small to medium.

N. marliacea varieties vary from pure white to rose pink and there's a yellow too, 'Chromatella'. Some varieties are fragrant and some have attractive, reddish brown marking on the leaves. Medium to large.

'Mrs Richmond' produces pale rose-pink flowers. Medium.

N. odorata bears fragrant, white flowers, and the variety 'William B. Shaw' is pale pink, deepening towards the centre. Medium. The variety 'Minor' is white and suitable for a very small pool; 'Sulphurea' has canary-yellow flowers. Small.

N. pygmaea varieties are excellent miniatures. 'Alba' is white; 'Helvola' is yellow and 'Rubra' is red. Small.

'Rose Arey' is one of the best pinks, bearing deep pink flowers with striking orange stamens. Medium.

'Sioux' opens yellow flushed red and gradually changes to coppery red. Medium.

'Solfatare' has pale yellow flowers flushed with pink and leaves blotched with red. Medium.

Orontium aquaticum Golden club
The leaves of this plant grow in large rosettes and have a silvery sheen . Poker-like yellow-and-white flowers are produced in late spring. Plant 10–45cm (4–18in) deep.

OXYGENATING PLANTS

In order to create a natural balance in the pool it's important to grow plants that will provide a supply of oxygen. There are several available at water garden centres, but some are too invasive for most garden ponds. It's best to stick to the one, *Elodea crispa*, which will not be too difficult to control.

Nonetheless, you'll still have to remove some from time to time. Do it with great care. A pond slightly choked with weed allows tadpoles and young adult frogs and newts to hide from their predators, so avoid removing it in spring, taking tadpoles or adults with it. Wait until early summer when they've left the pond, and even then pile the weed in shallow water for a week to allow anything trapped in it to escape.

MARGINAL PLANTS

Marginal plants grow at the edge of the water with their roots just below the surface.

Acorus Sweet rush
A grassy plant, some varieties of which have variegated foliage.

Acorus calamus 'Variegatus' grows to about 75cm (30in) and bears attractive, green-and-white-striped leaves.

A. gramineus 'Variegatus' has silver-and-white variegations and grows to 30cm (1ft).

A. g. 'Oborozuki', a superb plant with bright yellow variegations, grows to 30cm (1ft), while 'Yodonoyuki' is pale green and silver.

An idyllic country dew-pond, complete with ducks and surrounded by native marginal plants like the yellow flag irises.

Alisma plantago **Water plantain**
This reaches 60cm (2ft) with large, spinach-like leaves and tall spikes of pink-and-white flowers.

Butomus umbellatus **Flowering rush**
A native plant, this forms tall clumps of graceful foliage and 1.2m (4ft) stems of pretty, pink flowers.

Calla palustris **Bog arum**
A low-growing, creeping plant with white flowers and bright red berries.

*Both the kingcups (*Caltha palustris*) in the foreground and the large-leaved skunk cabbage (*Lysichiton americanus*) behind it have brightgolden flowers in spring.*

Caltha palustris **Kingcup/marsh marigold**
A European native which produces bright yellow, buttercup flowers on 30cm (1ft) stems. The variety 'Alba' has white flowers and is a little taller, while 'Plena' has striking, double flowers. 'Polypetala' is a taller plant, growing to 60cm (2ft), with yellow flowers and larger leaves.

Carex
These grasses will grow in damp soil or in about 5cm (2in) of water. *Carex elata* 'Aurea' is bright yellow and grows to about 30cm (1ft), while *C. riparia* 'Variegata' has silver stripes. *C. pendula* reaches about 1.2m (4ft), with stout stems terminating in drooping sprays of flowers.

Houttuynia **'Chameleon'**
I hesitated before including *Houttuynia*, because the green-leaved variety can become invasive. This one, however, shouldn't cause problems and has such striking red-, yellow-, green-and-cream leaves that it really deserves its place. It has rather insignificant, white flowers and grows to 30cm (1ft).

Iris
The types listed below are true water irises and grow best in about 15cm (6in) of water.
   Iris laevigata (Japanese iris) is one of the best of all irises. It has mid-blue flowers in early summer and sometimes again in late summer. Most varieties grow to about 75cm (30in). 'Alba' is white, slightly speckled with pale blue; 'Colchesteri' is double white marked with blue; 'Midnight' is a deep blue double; 'Mottled Beauty' is a single blue marbled with white; 'Richard Greany' is sky blue and single; 'Rose Queen' is pink; 'Snowdrift' has very large, pure white flowers; 'Violet Garth' is a violet single; and 'Weymouth' is a vivid blue single.

The yellow flag iris reaches a height of 60–90cm (2–3ft). The species is not worth growing, but some varieties are. 'Bastardii' has pale sulphur-yellow flowers; 'Variegatus' bears superb, yellow-variegated leaves which fade somewhat in summer; 'Ecru' has pale yellow flowers marked with black; and 'Ivory' is creamy white.

Iris versicolor grows to 45cm (18in) and has blue-mauve flowers. There's also a purple and a rose-pink form, and 'Kermesina' has flowers of rich claret-red.

Lysichiton americanus Bog arum/skunk cabbage

In spring this beautiful plant produces great spathes of arum-like flowers in rich yellow. *Lysichiton camtschatcensis* is similar, but with white flowers. It grows to about 60cm (2ft).

Mentha aquatica Water mint

A spreading plant, reaching about 30cm (1ft), with aromatic, purple-tinged foliage and small, rounded flowers of lilac-pink in summer. They are very attractive to bees.

Menyanthes trifoliata Bog bean

A creeping plant growing to about 23cm (9in) with bean-like leaves and very pale pink flowers.

Myosotis scorpioïdes Water forget-me-not

Forming floating mats of foliage studded with small, blue, forget-me-not flowers in early to mid-summer, this grows to 30cm (1ft). Look for the newer variety 'Mermaid', which is more compact and has larger flowers. 'Pinkie' is a pink-flowered form.

Peltandra undulata

From bold, shield-like leaves arise yellow-green, arum-like flowers followed by red berries. It grows to about 45cm (18in).

Pontederia cordata Pickerel weed

This forms neat clumps of lush, green foliage from which arise in late summer 75cm- (30in-) tall spikes of blue flowers. The variety 'Alba' has white flowers, while 'Lancifolia' is taller with spear-shaped leaves.

Sagittaria sagittifolia Arrowhead

A vigorous plant growing to about 90cm (3ft) with attractive, arrow-shaped leaves and spikes of white flowers in summer. For a smaller pool, look out for the less vigorous 'Leucopetala' with white and yellow flowers which grows to about 45cm (18in), or 'Flore Pleno' with double white flowers at about the same height.

Saururus cernuus Swamp lily

The green, heart-shaped leaves develop attractive autumn colour and from them in summer arise pendulous spikes of catkin-like, white flowers. It grows to about 45cm (18in).

Schoenoplectus tabernaemontani 'Zebrinus' Zebra rush

A completely unpronounceable name for what used to be called *Scirpus zebrinus* and is still sometimes sold as such for understandable reasons! The 75cm (30in) reeds have horizontal stripes of green and white, making it a very decorative variety for a small pool. The variety 'Albescens' grows to 1.2m (4ft) and has longitudinal stripes of green and white.

Typha Reed mace

Typha latifolia (greater reed mace) is too invasive for most pools and to be avoided. *T. angustifolia* (lesser reed mace) grows to 90cm (3ft) and is the better choice for a large pool. Like all the reed maces it carries brown, bulrush-like heads. The smallest, *T. minima*, grows to only 60cm (2ft) and is much less invasive, so is suitable for small pools.

Veronica beccabunga Brooklime

A pretty, creeping plant with white-eyed, blue flowers throughout the summer. Cut it back hard in spring to stop it becoming straggly. It grows to about 20cm (8in).

Zantedeschia aethiopica Arum lily

A frost-tender plant that will generally escape damage if it's planted in 15cm (6in) of water to protect the crown in winter. Still success is not guaranteed, but the flowers are so outstanding that it has to be worth a try. In warmer areas this is best grown in the bog garden. Alternatively grow it in a pot, submerged in the water, and overwinter it in a greenhouse. Look out for the varieties 'Crowborough' with 90cm- (3ft-) tall, white, arum-lily flowers, and 'Green Goddess' with superb, green flowers to 75cm (30in).

Moisture-loving Plants

The following list includes plants that can be grown in wet soil in the bog garden.

Arisarum proboscideum
Mouse-tail arum

A curiosity, this tuberous plant produces carpets of arrow-shaped leaves and, in mid-spring, chocolate-coloured flowers which look for all the world like a small mouse diving for cover. It grows to about 10cm (4in).

Aruncus dioicus Goat's beard

A handsome plant with broad, fern-like leaves, topped in mid-summer by great spikes of small, starry, cream flowers, it reaches a height of about 1.5m (5ft). The variety 'Kneiffii' is slightly smaller with a finer leaf, and 'Glasnevin' is a dwarf growing to 60cm (2ft). For really tiny spaces *Aruncus aethusifolius* grows to just 30cm (1ft).

Astilbe arendsii

With fern-like, divided foliage and plumes of striking flowers, astilbes make a fine show all season. There are many good varieties, so a trip to the nursery is essential. Among my own favourites are 'Amethyst', which bears magenta flowers; 'Bridal Veil', which is white; 'Bronze Elegance' with bronze foliage and pink flowers; 'Fanal' with bronze leaves and dark red flowers; and 'Perkeo' and 'Sprite', both which both bear bright pink blooms. They can vary in height between 30–90cm (1–3ft).

Astilboïdes tabularis

A wonderful foliage plant with huge, circular leaves and sprays of white flowers in summer. It grows to about 90cm (3ft) in sun or shade. It was and is sometimes sold as *Rodgersia tabularis*.

Camassia leichtlinii Quamash

A bulbous plant that, in summer produces 1.2m- (4ft-) tall spikes of deep blue, star-shaped flowers. 'Alba' has cream flowers and 'Atrocaerulea' is deep blue-purple.

Cardamine pratensis 'Flore Pleno'
Lady's smock

This forms 20cm (8in) clumps topped by pretty, double, lilac-pink flowers in spring. *Cardamine raphanifolia* grows to 45cm (18in) and has single, mauve flowers rather like those of honesty.

Cimicifuga racemosa Bugbane

A tall plant with 1.8m (6ft) spires of pure white, branching, bottle-brush flowers held over superb, divided, ferny foliage of bright green.

Cimicifuga simplex is another superb plant, growing to about 1.2m (4ft). Look for the variety 'Elstead' which has the purest white flowers opening from purplish buds.

Darmera peltata Umbrella plant

Confusingly, this plant became well known as *Peltiphyllum peltata*. It's a superb architectural plant with large, rounded leaves topped by flat heads of pink flowers on 90cm (3ft) stems. Its creeping, rhizomatous stems can easily be divided for propagation.

Filipendula Meadowsweet

From robust clumps of fern-like foliage arise frothy flowers on tall stems in summer. *Filipendula palmata* 'Elegantissima' grows to 90cm (3ft) and has red flowers; *F. purpurea* reaches 1.2m (4ft) and bears cerise flowers; *F. rubra* towers above them at 2.1m (7ft) and has pale pink flowers; *F. ulmaria* 'Aurea' is a very attractive foliage plant in spring with finely cut, yellow leaves and white flowers, growing to 30cm (1ft).

Geum rivale Water avens

A low-growing, clump-forming plant with nodding, cup-shaped, pink flowers in summer, this grows to 30cm (1ft). Look out for 'Leonard's Variety' with coppery flowers; 'Lionel Cox', with pale yellow; the taller 'Marika' with peach-pink flowers; and the 15cm (6in) tall 'Alba' with white.

Gunnera manicata Giant rhubarb

A huge and imposing plant only for large bog gardens or where the roots can be restricted to keep it smaller. Unrestricted it'll grow to about 2.4m (8ft) with enormous, rhubarb-like leaves. In winter protect the crown by bending the leaves over it.

Hosta Plantain lily

A superb plant for both foliage and flower, but unfortunately rather subject to slug damage – and it has to be said that slugs are very much at home in the bog garden. Hostas repay perseverance, however.

There are hundreds of varieties to choose from, so either visit a nursery or get hold of a specialist catalogue. My favourites include the following varieties: *Hosta fortunei* 'Albopicta' with yellow leaves edged green and lilac flowers, growing to 75cm (30in); *H. fortunei* 'Marginata Alba' with green leaves edged white and lilac flowers; *H. fortunei* 'Obscura Marginata' with green leaves edged bright yellow; 'Krossa Regal', which produces a dome of bluish foliage 1.5m (5ft) tall with lilac flowers in late summer; *H. plantiginea* 'Grandiflora', a Japanese variety with 60cm- (2ft-) tall clumps of arching, heart-shaped leaves and pure white, heavily perfumed flowers; 'Frances Williams' with gold-edged green leaves, growing to 75cm (30in); 'Great Expectations', which bears broad, green leaves splashed and veined with yellow; 'Halcyon' with thick,

Lush variegated hostas look super near water.

bluish leaves less troubled by slugs; 'Honeybells', 90cm (3ft) tall with wavy-edged, green leaves and scented, pink flowers in summer; 'Thomas Hogg' growing to 60cm (2ft) with smooth, pointed leaves, dark green with a white edge, and spires of lilac flowers; *H. undulata* 'Erromena', which reaches 1.2m (4ft), producing lovely mounds of broad, shiny green leaves and tall spires of lilac trumpets in summer; and *H. ventricosa*, which also grows to 1.2m (4ft) with very shiny leaves and spires of bell-shaped, violet flowers.

Iris
True water irises are covered on page 128; the following will grow happily in moist soil.

Iris chrysographes is a small iris growing to about 45cm (18in) with purplish flowers. A form sold as 'Dark Form' is very nearly black, while 'Rubella' has deep velvet-red flowers.

There are dozens of varieties of *I. ensata* (clematis-flowered iris), a superb Japanese plant which used to be called *I. kaempferi*: get hold of a specialist catalogue. They form clumps of stiff, narrow leaves topped in summer by beautifully shaped flowers in various colours, and grow to 75cm–1.2m (30–48in). My favourites include: 'Apollo', single white; 'Blue Peter', deep blue double; 'Chitose-no-tomo', cobalt blue double; 'Galatea', blue double with white veins; 'Glitter and Gaiety', single deep purple with a white border; 'Hokkaido', pale violet with purple veining; 'Magic Opal', pink with a blue halo and veins; 'Narihiri', deep maroon double; 'Royal Crown', white with deep red borders and a white crest; 'Rose Queen', deep pink; and 'Taga-Sode', fuchsia veined white.

I. sibirica offers another wide range but with narrow, grassy leaves forming lax clumps and topped by many smaller flowers to make a striking overall effect. They grow to about 60–90cm (2–3ft). There are many good

varieties including: 'Flight of Butterflies', blue and white; 'Mrs Rowe', pale lilac; 'Mrs Saunders', blue with a white edge; 'Navy Brass', dark blue and gold; 'Perry's Favourite', lavender-blue with a honey centre; 'Pink Haze', pink and white; 'Roger Perry', blue splashed purple; 'Snow Queen', white; and 'Southcombe White', white flushed blue.

Ligularia dentata
This 1.2m- (4ft-) tall plant has striking, rounded foliage and spikes of brilliant orange flowers. Look out for 'Desdemona' which is more compact and has red undersides to the leaves, and 'Othello' which is slightly paler. *Ligularia przewalskii* has deeply cut leaves, black stems and yellow flowers and grows to about 1.8m (6ft), while *L. veitchiana* has rounded, green leaves and yellow flowers and reaches 1.2m (4ft).

Lobelia
Fine, upright plants with striking foliage and flowers. Some tend to be a bit tender, but they're very easy to propagate from cuttings to overwinter inside. They can also be raised from seed.

There are many named varieties as well as the species. A good selection includes: *Lobelia cardinalis*, which grows to 60cm (2ft) and has green leaves and spikes of brilliant scarlet, bell-shaped flowers; *L. fulgens*, which bears reddish leaves and scarlet flowers; *L. siphilitica*, which has green leaves and blue flowers and grows to 90cm (3ft); 'Bee's Flame' with beetroot-red foliage and scarlet flowers; and 'Pink Flamingo' with green leaves and pink flowers.

Lythrum salicaria Purple loosestrife
A native European plant and a little invasive where it's suited. Nonetheless it's well worth

growing for its 1.2m (4ft) spikes of pink flowers in summer. Look out, too, for 'Firecandle' with intense rose-red flowers and the rose-pink 'Robert' or 'The Beacon'. Slightly smaller and daintier are *Lythrum virgatum* 'Rosy Gem' with clear violet-pink flowers and the deep rose-pink 'The Rocket'.

Persicaria Knotweed

Previously known as *Polygonum*, the knotweeds are easy-to-grow plants which can be rampageous though not difficult to control with a spade. *Persicara affinis* 'Superba' is the best of this species with upright flower spikes which open white and turn to crimson. It grows to about 23cm (9in). *P. amplexicaulis* is much taller, reaching 1.2m (4ft). It makes good clumps of leaves topped with erect spikes of many flowers from early summer to the first frosts. 'Alba' is pure white; 'Atrosanguinea' is deep crimson; 'Firetail' is red and a little shorter; and 'Rosea' is pale pink.

Podophyllum hexandrum

An intriguing plant for a shady spot. It comes through the ground like folded umbrellas and the leaves uncurl to form three, brown-mottled lobes topped by cup-shaped, pinkish white flowers in summer. They're followed by shining, red fruits.

The variety 'Majus' is larger and stronger and *Podophyllum hexandrum chinense* has rose-pink flowers.

Primula

What would a pondside be without primulas? They're the mainstay of the garden and come in a wide range of flower shapes and colours. Most will thrive in shade and don't mind sun provided they're not allowed to dry out.

Primula alpicola grows to 30cm (1ft) with nodding, pale yellow flowers. *P. alpicola alba*

Reddish-pink candelabra primulas with kingcups, irises and ferns.

is ivory-white and *P. alpicola violacea* is soft lilac. Both these are sweetly scented.

P. beesiana is a 60cm- (2ft-) tall candelabra type with lilac flowers arranged in whorls up the stems.

P. bulleyana is similar to the above but with orange flowers. Hybrids are also available in a mixture of oranges and pinks.

P. denticulata is the well-known drumstick primula which produces spherical heads on long stems like drumsticks. One of the first to flower in spring and very reliable, it comes in a variety of colours including mauve, white and red and reaches 30cm (1ft) in height.

P. florindae is a superb plant, flowering in summer for many weeks. From strong clumps of rounded leaves it produces fragrant, drooping heads of clear citron yellow. It spreads well to make outstanding mats of colour.

P. japonica is another candelabra type, flowering in early summer and growing to about 45cm (18in). The flowers of the species are pink, but look out too for 'Postford White' and 'Miller's Crimson'.

P. sikkimensis is another excellent subject for the bog garden, producing yellow, nodding flowers in profusion in early summer. It grows to about 60cm (2ft).

P. vulgaris (common primrose) is much to be desired in this type of garden. Apart from the normal yellow form, there are many others with green, white and lilac flowers, plus single and double hybrids.

Rodgersia Bog sage

A range of wonderful, imposing foliage plants with the bonus of striking flower heads in summer, towering above the leaves to 90cm–1.2m (3–4ft). *Rodgersia aesculifolia* has shiny, bronze-tinted leaves topped by large heads of small, pink-tinted, white flowers.

R. pinnata bears pairs of burnished leaves with pink flowers. Look out for the variety 'Superba', which has extra-shiny leaves and brilliant pink flowers.

R. podophylla has large, jagged leaves, bronze when young, turning green and then copper-coloured in autumn. The cream flowers are not as striking as most.

Salvia uliginosa

One of the few salvias that thrives in boggy conditions, this makes a lovely, airy plant with waving sprays of clear blue flowers to 1.5m (5ft). It may not be hardy in cold areas, but it is easily raised from seed to flower in the same year.

Sambucus Elder

This makes a large shrub up to about 3m (10ft), but the foliage is best on young growth, so keep the plant small with annual pruning back to two buds of last year's wood. Still it should be planted near the back of the bog garden and allowed a spread of at least 1.8m (6ft).

The varieties I would recommend are *Sambucus nigra* 'Aurea' with acid-yellow foliage; *S. nigra* 'Guincho Purple' with purple-bronze leaves; and *S. racemosa* 'Plumosa Aurea' with finely cut, serrated, golden leaves.

Scrophularia auriculata 'Variegata' Water figwort

A fine foliage plant with leaves splashed and striped with cream. The flowers are not noteworthy and should be cut off before they seed to prevent rapid spreading. Water figwort prefers a shady spot and grows to about 90cm (3ft).

Trollius Globe flower

No bog garden should be without this superb plant. It forms stalwart clumps of shiny, divided foliage from which arise large, spherical flowers in brilliant colours. *Trollius chinensis* is an outstanding species, growing to 90cm (3ft) and producing wonderful clumps of brilliant orange flowers. *T. cultorum* produces large, yellow or orange flowers like double buttercups about 90cm (3ft) tall. Above all don't miss the slightly shorter variety 'Alabaster' with superb, ivory-tinted flowers.

T. europaeus is the more commonly grown globe flower which has been seen in gardens in Britain since the sixteenth century. Look for the variety 'Superbus' with delightful, cool lemon-yellow flowers which grow to about 60cm (2ft).

DRY 'BOG GARDENS'

In many gardens there simply isn't the space for a separate bog garden around the pond and that's the case here with the one in the country garden. Because the water is held by a liner, nothing overflows into the soil around, so it can be as dry as dust. Still the pond needs to be incorporated into the whole design or it'll stand out like a sore thumb.

To make the pond look as if it's meant to be there it's necessary to plant around it plants that look as if they could be the lush, soft-foliaged types you'd expect to find in a bog garden. Since most suitable plants would still prefer a soil that doesn't ever dry out completely, it's worth incorporating plenty of organic matter before planting and mulching annually to maintain it.

There are several plants that fit the bill and the following list includes those that I selected for my own country garden.

Aconitum Monkshood

An erect plant with rich, divided foliage and hooded flowers that give it its common name, monkshood has been grown in Britain since the sixteenth century. The roots in particular are very poisonous, so don't plant it where it's likely to be dug up and eaten, perhaps by a young child or even a dog. *Aconitum carmichaelii* is one of the finest, growing to 1.2m (4ft) with light blue flowers. 'Barker's Variety' and 'Kelmscott' have violet-blue flowers.

A. japonicum bears lavender-blue flowers of exceptional quality over a long period, but tends to be somewhat variable; it grows to 90cm (3ft).

A. napellus (common monkshood) is taller at about 1.5m (5ft) with indigo-blue flowers. The variety 'Carneum' is pink and well worth searching out.

Aegopodium podagaria 'Variegatum' Variegated ground elder

Ground elder is a name that strikes terror into the hearts of gardeners, but the variegated type is nothing like as invasive as its green cousin and is easily controlled with a spade. It's certainly well worth growing for its ground-hugging, fresh green-and-white foliage. The insignificant flowers are best cut off.

Ajuga reptans Bugle

An excellent ground-coverer with coloured foliage and mainly blue flowers borne on 8cm

The lush-looking leaves of Brunnera macrophylla *make it a good choice for a dry 'bog garden'.*

(3in) stems. 'Alba' produces green leaves and white flowers; 'Braunherz', with blue flowers, is the best of the bronze-leaved forms; 'Burgundy Glow' bears cream-and-pink-variegated leaves and blue flowers; 'Jungle Beauty' has green leaves and blue flowers; and 'Pink Elf' bears green leaves and pink flowers.

Brunnera macrophylla

A fine, leafy plant requiring some shade. In spring it produces airy sprays of vivid, forget-me-not-blue flowers to about 45cm (18in). The foliage suppresses weeds and looks attractive all season long. There's also a good variety with cream-bordered leaves, 'Hadspen Cream'.

Corydalis

A delicate plant with delightful, lacy foliage. It needs some shade and dies down in mid-summer, so you need to know where it is to avoid digging up the small tubers. *Corydalis cava* and *C. solida* grow to about 23cm (9in) and, from mounds of lovely, divided foliage, produce spikes of tubular flowers of lavender-grey in early spring. There are several good varieties of *C. flexuosa*, the best of which is 'Père David' with masses of delightful, Wedgwood-blue flowers in spring.

Dicentra Bleeding heart

This popular cottage-garden plant prefers a moist, slightly shaded spot where it'll flower longer than in sunshine. All the forms have the most delicate, divided foliage, which is often bluish in colour. The strangely shaped flowers hang like lockets on arching stems. Most species and hybrids are worthwhile; most grow to about 45cm (18in).

Dicentra formosa forms lovely, ferny hummocks of finely cut leaves over which dangle mauve-pink flowers in late spring. A selection from it, 'Stuart Boothman', is slightly shorter and produces blue foliage and pink flowers; 'Bacchanal' has finely cut foliage and dark red flowers; 'Langtrees' has cream flowers with pink tips; and 'Luxuriant' is rose-pink.

D. spectabilis is commonly known as bleeding heart, Dutchman's breeches, or lady-in-the-bath. It's well worth growing, out of cold winds, for its striking, pendulous sprays of rose-pink-and-white flowers. The white form 'Alba' also deserves a place. It grows to 60cm (2ft) and dies back in mid-summer.

Dierama pulcherrimum Wand flower

A graceful plant with evergreen, grassy foliage and graceful, arching stems up to 1.5m (5ft) tall which erupt with pink, bell-shaped flowers in late summer.

Euphorbia Spurge

A wide range of varied plants, all with outstanding foliage and attractive heads of mainly green or yellow flowers. All are excellent subjects for the poolside, revelling in full sun or part-shade. Some have invasive roots, but they're easily controlled.

Euphorphia amygdaloïdes robbiae forms rosettes of dark green leaves with flat, green flowers in spring. It has a creeping habit and may need controlling. It grows to 60cm (2ft). The variety 'Purpurea' produces purple-mahogany leaves and yellow flowers.

E. characias wulfenii grows to 1.2m (4ft), producing great spikes of yellow flowers; one of the best varieties is 'Lambrook Gold' with large, more intense flower heads.

E. griffithii 'Fireglow' runs through the soil, but is easy to control and well worth a little trouble. It produces bright red flowers on 90cm (3ft) stems over attractive foliage in early summer.

E. myrsinites forms 15cm- (6in-) tall mats of long, trailing, grey-green stems terminating with starry, yellow flowers fading to pink.

E. palustris is a wonderful spring flowerer, producing great heads of yellow flowers on 90cm (3ft) plumes of green which turn yellow and orange in autumn.

E. polychroma makes a perfect, 45cm (18in) dome of yellowish green foliage topped by flat heads of yellow flowers for many weeks. Grow it singly to maintain the shape.

Hemerocallis **Day lily**

An excellent, easy-to-grow plant with flowers in many colours: new American hybrids have greatly extended the range. It forms a grassy clump of arching leaves about 60cm (2ft) tall and the flowers are perfumed and lily-like.

Recommended hybrids include: 'Anzac', pure red; 'Black Magic', deep maroon; 'Bonanza', orange with an amber centre; 'Burning Daylight', orange; 'Canary Glow', yellow; 'Chicago Royal Robe', deep purple; 'Franz Hals', with orange-and-red stripes; 'Hyperion', scented yellow; 'Luxury Lace', pink with ruffled petals; 'Pink Damask', pink; and 'Varsity', pink with a maroon centre.

Lysimachia **Loosestrife**

A somewhat invasive group of plants, but easily controlled with a spade. *Lysimachia ciliata* spreads to make fine stands of erect, 1.2m (4ft), bronze-leaved stems topped by nodding flowers of clear yellow in summer. *L. clethroïdes* produces 90cm (3ft) arching spikes of white flowers like ducks' heads. *L. nummularia* 'Aurea' (creeping Jenny) is a completely different plant. It grows to just 10cm (4in) and creeps between other plants to make a mat of golden leaves topped by yellow flowers: well worth growing.

Milium effusum **'Aureum'** **Bowles' golden grass**

A wonderful grass, growing to about 45cm (18in), its golden leaves light up the garden and in summer they're topped by yellow seed heads. It seeds itself freely among other plants but is never a nuisance.

Polygonatum **Solomon's seal**

A superb foliage plant that likes a cool root run but will grow in shade or sunshine provided the soil doesn't dry out. The lush foliage is perfect for the poolside and the pendulous, greenish white flowers impart a cool, woodland feel.

Polygonatum hybridum is the commonest species, reaching a height of 90cm (3ft). Two varieties of it are well worth growing. 'Flore Pleno' has double flowers, while 'Variegatum' bears creamy-white-striped leaves. *P. canaliculatum* is a wonderful plant resembling *P. hybridum*, but in good soil achieving about twice its size.

Rheum **Ornamental rhubarb**

Unlike the *Gunnera* described on page 131, this is a true rhubarb, but not edible. It's grown for its large, decorative leaves, though the tall spikes of white or reddish flowers are also worthwhile.

For large pools, *Rheum palmatum* 'Atrosanguineum' is the one to grow. It makes large, jagged leaves, red when they appear, but turning greener on top, though retaining the blood red colour underneath. It grows to 1.8m (6ft) with spikes of rather untidy, red flowers, but is still quite a sight. For smaller pools it's best to stick with the 90cm (3ft) 'Ace of Hearts', which has heart-shaped leaves of similar colour and pink flowers.

Chapter six

GARTHS AND FLOWERY MEADS

The most restful of colours, soothing the eyes and calming the spirit, is green. That's a fact that has been recognized for centuries. In the Middle Ages every monastery had its cloister garth, an area of nothing but turf with perhaps a fountain or pool, used by monks for contemplation, prayer and study. Every pleasure garden of the time included an area of plain grass for relaxation, *al fresco* meals and conversation, just as we use our own lawns today. According to Hugh of Fouilloy, quoted by Sylvia Landsberg in her book *Medieval Gardens*: 'The green turf which is in the middle of the material cloister refreshes encloistered eyes and their desire to study returns. It is truly the nature of the colour green that it nourishes the eyes and preserves their vision.'

Naturally, exactly the same rules apply today, and that 'nourishment' of the eyes and the contemplative mood thus engendered are the very essence of what we require from our own gardens. In modern gardens lack of space and our desire for colour mean that purely green areas are rare, but few British gardens are without a lawn and we still use grass as the best of foregrounds for our more colourful borders.

In the kind of sanctuary garden we're interested in, an area of grass, while not essential, will certainly serve to calm the brighter borders and will also find constant use as a place to sit or sunbathe, as well as for contemplation and study, just as it did in medieval times.

Making a Cloister Garth

The easiest and cheapest way to make a new lawn is with seed and that's how I made mine in the country garden.

First cultivate the soil by single digging or rotavating and, during a dry spell, level it roughly and then consolidate it firmly by treading over every centimetre with your

---

This wildflower border blending into the lawn proves that, left to themselves, the flower colours of native plants combine in perfect harmony.

weight on your heels. Thorough firming is absolutely vital if the lawn is not to sink locally.

Scatter an organic fertilizer sparingly over the entire surface, and rake it level and to a fine, crumbly consistency. Now it is ready to sow.

LEFT *When the soil has been dug over, firmed and levelled, rake the surface lightly to open it up ready for the grass seed.*

BELOW LEFT *Once you know roughly what 50g of grass seed per sq. m (1½ oz per sq. yd) looks like, you can sow the rest either by hand or using two flowerpots to make a simple shaker.*

BELOW *Using a spring-tine rake, aim to cover approximately half the seed with soil.*

Choose a seed mixture that contains rye grass or even use a single variety of rye grass. It's much easier to manage and generally more drought-resistant than the really fine grass mixtures, and modern varieties will produce a fine enough finish to suit most tastes.

The seed should be sown at about 50g per sq. m (1½oz per sq. yd), but the amount is not critical. Just get an idea of what the right rate looks like by weighing out one lot of 50g and spreading it over a rough metre. Then distribute it with two large flowerpots – about 23cm (9in) diameter – one inside the other. Twist the inside one so that it almost covers the holes of the outside one and fill with seed. You'll find that when you shake the pots over the soil, it's easy to get a very even distribution.

Rake the seed in with a spring-tine rake (usually used for removing moss and thatch from the lawn). It will cover the seed without altering your carefully achieved levels. Aim to cover about 50 per cent.

Make sure that the soil doesn't dry out, but try not to water until after germination if you can since this could wash the seed into patches.

When the new grass is about 5cm (2in) high, mow it with the mower set to its highest cut. Then gradually lower the blades over successive cuts.

Maintenance should be kept to a minimum. In a country garden, when you cut the grass it's best to leave it no shorter than 1cm (½in) and the odd daisy or dandelion should serve only to cheer you up. If you insist on worrying about them, cut them out with a knife.

A wildflower meadow with ox-eye daisies, campion and grasses all growing happily together.

The Flowery Mead

Medieval tapestries and paintings of garden scenes invariably included a wide range of flowers set in grass. It was the height of fashion then to grow wild and cultivated plants in this way, but the practice began to disappear with the coming of the Renaissance in the late fifteenth century. It didn't resurface until quite recently when conservation-minded gardeners began to encourage wildlife into their gardens by growing wildflowers.

Our modern wildflower meadows are very reminiscent of the 'courtly gardens' of the Middle Ages, used for socializing and relaxing and as trysting places. Very similar were the more religious 'Mary gardens' dedicated to the Virgin Mary, worship of whom was a widespread cult at the time.

Much of our knowledge of medieval garden style comes from paintings and tapestries and, of course, the artists used a little licence. Don't expect to be able to recreate a flowery mead exactly as it's represented in an ancient painting, because the custom was to include all the flowers that would be seen there throughout the year, even though they certainly wouldn't have all flowered at the same time.

Bear in mind that the grass can be cut only once or twice a year, so a flowery mead is quite a different proposition from a fine lawn. Because the soil is kept poor, the grass won't grow quite as long and lush as in an unmown lawn, but neither will it be trim and neat. However, once you've seen it in all its flowery splendour you won't be disappointed.

Soil preparation needs to be done thoroughly to get rid of weeds and weed seeds. Ideally do it the organic way by covering the soil with black plastic to exclude light. Unfortunately this process takes many months and even then is not guaranteed to eliminate everything. In my view a better organic alternative is to start by digging out the perennial weeds and follow this by digging the ground over, removing all the weeds you can. Then allow a few weeks for ungerminated seeds to grow and hoe them off. One more hoeing a few weeks later just before sowing should do the trick. Alternatively, if you're happy to live with chemicals, simply spray with a glyphosate weedkiller twice with about four weeks in between. If you have existing turf, there's no better way than to strip it off with about 5cm (2in) or more of topsoil and sow directly into the poor soil underneath. Wildflowers will love it.

Four seasons of flowers captured by the embroiderer's needle in this sixteenth-century French tapestry.

Then the preparation is exactly the same as I've described for lawn-making with one notable difference. The essence of a good wildflower meadow is that the soil should be poor. If it's fertilized, the grass will grow long and lush at the expense of the wildflowers, all of which much prefer poor land. So do everything else but sprinkle fertilizer, and if the soil is a bit rough and poor to start with, so much the better.

Sowing should be done in the spring or autumn, when there is a better chance of showers. Autumn sowing is preferable if the mixture includes seeds like primroses and cowslips which need a cold spell to trigger germination. If you sow in spring when there might be a dry spell, ensure that you have a means of watering just in case.

For large areas in particular it's best to buy the seed mixture from a specialist. Tell him/her what kind of meadow you want, where you live and the nature of your soil, and he/she should be able to tailor the mixture to suit your needs. If, on the other hand, you have only a tiny space to sow, one of the mixtures from a seed catalogue will suffice.

An important fact to check before buying is that the seed actually comes from the country you live in. We need to protect indigenous species the world over; so, if you live in Britain, don't buy Dutch seed and *vice versa*. The species may be the same, but the strain of seed and thus the characteristics of the plants could be very different.

Sowing rates are quite different from those for plain grass seed. Wildflower seed is expensive and generally very small indeed, so it's sown at something like 4–5g per sq. m (0.14–0.17oz per sq. yd), less than a tenth of the rate for grass seed. Naturally it's quite difficult at that rate to get an even spread. The way to do it is by mixing it with a carrier just as you would when sowing small flower

seeds in the greenhouse. Some people use dry sand, but this has the disadvantage that the smallest seed tends to sink to the bottom, so when it germinates, you find the small-seeded species concentrated in one spot. A much better carrier, and the one used by landscapers sowing very large areas, is barley meal. You might, as I did, find that difficult to get, so instead use ordinary layers' mash sold at pet or animal-feed shops for feeding chickens. It does exactly the same job. Mix it at 4 parts to 1 of seed, or more if you have a very small area to sow. It'll need very thorough mixing, so put half the mash in a bucket, add the seed and the other half of mash and then stir it around really very well.

ABOVE *Since wildflower seeds are often tiny, mix them with a carrier like layers' mash bought from a pet shop to ensure that you spread them evenly when you sow.*

BELOW LEFT *Scatter handfuls of the mixture over the soil. Go over the area twice, spreading it quite thinly the first time to see how far it goes.*

BELOW RIGHT *Use a light garden roller to press the seed on to the soil. In a very small area simply tap it down with the back of a rake.*

When you ordered the seed, you will have told the supplier the area you had to cover, so sowing is just a matter of spreading the mixture by hand evenly over the whole area. Of course that's easier said than done, so aim to go over it twice, fairly thinly the first time and then a bit more thickly when you see how much you have left. Because the seed is

so small, it's not a good idea to rake it in for fear of burying it too deeply. Roll it in with a light garden roller or, if the area is very small, tap it into the surface with the back of a rake.

Then just stand back and wait for results. In about three or four weeks you'll see a thin carpet of green and, as the weather warms up, it'll grow away very fast. When it reaches about 25cm (10in), cut it down to 8cm (3in) and continue to cut it regularly to prevent the grass overwhelming the wildflowers and to give them a chance to establish in better light conditions.

The following spring trim it again to 8cm (3in), and then it must be left to flower. Cut it after the seed pods have shed their contents, in late summer. A rotary mower should do the trick or, for very small areas, you could try getting the hang of a scythe. It's not as easy as it looks! After every cut, because the soil must be kept poor, the grass cuttings should be raked off and put on the compost heap. Of course, you never feed or weedkill a flowery mead.

Over the years the wildflower population is bound to change somewhat as the more vigorous species swamp the weaker growers. This is a perfectly natural phenomenon, but if you want to control it and you have the time, you could cut off the flower heads of some of the more strongly growing species before they set seed. You may find that more vigorous weeds (which are, after all, no more than wildflowers) invade the area and threaten the less aggressive species, so a certain amount of 'umpiring' will be required. Simply pull out intruders like docks, nettles or fat hen by hand. Smaller weeds are rarely a problem and, of course, flowering types like dandelions and daisies are positively welcome. You'll free yourself from all the worry and hassle of a bowling-green lawn at a stroke.

Types of Mixture

Several different mixtures are available to suit all kinds of conditions and soil types. It's important to match the right mixture to your particular soil type since the species included can vary considerably. A specialist seeds merchant will be able to offer mixtures for the following conditions and uses: heavy clay soil; sandy soil; medium loam; wet soil; acid soil; limy soil; partial shade; hedgerows; waterside; for attracting butterflies; early flowering; late flowering; cornfield annuals.

Planting Existing Grass

If you don't want to go to all the bother of stripping an existing lawn and resowing with a grass/wildflower mixture, you can very successfully plant wildflowers from pots. Specialist nurseries and some garden centres sell ready-grown plants, but it's really quite easy to grow your own. You can buy seed in separate varieties, though that could be an expensive way of planting a small area. A mixed packet is cheaper and, since they all require the same treatment, just as successful.

Start in mid-spring by sowing the seeds on the surface of a pot of coir compost. Water the compost before sowing and afterwards cover the seeds with vermiculite and the pot with a piece of clear polythene. They need no heat for germination, but you'll get quicker results if you put them in a coldframe or cool greenhouse or on the windowsill.

When they germinate, remove the polythene and after three days or so put them in a closed coldframe. When the seedlings are large enough to handle, you can transfer them to wide spacings in another seed tray, though a much better method is to use plastic modules. These are simply seed trays divided into a number of separate cells about 3cm (1¼in) square. With one plant per cell, you'll be able to grow them on to the planting-out stage with no further disturbance.

If you're really stuck for time, an alternative method is to sow direct into modules. Big seed is placed singly, one per cell, and small seed in the tiniest of pinches you can manage. There's no need to transplant the seedlings or to thin them out, even if several come up in the same cell. Just plant them out as if they were a single plant.

The best way to handle the watering of modules is to put them onto a piece of capillary matting or a bed of sharp sand which is kept moist. The plants can then take up water as required, though you may need to water over the top in very dry weather.

As the plants grow, the coldframe should be progressively ventilated until, by planting-out time in late spring, they are fully acclimatized to the outside temperatures day and night.

Always cut the grass before planting and never use fertilizer. Planting is just a case of making a hole and stuffing the plants in. The ideal tool is a bulb planter, but you should have no difficulty planting with a hand trowel at that time of year since the soil should be reasonably wet and soft. If not, wet it locally with a watering-can rather than wetting the whole area with a sprinkler.

Bear in mind from now on that your plants will be in a very competitive situation. The grass is well rooted and feeling at home, while the wildflowers have to acclimatize, so help them out by ensuring that they never dry out. Watering, I'm afraid, has to be done by hand to ensure that you give plenty to the wildflowers but none to the grass. Once they're rooted, they'll quite happily look after themselves. After that, treat the lawn as suggested for the *second* season to give the wildflowers a chance to seed.

A Variation on a Theme

Far be it from me to discourage you from growing wildflowers. They offer a perfect alternative habitat for insects, including hover-flies, butterflies, lacewings and many more, all of whom are our allies. They often provide food for birds too when the flowers ripen their seeds. And the sight and smell of the flowers will fill your heart with joy. Do it if you can.

However, with my gardening hat on, I have to say that this kind of feature may not be that suitable for small gardens. When the flowers are blooming, they look nothing short of breathtaking, but at other times you may be disappointed. If you have a lot of space, I urge you to find room for a flowery mead, but in a pocket-handkerchief plot you may prefer my variation on the theme.

In my country garden I substituted the grass with low-growing ornamental grasses, which were planted in large drifts to form a tapestry of background colour. Between these I planted herbaceous perennials of a type that wouldn't swamp the grasses, and hardy annuals which would seed themselves. The result is a new kind of flowery mead which flowers throughout the spring, summer and autumn with a background of grasses that are colourful and interesting most of the year.

There's one major difference with this method which you may see as a disadvantage. You can't use it for sunbathing and even walking on it is difficult and damaging to the plants. To solve the problem of access I installed a winding path of stepping stones made from cut-up tree trunks obtained from the local woodyard. They're roughly 30cm (1ft) in diameter and 15cm (6in) thick. Their rustic look blends well with the rest of the garden, but they have the disadvantage that when wet they can become slippery and naturally quite dangerous.

Slices of tree trunk, wrapped in chicken wire to prevent them becoming slippery when wet, make a suitably rustic path through this new-style flowery mead.

Ensure that the top of the wooden 'stepping stone' is level with the surface of the soil, then tread it down firmly to make it stable.

So I covered each one with a piece of wire netting stapled to the sides. They're then simply set on the soil so that the top is level with the soil surface. After a month or so the wire netting weathers and is hardly noticeable.

PREPARATION AND PLANTING

Preparation should be thorough. Carefully dig out all perennial weeds first, and incorporate plenty of coarse grit on heavy land, plus manure or compost regardless of the soil type. I would also include a little organic fertilizer at planting time, but there should be no need at all for feeding afterwards.

If you're the kind of meticulous gardener who can draw up a planting plan and work to it, you'll have no problem planting. Make wide drifts of grasses, matching or contrasting colours to your taste, and allow space for the herbaceous plants in between. I'm anything *but* meticulous and find planting to a detailed plan onerous. So I simply worked it out as I went along. It took a bit of head-scratching and a lot of standing back, viewing and thinking, but it worked out pretty well in the end.

I plant small plants with my hands, forking over the soil lightly before planting each section to remove the footmarks I've made when planting the previous one. You may prefer to plant with a trowel and indeed, on stony soil, that may be the only way.

GRASSES

Acorus gramineus 'Ogon'
A Japanese grass forming low tufts of brilliant yellow that are especially effective in winter. It grows to 30cm (1ft).

Agrostis canina 'Silver Needles'
A delightful, spreading grass growing to no more than 8cm (3in). It has very narrow, white-margined blades.

Carex Sedge
Carex berggrenii is a dwarf, slowly spreading sedge with bronze leaves and small, brown flower spikes; it grows to 8cm (3in).

Ornamental grasses like the silver-blue Festuca glauca *and the bright variegated* Carex oshimensis *'Evergold' can provide interest for most of the year in the 'alternative' flowery mead.*

C. conica 'Snowline' is much the same height, but with deep green, evergreen leaves with a white edge.

C. oshimensis 'Evergold' grows to 23cm (9in) and has striking, green leaves with a bright yellow midrib. C. siderosticha 'Variegata' grows to about 20cm (8in), forming slowly spreading clumps of white-margined leaves, slightly reddish at the base.

C. petriei makes clumps of narrow, pinkish brown leaves, curled at the tip, and grows to 25cm (10in).

C. plantaginea (plantain-leaved sedge) bears broad leaves flushed red at the base and yellowish flower spikes in spring; it grows to 15cm (6in) and prefers shade.

Deschampsia flexuosa Wavy hair grass
This has narrow, bright green leaves and graceful purple-and-silver flowers. Deschampsia flexuosa 'Tatra Gold' bears superb yellow leaves if grown in sunshine.

Elymus magellanicus
A low-growing grass with pale blue leaves, evergreen but less blue in winter. It grows to 15cm (6in) and can be invasive.

Elymus scabrus grows to 45cm (18in), so can be used only as a 'spot' plant. It's well worth growing, though, for its superb blue leaves.

Festuca glauca
The best-known of the blue-leaved grasses, forming attractive, rounded tuffets about 20cm (8in) high. There are several selections like 'Azurit', 'Blauglut' and 'Elijah Blue', all of which are worthwhile.

OPPOSITE *The flowery mead 1990s-style, one season on, has combined cultivated perennials, annuals and grasses in a completely naturalistic way.*

Hakonechloa macra 'Aureola'
This gradually forms mounds of arching, yellow leaves with green stripes.

Holcus mollis 'Albovariegatus'
A carpeting grass growing to 15cm (6in), bearing creamy white leaves with a narrow central green stripe.

Imperata cylindrica 'Rubra'
Japanese blood grass
A striking grass for warmer areas. It produces 25cm- (10in-) tall leaves with blood-red tips.

Milium effusum 'Aureum'
Bowles' golden grass
This has 30cm (1ft), floppy leaves of soft yellow, growing greener as the season progresses. It seeds itself happily between other plants.

Ophiopogon planiscapus 'Nigrescens'
A grass which forms slowly spreading, loose tufts of jet-black leaves about 15cm (6in) tall.

OTHER GROUND-COVERERS

Of course, you don't have to stick entirely to grasses. There are dozens of suitable ground-cover plants that would do as well and, indeed, would look very good alongside the grasses. It would be a mistake, though, to use exclusively ground-cover plants at the expense of grasses since this would change the natural look of the feature completely.

Acaena 'Blue Haze' **New Zealand burr**
A plant which will rapidly cover large areas. Its blue-grey, divided foliage is a foil for bristly, brown flower heads, but it may need controlling from time to time. The stems are reddish in winter.

Ajuga reptans **Bugle**
This and other varieties of the rapidly colonizing bugles are suitable and in the country garden I included the shiny, purple *Ajuga reptans* 'Braunherz', which blends well with the blue grasses. See page 136.

Thymus serpyllum **Common thyme**
This thyme and its varieties hug the ground, forming mats of grey-green foliage topped by small flowers, and have the advantage that they can be walked on, when they give off a pleasant fragrance. Varieties like *Thymus citriodorus* 'Silver Posie' and 'Anderson's Gold' are slightly more shrubby and grow to 15cm (6in), but make a bright show and should certainly be considered.

Trifolium repens 'Purpurascens'
Maroon clover
An excellent foil for the grasses, as are the yellow-leaved varieties like *Trifolioum repens* 'Aureum'.

HERBACEOUS PLANTS

The herbaceous plants to form the flowery part of the mead must be carefully chosen. Use only varieties that will not completely swamp the grasses. Even then, you'll certainly have to spend a little time clipping and cutting to keep them in check during the growing season. Because you'll have your nose down among the flowers and the perfume, it'll never become an arduous task. The following list includes those plants I have found particularly desirable, but I'm sure you could add to it without difficulty.

Aquilegia **Columbine**
The hybrid strains are the most popular, growing to about 60cm (2ft) but never

becoming overpowering. The ferny foliage is topped in early summer by graceful heads of superbly shaped, spurred flowers in various colours. The form 'Hensol Harebell' is more like the old 'granny's bonnets' in shades of pink and blue, and seeds itself quite freely, as does *Aquilegia vulgaris* (common columbine).

Convallaria majalis **Lily-of-the-valley**
A lovely but somewhat invasive plant which would certainly have been grown in medieval flowery meads. It reaches no more than about 15cm (6in) in height and in spring produces delicate spikes of highly perfumed, white flowers. From time to time you may have to control it.

Corydalis flexuosa
A lovely plant about 40cm (15in) tall with delicate foliage and superb, intense blue flowers in spring to early summer. It'll bloom for longer in light shade and becomes dormant in summer after flowering.

Dicentra **Bleeding heart**
See page 136.

Dierama pulcherrimum **Venus' fishing rod**
Arching, grassy leaves 90 cm (3ft) in length send forth showers of silvery pink blooms in late summer.

Fragaria **Strawberry**
Wild strawberries were widely used in medieval flowery meads, and what could be better? The white flowers in spring are very decorative and they're followed by attractive, red fruits in summer which are, of course, edible. There are large-fruited varieties like 'Sweet Sensation' which can be grown from seed; or, alternatively, raise alpine strawberries like 'Baron Solemacher' which have much smaller fruits.

Gypsophila **Baby's breath**
Don't let the twee common name put you off. It makes a 60cm (2ft) mound of tiny, white or pink flowers in summer through to autumn. The varieties 'Festival White' and 'Festival Pink' are worth looking out for.

Heuchera **Coral flower**
This is in a slightly different category in that it will form clumps of quite large leaves which will certainly cover other lower plants. However, if you choose varieties like the purple-leaved 'Palace Purple' or the silver-and-purple 'Pewter Moon', both of which produce airy, white, bell-shaped flowers to a height of about 30cm (1ft), you get the best of both worlds since the leaves are more or less evergreen. Alternatively you could use one of the more vivid varieties like the brilliant red 'Rosemary Bloom' which has green foliage.

Meconopsis cambrica **Welsh poppy**
A wonderful 'weed' which makes clumps of ferny foliage over which bright orange or yellow, single flowers sway gracefully on wiry stems in late spring. It seeds prolifically, but is easy to weed out where it's not wanted. It grows to 45cm (18in).

Nepeta govaniana
A beautiful, 90cm (3ft)tall plant producing airy sprays of clear yellow, tubular flowers in summer. It likes a cool position and it may not be entirely hardy everywhere. It's easily raised from self-collected seed, however, so it's not difficult to replace.

Papaver nudicaule **Iceland poppy**
Often listed as a biennial, this delightful plant is in fact a short-lived perennial. I grow mine for two years running and collect the seed for new plants each year. The single, silky flowers are available in many shades

The autumn-flowering
Schizostylis coccinea.

including pink, orange, red and white. The plant grows to about 45cm (18in).

Schizostylis coccinea **Kaffir lily**
Something like a small gladiolus, this autumn-flowerer produces 60cm (2ft) flower spikes from clumps of grassy foliage. It's available in various shades of white, pink and red.

Thalictrum aquilegifolium **Meadow rue**
A graceful plant with ferny foliage above which rise elegant spires of fluffy, lilac flowers to about 90cm (3ft). Even better is *Thalictrum delavayi* (often sold as *T. diptero-carpum*), with more delicate foliage and huge sprays of lovely, lilac flowers with protruding, cream stamens. It needs a somewhat sheltered spot and may need staking.

Verbena bonariensis
A tall, graceful, 'see-through' plant with a lovely, airy habit. It grows to about 1.5m (5ft) and produces sparsely leaved, branching stems, each one tipped with an intense blue, scented flower. It may not be hardy in all areas, so it's worth collecting seed which it will often spread and germinate without help too.

Veronica gentianoïdes **Speedwell**
Producing 40cm (15in) spikes of light blue flowers in late spring and early summer, this is easy to grow in a sunny spot.

Viola **Violet**
There are varieties of sweet violet in a range of colours in addition to the traditional deep mauve, allof which grow to about 15cm (6in). They will need some shade in summer, so plant them where taller plants will keep them cool.

Zigadenus elegans
A demure and charming plant with grassy leaves and spikes of greenish white, star-shaped flowers to about 60cm (2ft).

BULBS

Many bulbs are excellent flowery-mead material and most will keep coming back and increasing in size year after year. I have excluded those like the daffodils, for example, whose foliage has to remain, alas, looking scruffy for at least six weeks after flowering. Since the plants here are set very close together, it simply isn't feasible to lift them after flowering to heel in somewhere else.

OPPOSITE *The grapefruit-sized flowerheads of* Allium christophii.

Spring bulbs are planted in autumn, summer ones in spring and autumn-flowerers in summer. Plant with a trowel, covering the bulbs with soil to about two or three times their own depth. After several years you may want to lift overcrowded clumps, split them up and replant.

Allium Ornamental onion
Ranging from the low-growing, pink or pale purple-flowered *Allium schoenoprasum* (chives) to the 1.8m (6ft) *A. giganteum*, there are all kinds for all sizes and situations.

Starting in spring, I would choose the 15cm (6in) *A. triquetrum* with hanging, bell-shaped, white flowers with a green stripe. It should seed itself around too. *A. unifolium* grows to about the same height with large, flat, star-shaped, pink flowers in spring.

For summer, plant *A. aflatunense* which produces large, round heads of rich purple flowers held on 90cm (3ft) stems. *A. christophii* develops large, round heads of star-shaped, violet flowers on 60cm (2ft) stems with superb seed heads to follow. *A. flavum* has completely different, yellow flowers on loose heads which curve downwards in a very graceful way; it grows to 30cm (1ft).

A. giganteum is probably too tall for a flowery mead, but the slightly smaller *A. rosenbachianum* with its big, mauve drumsticks would not overpower a large area. *A. moly* is an easy-to-grow, yellow-flowered variety with star-shaped blooms on 23cm (9in) stems. The 60cm (2ft) *A. schubertii* resembles *A. christophii*, but its pink flowers are slightly smaller and borne on stems of different heights to dramatic effect.

Finally don't shun the herb *A. tuberosum* (Chinese chives), which forms clumps of garlic-flavoured leaves and in summer bears masses of lovely, white, star-shaped flowers on 45cm (18in) stems.

Anemone blanda
Very easy to grow with many petalled, daisy flowers of blue, pink, white or magenta on 10cm (4in) stems. It flowers in early spring.

Colchicum autumnale Meadow saffron
Also known as autumn crocus, this is, of course, not a crocus at all. It produces flowers that resemble the crocus in shape but are bigger and pink/white. It's a weak plant and needs the support of the grasses in the flowery mead. Plant in mid-summer.

Crocus
The perfect flower to herald spring and available in many colours. It grows generally to about 15cm (6in) tall with characteristic, trumpet flowers and has the great advantage of not leaving behind too much foliage but returning year on year. Choose the ordinary Dutch crocus for spring and then look to true autumn crocuses, like the purple *Crocus sativus* (saffron crocus) and the deep purple *C. serotinus* (Spanish crocus), for a later show. All are very easy to grow, needing only about 5cm (2in) of soil over them when they are planted.

Eranthis hyemalis Winter aconite
Flowering very early before there's much else about, the bright yellow heads of this plant, no more than 10cm (4in) tall, are a cheering sight. The small, knobbly tubers must be soaked before planting or they'll be disappointing.

Fritillaria meleagris Snake's head fritillary
Certainly this European native bulb would have been seen in the original flowery meads and, provided it won't get baked by the summer sun, it's still a prime candidate. It grows to about 45cm (18in) and in spring bears lovely, pendulous, bell-shaped flowers of pinkish purple conspicuously chequered with lighter purple. There's also a white form.

Snake's head fritillaries naturalize
very well in grass.

Galanthus nivalis Snowdrop

Too well-known to need description, the
15cm- (6in-) high, white, bell-shaped,
pendulous flowers of the snowdrop are one
of the early delights of the year. It's best
planted either when lifted immediately after
flowering or as a pot-grown plant.

Iris reticulata

A delightful plant growing to about 10cm
(4in) with delicate flowers in a range of blues,
reddish blues and white, all with attractive,
mainly yellow markings. It flowers very early
in spring.

Leucojum vernum Spring snowflake

Like a larger snowdrop, this grows to about
20cm (8in) with pendulous, white bells
tipped with green. It must have a slightly
shaded, dampish position.

Lilium Lily

Most lilies prefer to have the base of the plant
shaded and the flowering parts in the sun, so
the flowery mead should be ideal. Plant them
in the autumn or early spring as soon as
possible after you buy them. Above all keep
the bulbs out of the sun. All but *Lilium
candidum* (madonna lily), should be planted
deeply, covered with soil to three to four
times their own depth.

Some of the species lilies, like *L. martagon*
(Turk's cap), which produces tall stems of
nodding, rosy pink flowers, will naturalize
well, while nearly all the hybrids, with their
upward-facing flowers in many colours, will
thrive. They all flower in summer or early
autumn and can be left in the ground from
year to year.

Ornithogalum umbellatum
Star of Bethlehem

A clump-forming plant with narrow, white-
striped leaves and 20cm (8in) stems of starry,
white flowers in early spring. The flowers
won't open in shade, so give it a sunny spot.

Scilla Squill

Scilla sibirica (spring squill) is the best known,
producing deep blue to light blue or white
flowers on 15cm (6in) stems. It's easy to grow
anywhere but very hot, dry places. Look out
too for *S. litardierei* which flowers in late
spring or early summer with bluebell-like
heads of light blue 20cm (8in) tall.

Tulipa Tulip

Tulips really produce too much foliage for the
flowery mead, but I don't think I could resist a
few. The so-called cottage tulips, the lily-
flowered and the *viridiflora* types flower mid to
late season and have been the most successful
for me without lifting after flowering, an
impossible task in the flowery mead.

HARDY ANNUALS

With a more or less permanent cover of foliage on the flowery mead, it won't be possible to sow annual flowers into it and you won't want to leave spaces to plant either. After the initial planting it should, apart from odd replacements where plants fail, look after itself. Even annual plants, therefore, have to be self-perpetuating, which means that they have to be hardy annuals, since the half-hardies would succumb to frost in the first winter. There are several hardy types that will sow themselves year after year and it's these that should be used.

It's best to start by raising them in plastic modules in exactly the way described for starting wildflower plants (see page 145). Naturally, after the first year, the seedlings will appear where *they* want to grow and you'll have little control over that except, of course, that you can weed out seedlings where they're not wanted. This informal spread of plants helps the feature to look entirely natural and much less contrived.

The difficult bit is choosing annuals that'll seed themselves. Some will and others won't, and it's hard to know which are which in your part of the world. However, seed is cheap, so you can afford to experiment. The following list includes those annuals that I've found successful year on year in my own garden.

Calendula officinalis Pot marigold
The English pot marigold has been around since medieval days and is one of the easiest and brightest of cottage-garden flowers. It produces masses of large, yellow or orange flowers the season long and will always

reseed. Use varieties like the 30cm (12in) 'Fiesta Gitana'.

Eschscholzia Californian poppy
Lovely, silky, poppy flowers in a wide range of colours through red, orange, pink, yellow and cream are partnered by fine, divided foliage on plants 23cm (9in) high.

Limnanthes douglasii Poached egg flower
Compact, 15cm- (6in-) high plants produce dozens of bright yellow flowers edged white all summer. An excellent insect attractor.

Linaria Toadflax
The annual toadflax grows to about 23cm (9in) and is covered with small, snapdragon flowers in a wide range of bright colours. The native variety would have been used widely in medieval times and, if it happens to drift in from outside, is worth leaving.

Nigella Love-in-a-mist
The foliage is feathery and delicate and from it arise 45cm (18in) stems of deep blue, rounded flowers followed by attractive seed heads to prolong the season. There are pink, purple and white varieties too, generally sold as a mixture.

Papaver Poppy
Probably the best plant of all for this purpose. The lovely, silky flower heads waft gently over the background tapestry in a variety of colours, some pastel and some striking.

The best to grow are *Papaver rhoeas* 'Mother of Pearl' with superb, single flowers in pastel shades like faded Victorian ballgowns. *P. commutatum* 'Ladybird' has brilliant scarlet flowers with black blotches in the centre. The hybrids like 'Summer Breeze' bear superb flowers in orange, yellow and white, but unfortunately will not reseed.

OPPOSITE *The Iceland poppy,* Papaver nudicaule

Chapter seven

MOOD PLANTING

Nothing warms a gardener's heart more than a plant that's growing vigorously. Strong, shiny, unblemished foliage is a very cheering sight, meaning that all is well and you've done your job properly. The flowers come as something of a bonus. Of course, we all have our failures and, after gardening for a year or two, you can generally shrug your shoulders in the certain knowledge that things will be better next year. What's depressing is finding out that the failure is all your fault.

It's quite essential therefore to find out about your plants, preferably before you buy them and definitely before you plant them. Before you give a solitary thought to the *art* of planting, just make sure that you're putting your charges where they're going to thrive.

Soil type is important. On the heavy clay in my own garden, for example, I can't grow those plants, like pinks, that demand perfect drainage. I have to prepare special planting places with barrow-loads of coarse grit and even then I replace the plants with cuttings every two or three years. If you don't want that kind of commitment, grow something else that will thrive on heavy land.

I can't grow acid-loving rhododendrons, pieris or summer-flowering heathers either, because my soil's just on the limy side of neutral. I could build raised beds and fill them with acid soil, but in this case I prefer to grow lime-lovers. There are plenty of them.

Perhaps even more important is aspect. Sun-loving plants growing in the shade will probably produce perfectly good foliage but very little flower, while shade-lovers in the sun will simply shrivel up. Some golden foliage plants will turn green in shade; others will brown at the edges in too much sun.

Hardiness is another factor that will affect your choice of plant and position. Plants from warmer countries will often thrive in much colder conditions if they're given a south-facing wall and the drainage is improved so that their roots don't sit in water during the winter. Others, just a bit more tender, will have to be grown in pots and sheltered inside during very cold spells.

To make it easier to select plants, I've indicated in my lists whether they are sun- or

---

It takes courage to go for a single block of colour, but the smoky grey foliage and lavender blue flowers of the catmint against the warm buff gravel and brickwork looks almost Mediterranean.

The chalk white and pale pink of these roses forms a soft, easy colour combination that works very well against the mellow terracotta of the brick wall.

shade-lovers, whether they need special cold-weather insurance, and if they grow best on light, sandy soils. I've generally excluded the acid-lovers, which simply refuse to grow on limy soil.

Of course, you'll also have to take into consideration heights, spreads and flowering times. It's not a lot of good making the perfect combination of pink and purple flowers only to find that one plant flowers in June and the other in September.

There's a lot to think about and you shouldn't expect to get it absolutely right the first time – or the second, or the third. Indeed, I still make plenty of planting mistakes and I've been at it for about a hundred years. But you should never let mistakes worry you. Often they're serendipitous, with colours you didn't expect to combine well making the perfect match. Sometimes that plant you thought would grow to knee-height, but

which actually reaches your shoulder, looks very much at home rising out of the lower planting at the very front of the border.

If you do make an error that really screams at you every time you walk into the garden, all is not lost. Plants are very forgiving and will nearly always happily transplant somewhere else, even if they've been in a few years. Herbaceous plants positively thrive on being shifted and even shrubs and trees will move without damage and with only the slightest of checks to their growth, provided you do the job with care and at the right time of year. Remember the great truism of this garden: that as soon as you start to fret and worry about it, you've completely defeated its object.

MATCHING COLOURS

Cottage gardeners have no inclination or need to plan their planting schemes. They simply put plants where they'll thrive, producing a great jumble of colour that nonetheless few of us would deny always looks wonderful. It's the easiest planting style of all and one you may well wish to emulate in your own garden, or at least in part of it. Where you need an effect that will simply lift the spirits, you couldn't do better.

Other gardeners prefer to take the process a stage further and plan their planting, like they do their wallpaper and curtains, so that the colours of flowers match and complement, or contrast with, each other.

The great Victorian/Edwardian plantswoman Gertrude Jekyll was the

original inspiration for many later gardeners. She produced dozens of superb gardens herself, but must have inspired hundreds more throughout the world. She started life as a painter, but her poor eyesight ended her aspirations when she was quite young. Turning to gardening, she developed the technique of 'painting' with flowers to produce effects that had never been seen before. She had many keen disciples: notable gardeners like Vita Sackville-West, the creator of the fabled Sissinghurst Castle gardens, Margery Fish at East Lambrook Manor and many others, all of whom have developed the technique and added their own variations.

The White Garden at Sissinghurst Castle in Kent.

Jekyll relied heavily on the idea of the colour wheel, first conceived by Sir Isaac Newton and developed by French artist Michel Chevreul in 1854. Her principle was that, to blend colours into perfect harmony, you mix those that are adjacent to each other on the colour wheel. Jekyll simplified the wheel to six colours – red, orange, yellow, green, blue and purple – and, in all the examples I've seen, she planted a fairly long border where the principle could be used to good effect. The result is a continuous band of ever-changing colour, gradually blending from blue to purple, red to orange and so on, with never a jarring note.

To make the perfect contrast, on the other hand, you use the colours opposite each other on the wheel. Thus blue would make a perfect combination with purple and an acceptable contrast with orange.

If it's necessary to plant two unacceptable colours together, they should be separated with a neutral colour like white, grey or very dark green.

While these rules make a very good starting point, at the end of the day your own personal ideas of good colour combinations must naturally prevail. I, for example, find the combination of blue and yellow very acceptable, yet they would not fit with Jekyll's colour-wheel rule at all. Still, since the chances of her visiting my garden to complain are pretty remote, I have followed my own star and planted to suit myself. I promise that, if you decide to stray from my advice, I won't complain either. Indeed, quite the reverse.

However, the basic principle remains true and I have more or less followed it in the planting of my town garden.

Opposite the gazebo, where I'll be sitting in the evenings, enjoying a gin and tonic and doing no more than contemplating my navel,

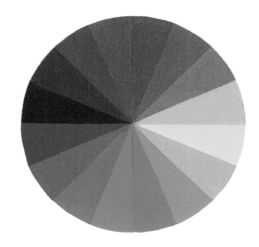

The colours of the spectrum merge gradually, so a softer effect is obtained if the above colour sequence is followed. But the creation of a border is very much a matter of personal preference and some gardeners will want to provide a 'shock' by using contrasting colours in certain situations.

I was after relaxing colours. So here I've planted all the deeper reds, blues and purples, lightened occasionally with white and dark green. Seeing these subdued tones across the reflections in the water has a powerfully soothing effect on jangled nerves and sets me up for a relaxed evening and a good night's sleep.

Moving anti-clockwise round the garden, the next plot, which I can also see from the gazebo without craning my neck, blends gently into the lighter blues and pinks. This is a subtle buffer-zone before the scheme gets busier and brighter with pale blues, yellows and orange in the border near the conservatory.

That one and the scented border are the most visible from the patio and the conservatory, both of which will be used for breakfast depending on the weather. They'll inspire me and remind me of all the good things we're blessed with before I go off to work. It's a far better tonic than the daily dose of gloom you'll get from the morning paper.

There is one difficulty with this otherwise very effective system. Jekyll would plant in long borders with plenty of space, and in my town garden I'm able to divide the borders with a path and a water-rill to make four separate beds. Both methods are highly successful, but in tiny gardens, where the only possibility is a very small border, it just doesn't work: all the plants tend to grow into each other and the graded effect is entirely lost. So simplicity must be the keynote.

I would advise sticking to a much more restricted colour combination here, using perhaps just purple, red and deep blue plants or only pinks, light reds and light blues. You could even use another Jekyll innovation and plant a single-colour border.

The major complication with co-ordinated planting, as I've mentioned, is that there's not a lot of point unless the plants flower at the same time. On the other hand, you can't afford, as they could in big gardens, to have a single border devoted to spring, another to summer and so on. It's inevitable, then, that you'll have some plants in the border that aren't flowering while others are in full bloom.

As I see it, that's not really a problem. Just plant all the reds in one place, followed by all the oranges and your border will blend all the time. There will also, of course, be plants grown especially for their foliage colour which will link the whole thing together as long as they keep their leaves. For the longest-lasting link, therefore, you obviously look to evergreens. I'm quite sure that, after a year or two, you'll want to ring the changes by planting a few contrasting colours as well, so hang on to that colour wheel.

As you'll appreciate, in a book of this size it's not possible to list all available plants, so I've restricted myself to my own favourites and those I feel you simply can't be without – well, provided you've got about 10 acres, that is!

The Reds and Purples

TREES AND SHRUBS

Acer palmatum Japanese maple
The reddest variety, 'Atropurpureum', makes a superb show of red foliage right through the spring and summer. In autumn the fiery colours light up the garden. The variety 'Bloodgood', which grows to 3m (10ft), is even better. 'Dissectum Atropurpureum' makes a lower, gracefully lax bush with very finely divided leaves. Look out too for 'Crimson Queen' and 'Garnet' which have even redder leaves; these will reach a height of about 1.5m (5ft). See page 82.

Berberis Barberry
Berberis ottawensis needs sunshine for the best colour and should be pruned hard every few years to rejuvenate it. *B. thunbergii* 'Atropurpurea', its smaller counterparts 'Atropurpurea Nana' and 'Bagatelle', 'Red Chief' and 'Red Pillar' are also recommended. See pages 90 and 98.

Buddleia davidii Butterfly bush
The variety 'Royal Red' is a deep red-purple. See page 99.

Chaenomeles Flowering quince
Chaenomeles speciosa 'Cardinalis' bears large, crimson flowers while 'Simonii' has double flowers of blood red. There are several red-flowered varieties of *C. superba*, including the orange-red 'Boule de Feu', 'Crimson and

Gold' with red flowers and yellow anthers, and many brilliant red varieties such as 'Firedance', 'Rowallane', 'Texas Scarlet' and 'Vermilion'. See page 77.

Corylus maxima **'Purpurea' Purple filbert**
A strong, vigorous bush growing to 4.5m (15ft) with large, deep purple leaves and red catkins in spring. It grows anywhere and benefits from hard pruning every few years.

Cotinus coggygria **Smoke bush**
The popular variety 'Royal Purple' has deep red-purple, rounded leaves, while 'Grace' has bigger, slightly lighter red foliage. See page 101.

The red of the potentilla against a backgroud of purple foliage is a rich, strong colour combination, while the addition of white both lightens it up and cools it down.

Crataegus laevigata **Flowering thorn**
The variety 'Paul's Scarlet' is massed with double, red flowers in late spring and early summer and followed by red berries in autumn. See page 84.

Cytisus **Broom**
Cytisus scoparius 'Killiney Red' is brilliant scarlet, while 'Windlesham Ruby' is deeper red. The hybrid 'Compact Crimson' will grow to 1.2m (4ft) with deep crimson flowers. See page 92.

Fuchsia
Recommended varieties include 'Mrs Popple', 'Alice Hoffman', 'Dr Foster' (violet and purple) and 'Riccartonii' (crimson and purple like the slightly smaller 'Tom Thumb'). See page 102.

Hydrangea
Of the dozens of suitable varieties I would especially recommend the lacecap 'Geoffrey Chadbund' which grows to 90cm (3ft) and the mop-heads 'Ami Pasquier' and 'Masja', both with deep crimson flowers. See page 103.

Lavandula stoechas pedunculata **French lavender**
See page 95.

Malus **Flowering crab**
There are several varieties with red flowers in spring, followed by red fruits in autumn. Among the best are *Malus purpurea*, and the hybrids 'Eleyi', 'Lemoinei', 'Red Sentinel' and 'Royalty'. The superb 'Profusion' could perhaps go in the red or the purple areas since the flowers and leaves are very dark red-purple. See page 85.

Photinia fraseri **'Red Robin'**
See page 96.

Prunus cerasifera 'Pissardii'
Purple-leaved plum
A small tree or large shrub noted for its deep purple-red leaves and white flowers opening from pink buds.

P. cistena (purple sand cherry) is a smaller shrub growing to about 1.8m (6ft), again with red foliage and white flowers. It makes an excellent hedge. The colours of both are best in full sun. See page 86.

Ribes sanguineum **Flowering currant**
Red varieties include the deep maroon 'Atrorubens Select'; 'King Edward VII' with deep crimson flowers; 'Pulborough Scarlet', which has lighter red flowers with white centres; and 'Red Pimpernel' with rose-red flowers. See page 107.

Rosa **Rose**
Good, red, scented varieties include 'Belle de Crécy', a 1.2m- (4ft-) tall Gallica rose with cerise flowers gradually darkening to violet; 'Arthur de Sansal', a repeat-flowering Portland rose growing to about 90cm (3ft) with crimson-purple flowers and 'Rose de Rescht' with purple-crimson flowers.

'Mme Isaac Pereire' is a Bourbon rose growing to about 1.5m (5ft) and bearing very large, cabbagy, crimson flowers.

The best of the red English roses include the bright crimson 'L. D. Braithwaite'; 'The Dark Lady', very deep red; and the deepest crimson 'The Prince'. All grow to about 1m (39in).

Not all the hybrid tea roses and the floribundas are fragrant, so choose carefully. Many of the newest ones, however, have a high degree of disease resistance. 'Royal William' and 'Velvet Fragrance' are excellent velvety red HTs. Of the floribundas I like 'Dusky Maiden' with almost single, crimson flowers with golden anthers, and 'Shocking Blue' which is more of a vermilion colour with a fine fragrance.

The wine-red foliage of the berberis and pure scarlet of the salvia are an eye-catching combination in the foreground, while the softer pastel shades behind them recede into the distance.

Syringa vulgaris **Lilac**
This large shrub is the perfect alternative to rhododendrons if you have limy soil. 'Souvenir de Louis Spaeth' has the darkest red flowers and grows to about 2.4m (8ft). See page 108.

HERBACEOUS PLANTS AND BULBS

Ajuga reptans **Bugle**
A ground-covering plant for the front of the border. It grows in sun or semi-shade, reaching about 15cm (6in) in height. The spring flowers are in fact blue, but both 'Atropurpurea' and 'Braunherz' have glossy, bronze-purple leaves.

Astilbe arendsii

A fine plant for semi-shade and moist soil. Recommended varieties are 'Aphrodite' with light red flowers and dark bronze leaves and 'Red Sentinel', which bears deep crimson flowers over mahogany spring foliage, though you will find many other varieties at the nursery. See page 130.

Bergenia cordifolia Elephant's ears

An excellent plant in foliage and flower, for the front of the border in sun or semi-shade. It blooms in spring and grows to about 45cm (18in).

'Abendglut' has deep magenta flowers and green-and-maroon leaves which turn deep maroon in winter; 'Purpurea' produces maroon leaves and deep magenta flowers; and 'Morgenröte' has deep carmine flowers over green leaves.

Crocosmia

Most crocosmias have orange or yellow flowers, but the hybrid 'Lucifer' produces spikes of brilliant red from clumps of tall, grassy leaves. It grows to about 90cm (3ft) and flowers in late summer. It does best in full sun.

Cyclamen

This would be at home in a red or a pink border or perhaps as the transition between the two colours. *Cyclamen pseudibericum* sports large, scented flowers of deep carmine in early spring. *C. coum* has deep carmine flowers in winter.

The planting scheme to the right of the path is cool, with whites, pale mauve-pinks, blue itself and blue-green foliage, while the pink rose to the left is much warmer in tone.

Dahlia

A half-hardy plant that needs lifting and storing in a frost-free place in winter. It's well worth the trouble. Dahlias are available in all shapes, sizes and colours, so you'll certainly need a colour catalogue from a specialist. They're generally sold in garden centres prepacked with a colour picture on the front, and you can also make a good choice from that.

The most popular for the red border is undoubtedly the old variety 'Bishop of Llandaff', which grows to 1.2m (4ft) and has brilliant scarlet flowers with rich purple leaves in late summer. 'Comet' is a deep maroon double reaching 90cm (3ft).

Dianthus Garden pink

There are several good red pinks including *Dianthus deltoïdes* 'Wisley Variety' with deep red flowers and the hybrids 'Brympton Red', a dark single, and 'Emperor', a double. They have a fine perfume and grow to about 25cm (10in). Give them a sunny spot on very well-drained soil in full sun.

Digitalis purpurea Foxglove

Really a biennial, but since it never fails to seed itself, you'll have plants every year. Many of them have dark purple-red flowers, but if you wish to keep this colour alone, you'll have to keep weeding out other colours as soon as they flower. They grow to 1.5m (5ft) and prefer dappled shade.

Echinacea purpurea Coneflower

Producing wonderful, large daisies in late summer in shades of pinkish purple, this is easy to grow in well-drained soil in sunshine and reaches about 90cm (3ft). The hybrid 'Magnus' has the darkest, almost purple flowers with the characteristic dark brown cone in the centre.

Epimedium **Barrenwort**

A superb ground-covering plant with heart-shaped leaves, often delicately marked, and topped by dainty spring flowers. Most varieties should be cut back hard in early spring to expose the flowers. They grow to about 30cm (1ft) and prefer a moist soil in semi-shade.

Epimedium grandiflorum has brownish leaves with mauve-pink flowers.

E. rubrum bears green leaves with red-brown markings and clusters of crimson flowers wih a yellow spur.

Euphorbia **Spurge**

Many varieties have excellent red foliage that lasts all year.

---

*The soft blues of the forget-me-nots
and the bluebells create
a restful effect.*

Euphorbia amygdaloïdes 'Purpurea' (often sold as 'Rubra') has yellow flowers with purple stems and leaves. It grows to 30cm (1ft).

E. dulcis 'Chameleon' bears yellow flowers flushed purple over rich purple foliage and also grows to 30cm (1ft).

E. griffithii 'Fireglow' is the odd man out. In early summer it produces brick-red flowers over green-red foliage and it makes excellent autumn colour too. See page 136.

Foeniculum vulgare **'Purpureum' Fennel**

This fine foliage plant grows to about 1.8m (6ft), making a statuesque clump of deep bronze, ferny foliage. It prefers a well-drained soil in sun.

Fritillaria imperialis **Crown imperial**

This tall, stately plant is most often seen in the yellow form, but the variety 'Aurora' is brick-red and very handsome. Plant in the autumn 20cm (8in) deep to ensure continued flowering. It'll grow to 90cm (3ft).

Geranium **Cranesbill**

An accommodating, low-growing plant, some varieties of which will spread to form mats of flower and foliage, while others are clump-forming. Most have a very long flowering period and are never mean with their flowers.They'll grow in sun or part-shade, a few in deep shade and in any soil.

'Ann Folkard' has magenta flowers; 'Kashmir Purple' produces large, purple-red flowers; 'Russell Prichard' has a sprawling habit, growing to only 15cm (6in) in height, and is covered in magenta flowers all summer; Geranium phaeum has dark maroon flowers and does very well in shade; while G. sanguineum forms hummocks of vivid magenta flowers.

G. nodosum has lilac-red flowers and evergreen foliage and thrives in deep shade.

Geum Avens

An easy-to-grow, sun-loving plant that does better if divided every three years. Most forms reach 30cm (1ft) or more with graceful, cup-shaped flowers in summer.

Geum chiloense has scarlet flowers; 'Rubin' is a semi-double, crimson-flowered hybrid; and 'Mrs Bradshaw', though short-lived, is bright brick-red and easily raised from seed. See page 131.

Helleborus orientalis Lenten rose

An early-flowering perennial with wonderful, nodding, cup-shaped flowers in a variety of colours. There are some excellent, dusky reds, but make sure that you buy plants in flower because seedlings vary enormously. They grow to about 30cm (1ft) in deep or light shade and they prefer a retentive soil. Cut off the evergreen leaves in late winter to display the flowers to best advantage – new leaves will grow in spring.

Hemerocallis Day lily

Preferring full sun or part-shade, this plant is not fussy about soil. 'Anzac', 'Black Magic', 'Chicago Royal Robe', 'Franz Hals' and 'Stafford' (red with a yellow throat) all fit the bill from the point of view of flower colour. See page 137.

Heuchera Coral flower

See page 151.

Iris

There are several superb hybrids of the *Iris germanica* (flag iris) flowering in summer in deep red, purple and almost black. They grow to about 60cm (2ft) and like well-drained soil. Look out for 'Marshlander', which is mahogany-brown; 'Queechee', with deep garnet-red flowers; 'Sable', which is a rich, deep purple; and 'Tall Chief', mahogany-red.

I. chrysographes is smaller with grassy foliage, growing to about 45cm (18in). 'Rubella' bears burgundy-red flowers while those of 'Black Knight' are almost black. They prefer a retentive soil and all like full sun.

Lathyrus vernus Spring vetchling

A low-growing, mound-forming plant for the front of the border. In spring the ferny leaves are covered with dark purple flowers. It does best in retentive soil in half-shade.

Ligularia dentata

This striking plant needs a moist soil and will do well in a bog garden. In hot sun it tends to wilt, but soon recovers. The variety 'Desdemona' would be appropriate for the red/purple section of the border. See page 132.

Lilium Lily

The bulb catalogue will again be useful when choosing lilies since there are dozens of species and hybrids which are suitable. Varieties like 'Red Carpet' will brighten the border with vivid scarlet blooms, while the oriental hybrid 'Journey's End' is a more muted, deep carmine with darker spotting. Ideally grow them through lower-growing shrubs or herbaceous plants so that the bulb is shaded but the flowers are in the sun. Plant 15cm (6in) deep in the autumn or early spring.

Lychnis chalcedonica Maltese cross

An easy plant for well-drained but retentive soil in sun. The cross-shaped flowers are brilliant scarlet and look especially good brightening up a deep red or purple scheme. It grows to about 90cm (3ft) and flowers all summer.

Lychnis arkwrightii grows to 30cm (1ft) with brilliant scarlet flowers and purple-red foliage.

Lythrum salicaria **Purple loosestrife**
For this section of the border look out for the named varieties 'Firecandle' and 'The Beacon'. See page 132.

Monarda didyma **Bergamot**
A brilliant but short-lived herb growing to about 90cm (3ft) with large heads of sage-like flowers in late summer. 'Adam' and 'Cambridge Scarlet' are both bright red, 'Prairie Glow' is salmon-red and 'Prairie Night' is purple. They need a moist soil and a sunny spot.

Origanum laevigatum **Marjoram**
In late summer this attractive plant sends up 45cm (18in) spikes of purple flowers: invaluable for the front of the border.

Paeonia lactiflora **Peony**
In the sunniest spot in the garden, in retentive soil, peonies will give good value for many years. They produce large, exotic, cup-shaped flowers in summer. 'Félix Crousse' is a free-flowering, double red; 'Karl Rosenfield' is a double with wine-red flowers; 'Martin Cahuzac' has carmine-red, double flowers. They grow to about 75cm (30in).
Paeonia officinalis 'Rubra Plena' is the old-fashioned type with deep crimson, double flowers.

Papaver orientale **Oriental poppy**
A large, vigorous, sun-loving plant with huge, cup-shaped, papery flowers. It grows to about 75cm (30in) and should be cut back after flowering when it becomes floppy and untidy. You may need a potted plant to stand in its place while it regrows. 'Beauty of Livermere' is a blood-red single; 'Glowing Embers' is orange-red; 'Goliath' is a dark, glowing red; and 'Ladybird' is vermilion-red with a black centre. All flower in summer.

Penstemon
There are several good hybrids that produce their tubular flowers all summer and are well worth growing, though they may not be entirely hardy. Take cuttings in late summer and overwinter them on a windowsill. Leave the parent plant in to see if it's hardy.
They prefer a sunny spot and well-drained soil and most grow to about 60cm (2ft). 'Firebird' is bright red; 'Garnet' is wine-red; 'King George' is salmon-red with a white throat; 'Ruby' is blood-red and very free-flowering; and 'Cherry Ripe' is bright red. There are many more.

Persicaria amplexicaulis **Knotweed**
See page 133. 'Atrosanguineum', 'Firetail' and 'Taurus' – bright red and reaching only 60cm (2ft) – are appropriate choices. They all like a retentive soil in full sun or part-shade.

Phlox paniculata
An invaluable, strong-growing herbaceous plant for a sunny spot or dappled shade and a reasonably well-drained soil. If it is attacked by eelworm, there's nothing for it but to grow something else. In late summer, it produces large trusses on strong stems about 90cm (3ft) tall which may need staking. 'Border Gem' is violet-purple; 'Branklyn' is deep lilac; 'Franz Schubert' is lilac; 'July Glow' is crimson; 'San Antonio' is purple-red; and 'Marlborough' is purple with dark foliage.

Potentilla **Cinquefoil**
A marvellous, summer-flowering plant for the front of the border in sunshine or part-shade and excellent just trailing through shrubs or taller herbaceous plants. The prolific flowers are saucer-shaped and the plant grows to about 45cm (18in). 'Blazeaway' and 'Gibson's Scarlet' are brilliant red and 'Flamenco' is blood-red.

Primula

See page 133. There are also a few double primroses worth growing, like 'Roy Cope' with crimson flowers on 15cm (6in) stems, and *Primula vialii* produces dense, conical spikes of purple, red and blue flowers.

Pulsatilla vulgaris Pasque flower

A low-growing plant reaching about 23cm (9in). In spring the nodding buds open to dark purple-red, silky, cup-shaped flowers. These are followed by ferny, divided foliage and brown seed heads. It needs full sun and excellent drainage.

Rheum Ornamental rhubarb

Rheum palmatum 'Ace of Hearts' is an excellent foliage plant for a shady spot. See page 137.

Salvia officinalis 'Purpurascens' Purple sage

A summer-flowering, evergreen shrub with grey-green leaves flushed purple when young. It grows to 90cm (3ft) and produces purple-blue flowers. It likes a sunny spot and must have well-drained soil.

Schizostylis coccinea Kaffir lily

See page 152. 'Major' has deep crimson flowers.

Sedum Stonecrop

Many of the fleshy-leaved sedums are invaluable summer- or late-summer-flowerers. They reach from 15 to 60cm (6in to 2ft) and prefer a sunny or semi-shaded spot. 'Ruby Glow' forms rosettes of deep red flowers; *Sedum spectabile* 'Meteor' is a clump-forming plant with deep carmine-red flowers; *S. spurium* 'Schorbuser Blut' is a prostrate, creeping plant with purple-pink flowers and red-tinted leaves which turn crimson in winter; and *S. telephium* has purple flowerson lax stems.

The Pasque flower, Pulsatilla vulgaris.

Tricyrtis formosana Toad lily

The beautiful, orchid-like flowers, mauve with dark spots and a yellow throat, make this a plant that needs to be seen at close quarters. It prefers dappled shade and grows to 90cm (3ft). 'Stolinifera' has rich purple flowers and spreads rapidly.

Tulipa Tulip

There are tulips which flower from early spring to early summer in a wide range of reds and purples, from the brilliant red 'De Wet' to 'Black Swan', so dark purple that it really is almost black. Plant bulbs in late autumn or pot them up and plant in spring when you can see where the spaces are. They all prefer sun and a well-drained soil.

Viola labradorica Violet

While there are several hybrid violas with purple-red flowers, this one is a real gem. It forms low-growing mats of purple leaves topped with blue flowers in early summer. It seeds freely and will grow almost anywhere.

The Oranges and Yellows

TREES AND SHRUBS

Aucuba japonica **Spotted laurel**
'Crotonifolia' has large leaves blotched and spotted with gold, while 'Picturata' is one of the brightest with a bold yellow splash in the centre of the leaves. See page 90.

Berberis **Barberry**
Most of these valuable shrubs have yellow or orange flowers. See pages 90 and 98.

Catalpa bignonioïdes **'Aurea'**
Indian bean tree
See page 83.

Cestrum parqui
Willow-leaved jessamine
See page 99.

Coronilla valentina glauca
A lovely shrub producing bright yellow, pea-like flowers in late winter and spring. See page 92.

Cytisus **Broom**
Cytisus battandieri (Moroccan broom) produces large clusters of pea flowers strongly scented of pineapple.
  C. beanii is a prostrate, spreading form covered in yellow flowers in summer.
  C. praecox 'Canary Bird' has masses of brilliant yellow flowers.
  C. scoparius is more erect and grows to 1.5m (5ft); it bears brilliant yellow flowers. Its hybrid 'Cornish Cream' is creamy white and yellow; 'Luna' has two-coloured flowers of light and dark yellow. See also page 92.

Elaeagnus **Oleaster**
See page 92.

Forsythia
See page 102.

Genista
Genista tinctoria 'Royal Gold' forms a rounded bush 90cm (3ft) high. See page 103.

Gleditsia triacanthos **'Sunburst'**
Honey locust
See page 84.

Hamamelis mollis **Witch hazel**
See page 103.

Hypericum
See page 104.

Ilex **Holly**
Several hollies have yellow-variegated foliage and make excellent, tough trees or large shrubs, furnished with branches right down to the ground.
  Ilex aquifolium 'Golden Milkboy' is not easy to find, but is well worth searching out. The spiny leaves have a bold golden splash in the centre. 'Ferox Aurea' (hedgehog holly) is very spiny with a central gold splash and grows at about half the normal rate. See page 94.

Laburnum watereri **'Vossii' Golden rain tree**
See page 85.

Ligustrum ovalifolium **'Aureum'**
Golden privet
Wrongly much maligned, this makes a very bright bush with green-and-gold-variegated foliage and can be clipped to shape. See page 95.

Mahonia media
As well as the varieties listed on page 96, 'Buckland' is well worthwhile.

***Philadelphus coronarius* 'Aureus'**
Golden mock orange
One of the brightest golden foliage shrubs of
all in spring and early summer, turning pale
green later. See page 106.

Yellow, the dominant shade here, lights up the scene.

***Phlomis fruticosa* Jerusalem sage**
See page 96.

***Phormium* New Zealand flax**
Available in several colours, including some
varieties with bright yellow stripes. It makes
an excellent architectural contrast in a mixed
border. See page 96.

Physocarpus opulifolius **'Dart's Gold'**
See page 1060.

Potentilla fruticosa **Shrubby cinquefoil**
As well as the forms listed on page 106, look
for 'Coronation Triumph', which has brilliant
yellow flowers and grows to 1.2m (4ft);
'Goldstar', which reaches 90cm (3ft) with
large, yellow flowers; and 'Tangerine',
bearing copper-orange flowers.

Robinia pseudoacacia **'Frisia' False acacia**
See page 87.

Rosa **Rose**
There are dozens of very fine, yellow roses and,
as with the reds, you should look out for those
with good perfume as well as fine colour.
'Dutch Gold' is a vigorous hybrid tea with
well-formed, fragrant blooms; 'Pot o' Gold' has
clear yellow flowers and a good perfume;
while 'Sutter's Gold' is a rich gold flushed with
peach, and with an excellent perfume.

Of the cluster-flowered floribunda roses I
like 'Arthur Bell' with large, semi-double,
fragrant flowers; 'Chinatown', a very tall rose
with large, double flowers and good
perfume; and 'Mountbatten', another tall rose
bearing large, cupped blooms with an
excellent fragrance.

My all-time favourite English rose is
'Graham Thomas', which has rich butter-
yellow blooms and a superb fragrance. 'Jayne
Austin' has soft yellow, scented blooms; and
'Golden Celebration' has exceptionally deep
yellow flowers with a particularly fine perfume.

One of the best of the shrub roses is the
single-flowered 'Golden Wings', which
bears pale yellow, well-perfumed flowers
and red stamens.

There are several orange colours too. 'Pat
Austin' is a fine copper-orange English rose.
'Fellowship' is a bright orange floribunda

with a fine fragrance; 'Apricot Nectar' is
another floribunda but in a softer apricot
yellow. 'Apricot Silk', 'Mojave' and 'Beauté'
are apricot-orange hybrid teas, as are perhaps
two of the most popular, 'Just Joey' and
'Whisky Mac'.

Sambucus racemosa **'Plumosa Aurea'**
Golden elder
This is the best of the golden-leaved elders,
with copper-coloured buds which open into
fresh yellow leaves in the early spring. See
page 134.

Thymus citriodorus **'Aureus' Lemon thyme**
A low shrub growing to about 23cm (9in)
with small, yellow leaves. It needs a sunny
spot and excellent drainage.

Viburnum opulus **'Xanthocarpum'**
See page 110.

---

*The superb rich egg-yolk yellow of the English rose,
'Graham Thomas'.*

HERBACEOUS PLANTS AND BULBS

Achillea Yarrow

An easy-to-grow, tall plant with some fine, yellow hybrids. 'Moonshine' grows to 60cm (2ft) and produces flat heads of lemon-yellow above a clump of silver filigree foliage over a long period in summer. 'Anthea' is paler yellow and more erect, while 'Gold Plate' will grow to 1.2m (4ft) with large heads of brilliant yellow.

Alchemilla mollis Lady's mantle

This invaluable plant can spread rapidly, but is easy to pull out. Its rounded leaves catch drops of water which shine in the morning sunshine, and in summer it produces 45cm (18in) sprays of greenish yellow flowers. It's happy in sun or dappled shade in damp, dry and even waterlogged soil.

Anthemis tinctoria Ox-eye chamomile

For a brilliant display of yellow, this plant is hard to beat. After flowering it's important to cut it back to ground level to induce basal growth or the plant will be short-lived. Take basal cuttings in early spring to ensure con-tinuity. It prefers full sun and a well-drained soil and grows to about 90cm (3ft). The hybrid 'Grallach Gold' is deep yellow, while 'E.C. Buxton' and 'Wargrave' are a rather paler, primrose-yellow.

Caltha palustris
Kingcup/marsh marigold
See page 128.

Cephalaria gigantea Giant scabious

A huge plant for the back of the border producing a succession of yellow, pin-cushion flowers over a very long period. It grows to about 2.1m (7ft).

Coreopsis verticillata Tickseed

In late summer this easy plant produces masses of bright yellow daisies. It reaches about 60cm (2ft) and prefers full sunshine, though it'll grow in almost any well-drained soil. 'Grandiflora' has large, deep yellow flowers and those of 'Moonbeam' are pale lemon-yellow.

Crocosmia

These erect, spiky plants are invaluable late summer-flowerers. They like a sunny spot and good drainage and grow to about 75cm (30in). 'Bressingham Blaze' has brilliant orange flowers; 'Citronella' is slightly shorter than most with soft yellow flowers; 'Emberglow' is deep orange; 'Emily MacKenzie' is orange with a deep maroon throat; 'Jenny Bloom' has flowers of soft yellow; and 'Firebird' is brilliant orange. See page 167.

Crocus

Crocus angustifolius, known as 'Cloth of Gold', has bright orange-yellow flowers and *C. chrysanthus* 'E. A. Bowles' bears rich golden-yellow flowers in early spring. See page 154.

Doronicum austriacum Leopard's bane

This produces bright yellow daisies in early spring for a very long period. It grows in sun or part-shade in retentive soil. Look out for 'Harpur Crewe' which reaches about 90cm (3ft) and the shorter 'Spring Beauty'.

Eranthis hyemalis Winter aconite
See page 154.

Euphorbia Spurge

All the spurges are splendid for the yellow border, bringing a somewhat softer hue to tone down brighter colours. See page 136.

Filipendula ulmaria 'Aurea' Meadowsweet
The golden-leaved form of meadowsweet is
worth growing for its bright foliage which
needs sunshine or it loses its colour.
See page 131.

Fritillaria imperialis Crown imperial
As well as the yellow varieties, look out for
'Orange Brilliant'. See page 168.

Geum Avens
There are some excellent yellow and orange
varieties, including 'Borisii', which is early-
flowering with brilliant orange-red blooms;
'Coppertone', with arching sprays of copper-
orange flowers; and 'Lady Stratheden', which
is bright yellow and grows to 60cm (2ft). See
pages 131 and 169.

Helenium Sneezeweed
This well-known plant produces good
clumps of foliage and prolific yellow, orange
and red daisies with a central disc. It prefers
sunshine and may need staking. It flowers in
late summer and grows to about 90cm (3ft).
The variety 'Bressingham Gold' is deep
yellow; 'Butterpat' is clear yellow and rather
later flowering; and 'Coppelia' is copper-
orange.

Hemerocallis Day lily
There are many yellow hybrid day lilies
which flower in summer and grow to about
60–90cm (2–3ft). Look out too for the fragrant
species *Hemerocallis citrina* and *H. flava* and
for the orange *H. fulva*. See page 137.

Kirengeshoma palmata
This shrubby perennial thrives in moist soil
in sun or part-shade. It forms a bushy plant
with graceful, nodding flowers of pale
yellow. Growing to 90cm (3ft), it flowers in
late summer.

Kniphofia Red hot poker
This imposing plant rears above the border,
producing spikes of brilliant oranges and
yellows in summer. It likes full sun and a
well-drained soil. The foliage looks
somewhat untidy after flowering in
particular, so hide the bottom of the plant
among lower herbaceous plants.
  'Ada' grows to about 90cm (3ft) with
spikes of orange-yellow; 'Bressingham
Comet' is bright orange and grows to 60cm
(2ft); 'Fiery Fred' is orange-red and a little
taller; 'Goldelse' grows to 90cm (3ft) with
clear yellow spikes; while 'Shining Sceptre' is
orange-gold and about the same height.

Ligularia
See page 132.

Lilium Lily
Check out the garden centre or the bulb
catalogue for yellow and orange hybrid lilies.
See page 155.

**Lysimachia nummularia 'Aurea'
Creeping Jenny**
See page 137.

Meconopsis cambrica Welsh poppy
See page 151.

**Milium effusum 'Aureum'
Bowles' golden grass**
See page 137.

*While yellow and blue do not fit in with Gertrude
Jekyll's colour-wheel theory, the combination of bright
yellow* Coreopsis verticillata, *the pale sulphur of
helichrysum, the smoky blue of perovskia (Russian
sage) and the rich blue of salvia prove that nature
usually knows best.*

Narcissus Daffodil

The daffodils are well-known and need no description. They have the disadvantage of leaving a legacy of untidy leaves for some time after flowering, so plant them among herbaceous plants which will do a cover-up job with their own emerging foliage in spring

Oenothera Evening primrose

In well-drained soil and sunshine, this lovely plant produces large, trumpet-shaped flowers of clear yellow.

Oenothera missouriensis has a sprawling habit, reaching only 23cm (9in) though spreading much wider. Its yellow trumpets are produced over a long period in summer. The hybrid 'Highlight' grows to 60cm (2ft) with bright yellow flowers but may need staking, while 'Sonnenwende' has maroon leaves and buds which open to yellow on 45cm (18in) stems.

Origanum vulgare 'Aureum' Golden marjoram

The golden form of the well-know herb makes a good, low-growing carpet of yellow foliage from which arise purplish flowers in summer. To retain its colour it needs full sunshine. It grows to about 23cm (9in).

Papaver nudicaule Iceland poppy

See page 151.

Potentilla Cinquefoil

There are some valuable orange and yellow varieties, such as 'Firedance' with bright orange flowers; 'Goldkugel', which spreads less rapidly and bears fresh yellow flowers; 'William Rollison', which has brilliant orange blooms; and 'Yellow Queen', which produces silvery leaves and bright yellow flowers. See page 106.

Primula Primrose

Several of the primroses produce soft yellow flowers in early spring and can be grown among herbaceous plants or under deciduous trees and shrubs where they'll be in dappled shade in summer. See page 133.

Rudbeckia Coneflower

Among the best of the late summer perennials, the coneflower has brilliant yellow, daisy flowers with a deep brown central cone. Rudbeckia deamii bears greyish foliage and yellow flowers, but the best of all is the variety 'Goldsturm' with deep yellow flowers that continue for weeks, over dark green foliage. They grow to 75cm (30in). 'Goldquelle' is dwarfer and is covered in fully double flowers of sharp yellow.

Tanacetum parthenium 'Aureum' Feverfew

A fine, golden-leaved form of common feverfew. In spring the foliage is at its brightest and later the plant produces many white daisies and the leaves turn greener. It's happy in sun or shade and ordinary soil, growing to about 60cm (2ft). It seeds itself freely but never becomes a problem.

Thalictrum flavum Meadow rue

The yellow meadow rue grows to 1.5m (5ft) with green leaves and lovely, fluffy flowers in summer. The variety Thalictrum flavum glaucum has the added attraction of blue-tinted leaves. See also page 152.

Trollius Globe flower

See page 134.

Tulipa Tulip

A range of yellow and orange tulips will give a fine display from spring to early summer. Plant them among yellow or blue herbaceous plants. See page 171.

Verbascum Mullein

A tall, architectural plant that never seems to need staking, however tall it grows. It thrives in sunshine in well-drained soil. *Verbascum chaixii* grows to about 90cm (3ft) in height, producing lovely slender spires of yellow flowers with a mauve eye. There are several good hybrids too, including 'Golden Bush', which grows to 60cm (2ft) with several stems arising from the one clump, all packed with small, yellow flowers; 'Hartleyi', bearing darker yellow flowers with mauve centres; and 'Gainsborough', which is taller with woolly, felted leaves and spikes of yellow flowers.

The Pinks and Blues

I've combined these two colour groups because they complement each other perfectly. I have used them in my town garden borders in this way.

TREES AND SHRUBS

Acaena 'Blue Haze' New Zealand burr
A good ground-coverer for a sunny spot. See page 150.

Buddleia davidii Butterfly bush
'Empire Blue' is light blue with an orange eye; 'Lochinch' is violet-blue with an orange eye; 'Ile de France' is rich violet. See page 99.

Caryopteris clandonensis Blue spiraea
This small shrub needs a well-drained soil and a warm position. 'Ferndown' has violet-blue flowers; and 'Worcester Gold' bears bright blue flowers which form a good contrast with the greenish yellow leaves. See page 99.

Ceanothus Californian lilac
These are slightly tender shrubs which must be given a warm spot, preferably a south-facing wall. On heavy soil, improve the drainage too to help them through the winter. The evergreen varieties tend to be the less hardy and flower in spring, while the deciduous types flower in summer. See pages 76, 91 and 99.

Ceratostigma willmottianum Hardy plumbago
A sunny spot and good drainage are this shrub's preferred conditions. See page 99.

Cercis siliquastrum Judas tree
See page 83.

Chaenomeles speciosa Flowering quince
The variety 'Geisha Girl' has peach-pink flowers and is slightly shorter than most; 'Moerloosei' is a fine variety with delicate pink flowers; and 'Umbilicata' is coral pink. All grow to about 1.5m (5ft) and flower in late winter and early spring. There are also several good hybrids. 'Cameo' has double pink flowers; 'Coral Sea' is, naturally, coral pink; and 'Pink Lady' is red in bud opening to bright pink. See page 77.

Cistus Sun rose
'Grayswood Pink' produces masses of pink flowers and 'Peggy Sammons' has grey-green foliage and light pink flowers. See page 91.

Deutzia
Deutzia chunii grows to 1.5m (5ft) with pink, bell-shaped flowers with white inside and golden anthers in summer; the variety 'Pink Charm' is entirely pink. *D. rosea* 'Carminea' grows to only about 90cm (3ft) and has a spreading habit; red buds open to rosy pink flowers in early summer. See page 102.

Escallonia
See page 94.

Eucalyptus **Gum tree**
This is a fast-growing tree, many varieties of which have fine, glaucous, blue bark and blue foliage. In large gardens, forms such as *Eucalyptus pauciflora niphophila* make excellent, large trees, especially if grown multi-stemmed. But in this particular garden they would look decidedly foreign. On the other hand, if cut back hard each spring to keep it small, this species and the more common *E. gunnii* retain their rounded, juvenile leaves and make good evergreen shrubs. They grow to about 1.8m (6ft) and are not fussy as to soil or situation.

Hebe
'Margret' grows to 45cm (18in) and has blue flowers fading to white over a long period in summer; 'Midsummer Beauty' reaches 1.2m (4ft) and has a succession of lavender-blue flowers all summer; and 'Quicksilver' grows to 60cm (2ft) with silver-blue foliage and lilac-blue flowers over a long period in summer. There are several more, so check them out at the nursery. See page 94.

Helianthemum **'Wisley Pink' Rock rose**
A small, sun-loving shrub that thrives in poorish soil with good drainage. Trim the plant lightly after flowering. All summer it produces saucer-shaped, pink flowers which contrast well with silver-grey foliage.

Hibiscus syriacus **Mallow**
Slow-growing and late to leaf, this shrub needs patience. In a sunny spot on well-drained soil, it'll produce large, trumpet-shaped flowers in late summer. Prune it hard in early spring to encourage strong growth and good flowering. 'Ardens' is a lilac-purple

double; 'Blue Bird' is a single violet with a darker centre; and 'Violet Clare' is a double violet-blue. All grow to 1.5m (5ft).

Hydrangea
On chalky soil blue hydrangeas will turn pink or, at best, reddish blue. You can use a blueing agent to help blue varieties keep their colour. As well as the varieties listed on page 103 look out for 'Altona', which is pink or deep blue on acid soils, and 'Générale Vicomtesse de Vibraye', also pink or blue on acid soil.

Kolkwitzia amabilis **Beauty bush**
See page 105.

Lavatera **Tree mallow**
See page 105.

Malus **Flowering crab**
Several of the flowering crabs have good, pink flowers in early summer followed by coloured fruit in autumn. *Malus floribunda* grows to only 5m (17ft) and most of the hybrids will reach about 8m (26ft). 'Butterball' and 'Van Eseltine' both bear prolific, pink flowers, while 'Evereste' is smaller with pink-and-white blossoms. Don't forget the cultivated apples, too, which bear plenty of pink-and-white flowers. See page 85.

Parahebe perfoliata **Digger's speedwell**
An unusual dwarf sub-shrub with glaucous, blue, rounded leaves which encircle the stem. It grows to 45cm (18in) and produces violet-blue flowers in long clusters in late summer. It needs full sun and good drainage.

Perovskia atriplicifolia **'Blue Spire' Russian sage**
See page 106.

Prunus Flowering cherry

Many of the flowering cherries are suitable for quite small gardens. *Prunus sargentii* bears pale pink, single flowers and lovely, bronze foliage in spring and has good autumn colour too.

Prunus cerasifera 'Rosea' grows to about 8m (26ft) and has purplish leaves and small, pink flowers in profusion in spring. *P. subhirtella* 'Autumnalis Rosea' is a small tree, growing to about 6m (20ft) and producing flushes of pink flowers all winter and spring. There are many others, so make a visit to a good tree nursery. See page 86.

Rosa Rose

It really is necessary to get hold of a couple of good rose catalogues to make your choice, since there are dozens of excellent pink varieties, though of course no real blues. As with the other colours, make sure that your choices are fragrant and have a degree of disease resistance.

The best of the English roses include 'Heritage', a lovely blush pink; 'Sharifa Asma' with very pale pink flowers fading to white; 'Brother Cadfael' with large, darker pink flowers; and 'Gertrude Jekyll', a true deep pink. 'Abraham Darby' and 'Evelyn' have a touch of apricot in the very well-scented blooms.

Shrub roses to look out for include the Damask roses 'Ispahan' and 'Marie Louise', both 1.5m (5ft) plants with clear pink flowers. 'Fantin-Latour' is a 1.8m- (6ft-) tall Centifolia rose with lovely, cup-shaped blooms of blush pink deepening to shell pink at the centre. 'Comte de Chambord' is a darker, warm pink growing to 1.2m (4ft); 'Louis Odier' is one of the best of the Bourbons with warm pink flowers shaded lilac and a very strong perfume. 'Ballerina' is an almost continuous flowerer with small, pink blooms but alas no perfume to speak of. *Rosa eglanteria*,

The silvery olive-green foliage of Elaeagnus angustifolia *'Quicksilver' is the perfect foil for the warm, rich pink of this rose.*

(eglantine rose) is one not to be missed. In the mornings after dew, or after rain, it smells strongly of fresh apples, while the clear pink flowers light up the garden. They're followed by red hips in autumn. It grows to 2.4m (8ft).

Of the modern bush roses look for the hybrid teas 'Blessings', which is salmon pink; 'Prima Ballerina', rose pink; and 'Pristine', very pale pink. For floribundas I would choose 'English Miss', light pink; 'Escapade', violet-pink; and 'Pink Parfait', pink and cream, though with only a slight perfume.

Rosmarinus officinalis Rosemary

A well-known small shrub often grown in the herb border, but also very attractive with grey foliage and blue flowers in early summer. Probably the hardiest variety is 'Miss

Jessopp's Upright' with, as the name suggests, an upright growing habit to about 1.2m (4ft). For a more prostrate variety look for 'McConnell's Blue', which forms a 45cm-(18in-) high mound. They must have sun and excellent drainage.

Ruta graveolens 'Jackman's Blue' Rue

With deeply divided, ice-blue foliage, this small shrub is perfect for the front of a well-drained, sunny border. It grows to 90cm (3ft) and produces yellow flowers which detract from the appearance and should be pinched out. Be careful when you handle it, though, because it can cause a bad skin rash, especially in sunlight. Prune in spring, cutting out old shoots.

Syringa Lilac

There are several blue and, of course, lilac lilacs well worth growing for colour and perfume in early summer. As well as the varieties suggested on page 108 look out for 'Michel Buchner', a double-flowered lilac-blue.

Teucrium fruticans Shrubby germander

See page 79.

Viburnum

Viburnum burkwoodii 'Chenaultii' grows to 1.8m (6ft) and produces pale pink, very fragrant flowers in early spring. V. carlesii 'Aurora' grows to 1.5m (5ft) and has deep red buds opening to very fragrant, pink flowers in spring. See pages 97 and 110.

Vinca minor Dwarf periwinkle

A scrambling ground-coverer which can become a nuisance if not regularly controlled.

White and lavender-blue is a cool, soft colour combination.

It produces masses of small, bell-shaped, blue flowers in early summer. It will grow in dry shade, flowers better in good soil in the sun.

Weigela

The hybrid 'Boskoop Glory' is satin pink and 'Dropmore Pink' is deep pink; both grow to about 90cm (3ft). Taller varieties include the deep pink 'Rosabella', and 'Victoria' with dark purplish foliage and rose-pink flowers. See page 110.

HERBACEOUS PLANTS AND BULBS

Aconitum Monkshood

A very attractive plant producing 90cm (3ft) spikes of flowers a little like those of the delphinium. The hooded flowers give this poisonous plant its name. If you have young children or a puppy, make sure that they don't eat any part of the plant. Monkshood likes heavy, moisture-retentive soil and will tolerate some shade. It flowers in late summer and autumn.

'Bressingham Spire' has violet-blue flowers; Aconitum carmichaelii 'Arendsii' bears amethyst-blue flowers; and A. napellus 'Bicolour' is blue and white. See page 135.

Agapanthus African lily

This sun-loving plant produces tall stems topped by clusters of brilliant blue, lily-like flowers in late summer. It needs a well-drained soil, so dig in coarse grit on heavy land.

'Bressingham Blue' is the deepest blue, growing to 90cm (3ft), and 'Loch Hope' reaches 1.2m (4ft) with deep blue flowers. The Headbourne Hybrids come in a mixture of blue shades on 90cm (3ft) stems.

Allium Ornamental onion

The spiky onions with their large, round,

pink or blue flowers are all ideal for these borders. *Allium cernuum* is a 45cm- (18in-) tall, clump-forming plant producing drooping heads of lilac-pink in summer. It spreads rapidly. See also page 154.

Alstroemeria Peruvian lily
The Ligtu Hybrids are vigorous, even invasive plants, but easy to control. They don't like being moved, so buy pot-grown plants and put them in, a little deeper than they grew in the pot, in rich soil in sun. They have superb, pale pink, salmon-pink, yellow and orange flowers and grow to about 90cm (3ft).

Anemone
Anemone apennina and *A. blanda* are similar plants, growing to 15cm (6in) with ferny leaves and masses of rapidly spreading, bright blue or pink, daisy flowers in early spring: superb for naturalizing under deciduous trees and shrubs.

A. × *hybrida* (Japanese anemone) is a superb, autumn-flowering perennial which can become invasive once it's established, though it's easily controlled with a spade. Unfortunately it doesn't transplant well, so buy new plants pot-grown. It generally reaches a height of about 60cm (2ft) and produces large, beautifully shaped flowers with intense colouring, all with lovely, golden anthers. 'Hadspen Abundance' is deep rose pink and almost double; 'Lorelei' is deep pink; 'Lady Gilmour' has very large, almost double flowers in clear pink; and 'September Charm' is shorter with smaller, single flowers, but many of them.

Aquilegia alpina Columbine
A short-lived but delicate perennial growing to 30cm (1ft) with spurred, bell-shaped flowers of sky-blue in early summer. It likes

dappled shade in most soils. There are also several good hybrids that can be raised from seed, but they come in mixed colours so they would have to be pot-grown and planted out when they have flowered.

Aster Michaelmas daisy
Many varieties are subject to mildew so, since I don't want to spray, I stick with those that seem to be more or less immune. All prefer sun and well-drained soil, and flower in late summer and autumn.

Aster amellus grows to 45cm (18in), producing masses of blue daisies with a yellow eye. Look for the varieties 'King George' with violet-blue flowers; 'Pink Zenith', which is deep pink; 'Nocturne', lilac-lavender; 'Vanity', mid-blue; and 'Sonia', clear pink.

A. frikartii 'Mönch' is nothing short of superb, bearing lavender-blue flowers with a yellow centre for many weeks.

A. thomsonii 'Nanus' is very similar to 'Mönch', but grows to only 40cm (15in).

A. lateriflorus 'Horizontalis' reaches 90cm (3ft) and produces tiny leaves with a purplish hue at flowering time in late summer. The hundreds of small lilac-and-pink flowers form a haze of pinkish mauve.

Astilbe arendsii
Several of the invaluable hybrids have excellent pink flowers. 'Cologne' is shorter than most and pink; 'Düsseldorf' is cerise-pink; 'Mainz' is an early-flowering deep pink; 'Salland' reaches 1.8m (6ft) with imposing pink spikes; and 'Venus' is another tall pink, reaching 1.2m (4ft). See page 130.

Bergenia Elephant's ears
Several varieties have pink flowers and the leaves colour well in winter too. There are several good, pink hybrids including

'Ballawley' with rose-pink flowers;
'Bressingham Bountiful', which is light pink;
'Bressingham Salmon', which is, as you
would expect, salmon-pink; and
'Sunningdale', which is pink with attractive,
shiny leaves. See also page 167.

Brunnera macrophylla
See page 136.

Camassia leichtlinii Quamash
Plant the bulbs in late summer or autumn in a
sunny spot in the border so that the leaves of
other perennials will hide the ugly base of the
plants after flowering. See page 130.

Campanula Bellflower
Quite indispensable blue and pink flowers
for any sunny position.

Campanula carpatica is a low-growing
species for the front of the border. Growing to
no more than 30cm (1ft), its bright green
leaves are covered in blue trumpets in
summer.

C. glomerata is bordering on the invasive,
though easily controlled. It's quite variable,
growing to between 30 and 90cm (1 and 3ft),
with masses of violet-blue trumpets in summer.

C. lactiflora is one I wouldn't want to be
without. It produces 90cm–1.2m (3–4ft) stems
covered in light blue bells in summer.
'Prichard's Variety' is lavender-blue. 'Loddon
Anna' grows to 1.8m (6ft) and has pink flowers.

C. latifolia (giant bellflower) produces 1.2m
(4ft) spires of drooping, blue bells from a
sturdy clump of basal leaves. It can tolerate
some shade. The variety 'Gloaming' is an
attractive blue-grey.

C. latiloba makes good ground cover with
striking, violet-blue, cup-shaped flowers on
90cm (3ft) stems in summer.

C. persicifolia grows to about 90cm (3ft)
and has summer flowers ranging from light
to quite dark blue. 'Pride of Exmouth' is a

The golden eye of Anemone blanda
adds warmth to the cool blue of the petals.

light blue, double variety, while 'Telham Beauty' is a darker blue.

Centaurea dealbata Knapweed
An easily grown plant that thrives in a sunny spot. It reaches about 60cm (2ft) in height and bears pink, thistle flowers in early summer. 'Steenbergii' has larger, deeper pink flowers.

Centranthus ruber Valerian
A superb plant with clusters of small, deep pink flowers. It seeds itself freely and can become a nuisance, though plants are easily pulled out where they're not wanted. It grows to 90cm (3ft) absolutely anywhere.

Chionodoxa Glory of the snow
Small bulbs with brilliant blue, star-shaped flowers that grow to 15cm (6 in). Plant them in autumn in a sunny spot *en masse* to form a carpet of blue in early spring.

Chionodoxa luciliae is the most commonly grown, producing light blue flowers with a white eye; *C. sardensis* is a rich, deep blue.

Crocus
Crocus tomasinianus is a bright blue, early-flowering crocus that seeds itself freely. There are also several Dutch hybrids in blue. See page 154.

Delphinium
Among the most striking of all tall herbaceous plants, the delphiniums take a little trouble to grow but are well worthwhile. They need a sunny spot and good, retentive soil. They tend to be attacked by slugs, especially in the early spring when they're just coming through, and they need staking and regular tying.

Delphiniums are not difficult to raise from fresh seed, but named varieties should be propagated from basal cuttings taken in

spring. I grow the Avon Hybrids from seed, which produce a range of good blues on plants about 1.2–1.8m (4–6ft) tall. The Belladonna Hybrids are smaller and also in a good range of blues. 'Pink Sensation' grows to 90cm (3ft) and has rose-pink flowers but needs excellent drainage and a sunny spot to survive the winter.

Dianthus plumarius hybrids Garden pinks
Look out for hybrids like the single, pink 'Constance Finnis'; 'Dad's Favourite', which is pink with red blotches; the well-known 'Doris' with large, fully double, pink flowers; and 'Rose de Mai', which is pink with a red centre. They grow to 45cm (18in). See page 167.

Dicentra Bleeding heart
Dicentra spectabilis is the best-known variety with delightful, hanging lockets of pink and white. It grows to 45cm (18in). Plant it in a sheltered spot.

D. eximia and D. formosa have lovely, much-divided, greyish foliage and pink flowers on 60cm- (2ft-) tall plants. There are also several good hybrids, including the deep pink 'Luxuriant' growing to 25cm (10in). See page 136.

Echinops ritro Globe thistle
A handsome plant, reaching a height of 1.2m (4ft), with thistle-like heads of metallic blue in late summer. It likes poor, well-drained soil in full sun and comes easily from seed. 'Veitch's Blue' has lighter blue flowers.

Erigeron Fleabane
A bright-looking plant rather like a Michaelmas daisy and very easy to grow in well-drained soil in sun. There are several hybrids suitable for this border, including 'Adria', which is blue with a yellow centre and grows to 75cm (30in); 'Amity', slightly

shorter with single, pink flowers; 'Charity', which is pink and reaches 60cm (2ft); 'Dignity' with single flowers of deep blue; and 'Dimity' with large, pink flowers which grows to 30cm (1ft). All flower in summer.

Erigeron karvinskianus is a quite different plant, producing clumps no higher than 23cm (9in) smothered in white daisies which turn pink and then red as they age and go on all summer and autumn. It's a superb plant for the front of the border or between paving and is easy to raise from seed.

Eryngium Sea holly
A striking plant with gun-metal blue flowers reminiscent of the teazle and attractive, silver-blue foliage. It needs a sunny spot and very good drainage, so dig in plenty of coarse grit on heavy soil.

Erygium alpinum 'Slieve Donard' has 90cm- (3ft-) tall blue stems with steel-blue flowers.

E. oliverianum bears much-divided leaves and very vivid blue flowers for a long period in summer.

E. tripartitum has many-branched, 90cm (3ft) stems, each carrying a deep blue flower.

E. giganteum 'Miss Willmott's Ghost' is a biennial, but I include it because of its habit of freely self-seeding. It grows to 90cm (3ft) with shimmering, light blue flowers.

Erysimum 'Bowles' Mauve'
Perennial wallflower
A short-lived perennial for a sunny spot. It grows to about 60cm (2ft) and bears lilac-blue, wallflower-like flowers for a long period in summer. It's important to take cuttings every year to keep it going.

Erythronium dens-canis Dog's tooth violet
This bulbous plant is a delight in early spring with rosy-pink, cyclamen-like flowers above attractive, spotted leaves. It grows to 15cm (6in) and prefers a shady spot with plenty of organic matter in the soil.

Galega officinalis Goat's rue
An easy-to-grow plant with attractive foliage and 1.5m (5ft) spikes of lavender or pink flowers. 'Carnea' is a good, light pink and 'Lady Wilson' is purplish. It thrives in any soil in sun or part-shade.

Geranium Cranesbill
The geraniums are invaluable plants for the pink and blue borders. There are many varieties, so a trip to the nursery would be a good idea. *Geranium cantabrigiense* 'Biokovo' grows to only 20cm (8in), bearing pale pink flowers with darker centres, while the taller 'Cambridge' is rose-pink and does well in shade.

'Claridge Druce' is a 60cm- (2ft-) tall, clump-forming hybrid with bright pink flowers in summer; *G. endressii* 'Wargrave Pink' grows to 60cm (2ft) with clear pink flowers; *G. himalayense* is a clump-former with 30cm (1ft) stems of blue flowers veined red; 'Birch Double' has fully double flowers. The leaves of these varieties colour well in autumn, as do those of *G. macrorrhizum*, which is excellent in shade. The varieties 'Ingwersen's Variety' (pale pink) and 'Bevan's Variety' (deep pink), are improvements on the type.

There are some fine selections of the British native *G. pratense*. 'Mrs Kendall Clark' is blue and 'Roseum' is pink. A great favourite for a sunny spot in the front of the border is the deep pink hybrid 'Russell Prichard'. It spreads to form a 15cm- (6in-) high mat of silver-grey foliage covered in bright pink flowers all summer. *G. wallichianum* 'Buxton's Variety' is another fine plant for the front of the border with lavender-blue flowers with a white centre on 30cm (1ft) stems all summer and well into autumn. See page 168.

Hemerocallis Day lily

'Catherine Woodbury' is a deep pale pink; 'Cherry Cheeks' is cherry-pink with large flowers; 'Luxury Lace' is pink with ruffled petals; and 'Varsity' has large, peach-pink flowers. See page 137.

Hesperis matronalis Dame's violet

This is really a short-lived perennial, but I include it because it seeds itself freely, so you'll keep it from year to year. It grows to 1.2m (4ft) and has white, pink and mauve flowers which are sweetly scented. It grows well under trees or in full sun in almost any soil.

Heuchera Coral flower

Heuchera americana is a 45cm (18in) tall, frontal plant bearing delightful, copper-brown foliage with greenish markings topped by pale pink spires of flowers.

There are several excellent varieties of H. brizoïdes, which grows to 60cm (2ft) with clumps of green leaves topped by elegant spires of bell-shaped flowers. 'Pink Spray' is light pink, while 'Coral Cloud' has larger, deeper pink flowers.

There are several good hybrids too, including 'Charles Bloom' with large, pure pink flowers, 'Hyperion' and 'Pretty Polly', both with deeper pink bells. See page 151.

Hosta Plantain lily

There are a few superb hostas with rounded, blue leaves which will provide good foliage contrast in the pink-and-blue border. Blue-leaved varieties also seem to be less prone to slug damage. All need a moist soil and generally light shade, though some will do well in full sun. 'Blue Moon' is an excellent

hybrid, growing to 30cm (1ft) with many light mauve flowers in summer; 'Hadspen Blue' and 'Halcyon' reach a height of about 45cm (18in) with fine blue foliage and mauve flowers in summer. See page 131.

Iris

Two small, bulbous irises are invaluable for early spring colour. Iris histrioïdes and I. reticulata are both hardy and flower in late winter in brilliant blue. They need full sun and good drainage. Plant them in the autumn.

There are several forms of Iris germanica (bearded iris) suitable for the blue border, like the lavender-and-purple 'Braithwaite' and the light blue 'Jane Phillips'. See page 169.

I. sibirica varieties, like the light blue 'Papillon', the darker 'Persimmon' and the violet 'Tycoon', are all suitable in moist soil and sun. See page 132.

Lilium Lily

There are several pink lilies which will grace the pink-and-blue border. Lilium cernuum is a Turk's head type with nodding, pink flowers; 'Alpenglow' and 'Peach Blush' are Asiatic hybrids; while 'Devon Dawn' is a fine, deep pink hybrid. Again, get hold of a specialist catalogue. See page 155.

Linum narbonense Flax

A sun-loving perennial with 45cm (18in) stems carrying lovely, sky-blue, saucer-shaped flowers over a long period in summer.

Lychnis Campion

An easily grown plant for a sunny spot in any soil. Lychnis chalcedonica 'Rosea' is a pale pink form of the Maltese cross (see page 169).

Pastel shades create a soft misty effect and make the garden seem larger.

L. flos-jovis 'Hort's Variety' (flower of Jove) is a delightful plant, producing plentiful, pink flowers on 45cm (18in) stems over felty, grey foliage in summer for many months.

Lythrum **Loosestrife**
In moist soil and a little dappled shade, loosestrife produces good, pink flowers in late summer. See page 132.

Monarda didyma **Bergamot**
There are some good, pink varieties of this useful herb. 'Blue Stocking' is lavender; 'Croftway Pink' is rose-pink; and 'Melissa' is a large-flowered, pale pink. See page 70.

Muscari neglectum **Grape hyacinth**
Deep blue spikes of flowers are produced on 15cm (6in) stems in spring. This is an ideal plant for naturalizing under trees or shrubs and will spread rapidly. *Muscari armeniacum* is not so invasive and produces fat spikes of bright blue flowers.

Nepeta **'Six Hills Giant' Catmint**
An easy and very showy plant for a sunny spot in well-drained soil. It produces numerous 60cm (2ft) spikes of blue flowers which go on all summer.

Omphalodes cappadocica **Navelwort**
A low-growing plant bearing sprays of deep blue flowers in spring. It likes dappled shade and retentive soil and grows to about 15cm (6in). There's also an 'Irish Form' with a white cross in the centre of each small flower.

Paeonia lactiflora **Peony**
'Bowl of Beauty' has superb, large flowers of satin pink with white centres; 'Claire Dubois' and 'Sarah Bernhardt' are double pink; 'Edulis Superba' is double pink and scented; 'G. F. Hemerick' is deep pink; 'Shirley

The clear pink spikes of Persicaria bistorta.

Temple' is a large, deep pink double; and 'Solange' is a pale pink double touched with orange. There are many more. See page 170.

Penstemon
There are some good pink and some blue varieties of this sometimes tender perennial. 'Alice Hindley' is lavender and white; 'Apple Blossom' and 'Barbara Barker' are pink and white; 'Drinkstone' is deep pink; 'Evelyn' is rose-pink; 'Flamingo' is rose-pink with a creamy white throat; 'Macpenny's Pink' has small, pink flowers; 'Myddelton Gem' is carmine-rose; 'Stapleford Gem' is blue-shaded pink with a white throat; and 'Rose Blush' is pink grading to white at the base. See page 170.

Persicaria **Knotweed**
Persicaria affinis 'Dimity' grows to only 15cm (6in) and bears poker-shaped, pink flowers in summer; 'Donald Lowndes' reaches 20cm

(8in), but can look untidy as it fades. One of the best pinks is *P. bistorta* 'Superbum' with light pink flowers on 75cm (30in) stems over a long period in summer.

Phlox paniculata

There are several pink and a few blue varieties of this favourite cottage garden plant. 'Bill Green' is clear pink with a red eye; 'Caroline van den Berg' is blue; 'Eva Cullum' is about the best pink with a red eye; 'Mary Fox' is a deeper pink, again with a red eye; 'Rijnstroom' is a fine, clear pink; 'Skylight' is lavender-blue; and 'Windsor' is deep carmine with a darker eye.

The hybrid 'Chattahoochee' is quite different, growing to no more than 30cm (1ft) with delightful, light blue flowers in profusion over a long period. See page 170.

Pulmonaria Lungwort

A superb, spring-flowering perennial, often with evergreen, silver-spotted leaves and blue or blue-and-pink flowers. There are also good white and red forms available. Many of the named varieties are very similar, so it's best to buy from a nursery when the plants are in flower. They thrive in moist soil in dappled shade but will also grow happily in sun.

Pulmonaria angustifolia azurea 'Munstead Blue' loses its leaves in winter, but is the earliest to flower, with deep blue flowers opening from pink buds and green leaves; *P. longifolia* 'Bertram Anderson' has long, spotted leaves and deep blue flowers; while 'Roy Davidson' is my own favourite with lovely, light blue flowers. They all grow to about 45cm (18in). There are many more varieties to choose from.

Rodgersia

See page 134.

Saponaria ocymoïdes Bouncing Bet

A delightful plant for a sunny spot in the front of the border. It grows to about 45cm (18in) and produces clouds of small, pink flowers in summer.

Scilla sibirica Spring squill

Related to the bluebell, this plant is perfect for carpeting under trees or shrubs in moist, dappled shade where it'll form a carpet of blue (or white), nodding bells. See page 155.

Thalictrum Meadow rue

Thalictrum aquilegifolium and *T. delavayi,* both with mauve flowers, are suitable for this border. See page 152.

Tulipa Tulip

Pink tulips abound in nurserymen's catalogues. I have found the so-called cottage varieties to be most reliable, but it's hard to identify them these days. Generally the later-flowering types with elongated, egg-shaped flowers are the best. Examples are the rosy pink 'Smiling Queen' and the carmine-pink 'Halcro'. Lily, Darwin and Triumph tulips are also reliable for at least a few years. See page 171.

Veronica Speedwell

Three varieties of *Veronica longifolia*, 'Blue Peter', 'Blue Spire' and 'Foerster's Blue', have fine, deep blue flowers and grow to 90cm (3ft).

There are several good varieties of the clump-forming *V. spicata*. 'Blue Fox' is lavender and grows to 30cm (1ft); 'Lavender Charm' also produces spikes of lavender flowers, but reaches 90cm (3ft); and 'Saraband' is violet-blue and grows to 45cm (18in). *V. teucrium* 'Crater Lake Blue' forms a hummock of small, bright blue flowers 30cm (1ft) high, while 'Shirley Blue' is similar but lighter blue. See page 152.

The Whites

White-flowered plants can be used with any colour scheme and can make up complete borders or even whole gardens all on their own. The famous white garden at Sissinghurst Castle in Kent has been copied many times.

It's not quite a case of simply planting white plants together. A careful choice is needed so that, for example, a brilliant, clear white does not make a creamy white flower look dirty white. It really is a fine art and not one that I feel needs exploring in this context.

However, white flowers and foliage can be useful to break up and lighten an otherwise dark border. Among the purples and reds, for instance, a splash of white can lift the whole scheme like a n oasis in the desert.

TREES AND SHRUBS

Amelanchier lamarckii Snowy mespilus
One of the best of spring-flowering trees for the small garden and it can be grown as a large shrub too. See page 82.

Choisya ternata Mexican orange blossom
See pages 77 and 91.

Cistus Sun rose
See page 91.

Cornus Dogwood/cornel
A variable range of superb, white-flowered shrubs and trees for light shade, though some prefer an acid soil. See pages 83 and 99.

Crataegus Flowering thorn
See page 84.

Deutzia
See page 102.

Exochorda macrantha Bridal wreath
See page 102.

Hebe
Some hebes can be a bit tender but *Hebe pinguifolia* 'Pagei' has no such problems. A low-growing shrub reaching no more than 15cm (6in), it has attractive, silver-grey foliage and small, white flowers in summer. It likes well-drained soil in sun or part-shade. See also page 94.

Hydrangea
See page 103.

Magnolia
See page 85.

Malus hupehensis Flowering crab
This is one of the best of the flowering crabs. In early summer it's covered in pink buds which open out into white, well-scented flowers. It has a good autumn leaf colour and produces small, yellow fruits flushed with red. Buy one budded onto a dwarfing rootstock and it will grow to about 6m (20ft). See also page 85.

Olearia
Olearia scilloniensis, one of the toughest of the olearias, with attractive silver-grey foliage, is absolutely covered in small, white daisies in early summer. It never fails to flower, even when quite young. Growth varies depending on location, but 1.5m (5ft) is about average.

O. macrodonta is a superb shrub growing to 3m (10ft) with holly-like, evergreen leaves, grey-green above and silver below. The huge white, fragrant flower heads are borne in early summer.

Philadelphus Mock orange
See page 106.

Potentilla Shrubby cinquefoil
See page 106.

Prunus Flowering cherry
'Shimidsu Zakura' is a small, weeping tree growing to about 4.5m (15ft) with clusters of double, white flowers in spring. See also page 86.

Pyrus Pear
Pyrus communis (garden pear) produces fine, white blossom in spring followed, of course, by good, edible fruits. See also *P. salicifolia* 'Pendula' on page 87.

Rosa Rose
Of course there are dozens of varieties, so a trip to the nursery is essential. Of the English roses I would choose 'Fair Bianca', which grows to 90cm (3ft) and has cup-shaped blooms with an excellent perfume; and 'Glamis Castle', which is very special with strong, bushy growth and lovely old-fashioned-looking flowers with a strong fragrance. The shrub rose 'Boule de Neige' is a lovely Bourbon, white with a slight pink flush, growing to 1.5m (5ft). 'Blanc Double de Coubert' is a semi-double *rugosa* rose with pure white flowers; it grows to 1.8m (6ft). 'Little White Pet' is an unusual rose, growing to 60cm (2ft) and covered in clusters of white, pompon blooms.

Rosa pimpinellifolia is an upright, suckering shrub which slowly spreads. It has double or single, pink or white flowers in early summer. Of the hybrid teas 'Pascali' is one of the best with well-shaped, fragrant flowers on 90cm (3ft) bushes. Favourite floribundas are 'Margaret Merril' with dainty, high-pointed blooms lightly overlaid with pink and one of the finest fragrances of all; and 'Iceberg', an old variety but still one of the best with pure white, fragrant flowers on 1.2m (4ft) bushes.

The flowers of bridal wreath (Exocorda macrantha) are the purest white.

Sorbus Rowan/mountain ash
Sorbus hupehensis produces white berries tinged with pink. See page 87.

Spiraea
See page 108.

Symphoricarpos doorenbosii Snowberry
The common snowberry is a rapidly suckering shrub and therefore not really suitable for small gardens. Varieties of this species spread much more slowly and are easily controlled. Growing to about 1.5m (5ft) and happy in dry shade and any soil, they're noted for their large berries in late summer and autumn. 'Mother of Pearl' is white suffused with pink and 'White Hedge' has white fruits.

Syringa **Lilac**
See page 108.

Viburnum
There are several fine, white-flowered viburnums, both evergreen and deciduous. See pages 97 and 110.

Herbaceous Plants and Bulbs

Agapanthus campanulata **'Alba' African lily**
This is the white form of the lovely, normally blue bulb. See page 183.

Anaphalis triplinervis **Pearly everlasting**
Greyish leaves set off prolific, white, everlasting flowers in mid to late summer. It spreads well to make good ground cover. The variety 'Summer Snow' is freer-flowering and slightly whiter. It grows to 25cm (10in).

Anemone
Anemone nemerosa (wood anemone) is a European bulb which thrives in cool soil in woodland or under trees and shrubs, producing large, white flowers in early spring on 15cm (6in) stems. It seeds itself around as well as spreading through underground rhizomes. Mulch with compost or leaf-mould in autumn.

Of *A.* × *hybrida* (Japanese anemone), 'Luise Uhink' is probably the best pure white, though 'White Giant' is taller, reaching 90cm (3ft) with very large flowers. See page 184.

Anthemis punctata cupaniana
A sun-lover which makes mats of attractive, divided, silver-grey foliage topped by 75cm (30in) stems of handsome, white daisies with yellow centres over a long period from early summer. Divide the plants regularly or take basal cuttings in spring to rejuvenate them.

Aruncus dioicus **Goat's beard**
See page 130.

Aster divaricatus **Michaelmas daisy**
A somewhat floppy plant which Gertrude Jekyll grew behind bergenias so that the white daisies flopped over them and were supported. It likes a cool, shady spot and grows to 60cm (2ft), flowering in late summer.

Astilbe
Most astilbes are grown for their silvery foliage, which will do much the same job as will white flowers of lightening an otherwise dark border. But *A. lactiflora* (mugwort) is the exception with green leaves and tall spikes of impressive, creamy white plumes of flowers 1.5m (5ft) tall in late summer.

'Deutschland', 'Irrlicht' and 'Snowdrift' also produce attractive, white, summer flowers. See page 130.

Astrantia major **Masterwort**
A sun-loving plant bearing curious flowers with a domed centre surrounded by small florets and all encircled by a frill of bracts. The flowers are greenish white on 75cm (30in) stems in summer. The form 'Shaggy' (synonomous with 'Margery Fish') has larger flowers.

Bergenia **Elephant's ears**
The variety 'Silberlicht' has mid-green leaves and clusters of white flowers suffused with pink and grows to 30cm (1ft); *Bergenia stracheyi* 'Alba' is a smaller plant with attractive, rounded leaves and white flowers; it grows to 23cm (9in). Both flower in spring. See also pages 167 and 184.

Camassia leichtlinii **Quamash**
There is a creamy white form of this normally blue, bulbous plant. See page 130.

Campanula **Bellflower**

All the campanulas mentioned on page 185 have white forms worth growing. Look for the following varieties: *Campanula carpatica* 'Hannah' or 'Snowsprite'; *C. glomerata* 'Nana Alba'; *C. lactiflora* 'Alba' or 'White Pouffe'; *C. latifolia* 'White Ladies'; *C. latiloba* 'Alba'; and *C. persicifolia* 'Fleur de Neige' or 'Hampstead White'.

Centranthus ruber **'Alba' Valerian**

This is the white form of the better-known red variety and well worth growing for early summer flowers. See page 186.

The slightly different whites of valerian, foxgloves and epilobium look fresh against the dark green of the hedge.

Cerastium tomentosum **Snow-in-summer**

A well-known ground-coverer, making extensive mats of silver foliage covered in small, white flowers on 15cm (6in) stems in early summer. It spreads rapidly, but is easily controlled.

Convallaria majalis **Lily-of-the-valley**

See page 151.

Crambe cordifolia **Seakale**

A relative of the edible seakale, this rather handsome perennial reaches 1.8m (6ft), covering its widely branching stems with clouds of small, white flowers in early summer. It likes a sunny spot and good drainage.

Dianthus Garden pink
The old variety 'Mrs Sinkins' is a lovely double white and 'Haytor' is similar. See page 167.

Dicentra Bleeding heart
The various species and hybrids mentioned on page 136 also have white forms. Look for *Dicentra eximia* 'Alba', *D. spectabilis* 'Alba' and the hybrids 'Pearl Drops' and 'Snowflakes'.

Digitalis purpurea Foxglove
An indispensable flower for the back of the border, available in white forms as well as the more usual purplish colours. See page 167.

Erythronium revolutum Dog's tooth violet
The variety 'White Beauty' has white flowers in spring. See page 187.

Fritillaria meleagris Snake's head fritillary
There is a white form of this delicate plant. See page 154.

Galanthus nivalis Snowdrop
This needs sun in winter and part-shade in summer, so planting under deciduous trees or shrubs is ideal. See page 155 for further details.

Galtonia candicans Summer hyacinth
A late-summer-flowering, bulbous plant producing 90cm (3ft) spires of bell-shaped, scented, white flowers marked with green. It likes a sunny spot and good drainage. Plant the bulbs in spring.

The small pompon flowers of the double feverfew really do gleam, while these pink and yellow roses are all sufficiently pale to work well together.

Geranium Cranesbill
Geranium macrorrhizum 'Album', with white flowers on 25cm (10in) stems in summer, is an excellent white plant for dry shade.

G. pratense 'Album' has single, white flowers and 'Plenum Album' is double white. They reach 60cm (2ft) and also flower in summer.

G. sanguineum 'Album' has light green foliage and white flowers on 25cm (10in) stems all summer.

G. sylvaticum 'Album' forms good 60cm (2ft) clumps with white flowers in early summer. See page 168.

Gypsophila paniculata Baby's breath
The variety 'Bristol Fairy' has larger, double flowers, while 'Compacta Plena' also bears double flowers but on 45cm (18in) plants. It likes a sunny spot and good drainage.

Helleborus Hellebore
A number of hellebores have white flowers, some with attractive markings inside.

Helleborus niger (Christmas rose) flowers in late winter or early spring, producing charming, cup-shaped flowers of pure white. Look for named selections like 'Potter's Wheel' and 'White Magic'. They grow to 30cm (1ft).

H. argutifolius grows to 60cm (2ft) with greenish white flowers in spring. It's rather floppy in habit and may need support.

H. foetidus 'Westerflisk' is similar but with a purple edge to the flowers.

H. nigercors is a very handsome plant with large, creamy white, spring flowers which fade to pink. It grows to 30cm (1ft).

Some varieties of *H. orientalis* (Lenten rose) are white, generally marked and spotted inside, but since they hybridize so readily, either buy a named variety like 'Albin Otto' or buy the plants in flower. See also page 169.

Hesperis matronalis **Sweet rocket**

There is a white form of this normally lilac or pink, short-lived perennial. It flowers in early summer and is sweetly scented. See page 188.

Hosta **Plantain lily**

'Royal Standard' grows to 90cm (3ft) with large, shapely, green leaves and white, slightly scented flowers in late summer.

H. plantaginea 'Grandiflora' will need searching out and is best in warmer areas; however, where it can be grown well it produces 90cm (3ft) spikes of lily-like flowers with a superb fragrance. The leaves are fresh green.

Iris

Iris ensata 'Snowdrift' thrives in the bog garden in a sunny spot or will do well in the border, provided there's sufficient summer moisture.

The white flowers of Dicentra spectabilis *'Alba' really show up against dark green foliage.*

I. germanica 'Frost and Flame' is a 90cm (3ft) bearded iris bearing pure white flowers with an orange beard. 'The Citadel' is pure white; 'Stella Polaris' is white with a touch of cream; and 'Pegasus' is a tall, pure white.

I. sibirica 'White Swirl' forms a wide tuft of grassy leaves with 90cm (3ft) white flowers. See page 132.

Leucanthemum maximum **Shasta daisy**

A very easy-to-grow, reliable perennial forming an expanding clump of foliage from which 60–90cm (2–3ft) stems of white daisies with yellow centres arise in summer. The double form 'Esther Read' is outstanding and the single 'Snowcap' is a good, short variety only 40cm (15in) tall. They need a sunny spot on any soil and should be divided every three years.

Lilium **Lily**

Perhaps the most beautiful and certainly the most historic lily of them all is *Lilium candidum* (madonna lily). It bears large, waxy, white flowers in summer on strong, 90cm–1.5m (3–5ft) stems. Plant it in a sunny spot against a wall if possible and bury the bulb only 2–3cm (1in) deep.

The Martagon lily has a white form, L. martagon 'Album', with pure white, trumpet-shaped blooms in summer. It needs a rich soil and dappled shade.

L. regale likes similar conditions. Bearing very fragrant, large, white trumpets with sulphur yellow inside in summer, it grows to 90cm (3ft).

Lunaria annua **'Alba' Honesty**

This is in fact a biennial, but it seeds itself freely and is well worthwhile. It grows to 60cm (2ft) with white flowers in spring and is most at home in shrub borders or under trees.

Lysimachia **Loosestrife**
Lysimachia ephemerum is not as invasive as
most loosestrifes, forming good clumps of
1.2m (4ft) spikes topped by greyish white
flowers in late summer. See page 137.

Ornithogalum umbellatum
Star of Bethlehem
A 30cm (1ft) bulbous plant bearing spikes of
star-shaped flowers, each petal with a green
stripe, in spring.
   Ornithogalum nutans grows to 45cm (18in)
with nodding, bell-shaped flowers, again
with a green stripe in spring. They prefer sun
and retentive soil.

Paeonia lactiflora **Peony**
'Duchesse de Nemours' is a large, double
white; 'Festiva Maxima' is double white
flecked red; and 'Le Cygne' has very large,
double, white flowers. All grow to about
75cm (30in). See page 170.

Phlox paniculata
The variety 'Blue Ice' is white with a faint
blue blush; 'Fujiyama' is pure white; and
'White Admiral' has larger flowers than
normal. See page 191.

Polygonatum hybridum
Solomon's seal
See page 137.

Rodgersia
See page 134.

Sisyrinchium striatum
A plant with greyish, iris-like leaves and
spikes of small, cream flowers in summer. The
variety 'Aunt May' has creamy yellow-
variegated leaves. It likes sun or part-shade
and, though not long-lived, will self-seed
freely.

Smilacina racemosa **False Solomon's seal**
A shade-lover preferring a rich, moist soil,
this perennial has shiny, ribbed foliage and
fluffy, white flowers in spring with a
delicious lemon scent. It grows to 90cm (3ft).

Thalictrum aquilegifolium **Meadow rue**
There is a white form of this plant, 'Album'.
The white form of *Thalictrum delavayi*, which
is slightly taller and has larger flowers, is
perhaps a better plant. See page 152.

Tiarella cordifolia **Foam flower**
A shade-lover which forms 15cm- (6in-) tall
carpets of attractive, green leaves and sprays
of small, white flowers in early summer. It
spreads by underground runners and can
become invasive, though it's easy to control.

Trillium grandiflorum **Wake robin**
A delightful and much prized woodland
plant producing petals, calyces and leaves in
threes in spring. It likes a shady spot and
retentive soil and grows to 30cm (1ft). The
best of all is the double form 'Flore Pleno'.

Tulipa **Tulip**
There are dozens of white tulips to brighten
spring borders. 'Spring Green' is a late-spring-
flowering *viridiflora* type with 40cm (15in),
green-and-white streaked flowers; 'White
Triumphator' is a 60cm (2ft) lily-flowered
type, blooming in late spring; 'Shirley' is a
pearly white, late tulip, growing to 60cm (2ft);
'Purissima' is a 45cm (18in) *fosteriana* tulip
with creamy white flowers in early spring;
'Pax' is a pure white Triumph tulip, 45cm
(18in) tall, flowering in late spring; 'Cazzara'
is a 50cm- (20in-) tall cottage tulip, bearing
pure white flowers in early spring; 'White
Hawk' is a single early, 30cm (1ft) tall; and
'White Sail' is a Mendel tulip, with 40cm
(15in) flowers in mid-spring. See page 171.

Chapter eight

A PERFUMED GARDEN

Of all the senses, it's surely the sense of smell that's most evocative. I know that there are certain perfumes that glaze my eyes and send me into paroxysms of nostalgia.

My very first job involved growing thousands of chrysanthemums for cut flowers. I'd spend days disbudding millions of stems, working in mid-summer from dawn to dusk in the fresh Hertfordshire countryside and loving every minute. I still grow chrysanthemums, partly for the flowers but mostly because the smell of the leaves takes me straight back to those halcyon days.

The scent of daphne in late winter brings flooding back all the shyness and embarrassment of first love, and perfumed roses belong to my wife. I'll spare you the details.

But it's not just nostalgia that makes perfume such an important part of the pleasure of the garden. To sit in a honeysuckle-covered arbour in the evening, to stick your nose into the centre of a rose in the prime of its life or to walk in the garden at dusk past a border full of nicotiana takes you as near to heaven on earth as you're ever going to get.

Of course, flowers are not primarily perfumed for our pleasure. The strong smells they emit are designed to attract insects to perform the task of pollination, so a perfumed garden automatically equates with one that's alive with bees, butterflies and other insects – and they're a delight in themselves.

You don't have to confine the perfume to the garden. By cutting a bunch of flowers or drying a selection to make *pot-pourri* you can fill your house with the fresh smell of the countryside every day of the year.

If you plan to do that and you have the room, grow a few rows of plants especially for cut flowers in the vegetable plot. Then you'll be able to bring the garden into the house without robbing the borders.

Every seating area should be surrounded by scented plants: in this instance, climbing roses.

Smaller plants like lily-of-the-valley, which need regular dividing anyway, can be lifted in the autumn, a few roots potted into a clay pot and forced into early flower in a coldframe. They make superb, perfumed houseplants for early spring and simply couldn't be cheaper.

Of course, it isn't just flowers that are scented. Many leaves, when crushed, give off superb aromas. I have a plant of lemon balm growing just outside my back door so that, as I come in from a day's work in the garden, I can pick and crush a leaf to bring forth all the fresh, magical fragrance of spring. Other plants will release their perfume if you simply brush against them as you walk past.

My favourite aromatic leaf of all belongs to *Rosa eglanteria* (eglantine rose). During the filming of the television series connected with this book, I came across a hedge of it in a garden in Kent. Several plants had been planted against a fence of pigwire, which was completely hidden by the mass of foliage. In the early morning or after a shower of rain, the scent of fresh apples literally filled the whole garden. It's a perfume you would never tire of.

Siting Perfumed Plants

A few scented plants have the power actually to fill the garden with perfume. An area thick with garden pinks, for example, can be enjoyed from metres away. But generally, and especially with scented leaves, it's best to plant perfumed plants where you can get close to catch the full aroma.

Small plants can be grown in pots and set on low walls or on steps and, of course, containers and particularly windowboxes can be positioned to present the flowers at exactly nose level. Don't waste the opportunity. But I know that I also enjoy the perfume of many smaller flowers by getting down on my hands and knees and sticking my nose in among them. The areas where I grow violas and lily-of-the-valley are probably the best weeded in the garden!

Plants with aromatic foliage can be planted where you'll brush against them as you walk past, and it's a good idea to site some within picking distance as you'll not be able to resist picking a leaf or two and crushing them to savour their fragrance. Tougher ones, like thyme and chamomile, can be planted where they'll be trodden on to release their perfume.

Think too about the time of the year when plants flower. While it's a great joy to wander in the garden on summer evenings to savour its perfumes, it's not so much fun in an icy winter. So winter-flowering plants for perfume are best planted near the house where they'll be well within civilized sniffing distance.

LEFT *The subtle scent of cyclamen in winter invites closer inspection.*

OPPOSITE *Crush the leaves of herbs between your fingers to release the scent.*

*The Indian Bean Tree (*Catalpa bignonioïdes*)
has a sweet fragrance.*

Naturally anywhere you sit in the garden must be surrounded by perfume. Arbours should be covered with sweet-smelling climbers and seats surrounded by roses, perfumed shrubs and herbaceous plants. Indeed I simply won't buy plants that have, because of intensive breeding, lost their perfume. A rose or a sweet pea without a smell is, for me at least, only half a plant.

Finally remember that perfume is more likely to be released in warm, still air. So make the most of south- or west-facing areas to plant your perfumed plants, and if the site's exposed, plant other trees and shrubs on the windward side to allow the perfumes to linger in the air.

TREES

The list of trees with a worthwhile perfume is somewhat limited. Few have really strong scent, while others are simply too big for most gardens. *Catalpa bignonioïdes* (Indian bean tree), for example, has sweetly scented, white flowers in summer, but will grow much too big for small gardens. Certainly it can be pruned back annually to restrict it to a large shrub with superb leaves but, alas, by pruning you will lose the flowers.

Unless you have an overwhelming reason to plant scented trees, therefore, you may feel it best to go for species that give better value by producing good flowers, foliage and autumn colour too. There are, of course, exceptions to this rule, like my first choice, which no self-respecting garden should be without.

Cercidiphyllum japonicum **Katsura tree**
See page 83.

Conifers
All conifers have aromatic foliage reminiscent of pine woods. The leaves of some need to be crushed to release the aroma, but others, like the thujas, will waft it to your nose as you pass by. Conifer hedges are a delight to cut and you can use the clippings for paths, where they release their perfume as you walk on them.

Crataegus monogyna **Hawthorn**
The common, white-flowered hawthorn is not a popular tree, but it has a much better scent than its more highly coloured cousins. If you live in the country, you should certainly consider it as a hedge. See page 45.

Cydonia oblonga **Common quince**
The cooking quince has large, yellow fruits with a superb aroma. See page 84.

Eucalyptus **Gum tree**
This well-known Australasian tree has leaves whose aroma is rather reminiscent of cough medicine, but is none the less attractive. See page 180.

Halesia carolina **Carolina silverbell**
A delightful tree, producing masses of pendulous, white, sweetly scented bells in spring. In autumn the rounded leaves turn bright yellow. It grows on most soils to about 4.5m (15ft).

Laburnum watereri **'Vossii' Golden rain tree**
A well-known tree with softly scented, golden flowers. See page 85.

Magnolia
Several magnolias have superbly scented flowers, though they make quite large, spreading trees, so be careful how you choose. See page 85.

Magnolia hypoleuca bears enormous, saucer-shaped, cream flowers with a central boss of crimson stamens and a rich, fruity fragrance. It grows to about 9m (30ft).

M. loebneri 'Merrill' has well-scented white, spidery flowers, while the variety 'Leonard Messel' is pink. Both grow to about 8m (26ft).

M. salicifolia produces white, spring flowers which, together with the leaves, give off a sharp, lemony perfume. It grows to about 6m (20ft) and must have a neutral or acid soil.

Malus **Flowering crab**
Some varieties have a pleasant perfume, but you may have to stick your nose into the blooms to register it. *Malus floribunda, M. hupehensis* and the variety 'Golden Hornet' are particularly good. See also pages 164, 180 and 192.

Prunus **Flowering cherry**
Many of the flowering cherries give off a slight smell of almonds. The best are *Prunus yedoensis,* 'Shirotae' and 'Jô-nioi' which has single, white, spring flowers. See pages 181 and 193.

Ptelea trifoliata **Hop tree**
A lovely, small tree bearing clusters of small, greenish yellow flowers with a strong, rich perfume in summer. The leaves are also pungently hop-scented when crushed. It grows to 6m (20ft).

Styrax japonica **Japanese snowbell**
A small tree producing, in early summer, fresh, white, slightly scented flowers against attractive, green leaves. It grows to about 6m (20ft).

Shrubs

Aesculus parviflora Buckeye
The large, white clusters of flowers of this relative of the horse chestnut are heavily scented and could fill the garden with perfume. Well worth growing. See page 98.

Artemisia absinthum Wormwood
An attractive, silver-leaved shrub with aromatic foliage smelling of lemon when bruised, which may be used in *pot-pourri*. It needs a sunny spot and very well-drained soil. Prune it hard in spring. It grows to about 45cm (18in).

Berberis Barberry
Many varieties have a strong, honey fragrance. Among the best are *Berberis candidula*, *B. julianae* and *B. verruculosa*. See pages 90 and 98.

Buddleia Butterfly bush
All the buddleias have a scent of honey, some stronger than others. They need to be planted within sniffing distance, though the perfume is of course picked up easily by butterflies who swarm to it in their thousands. All varieties of *Buddleia davidii* are worthwhile (see page 99) though the white-flowered *B. fallowiana* is probably better scented. However this does need the protection of a south-facing wall.

Ceanothus Californian lilac
Many of the evergreen ceanothus have delicately scented flowers which attract insects by the thousand. See page 91.

Cistus purpureus Sun rose
This sun-loving shrub has hairs on its leaves that release a delicate perfume like incense. See page 91.

Cornus mas Cornelian cherry
In winter, the small, yellow flowers along bare branches can fill the surrounding air with sweet perfume. See page 101.

Cytisus Broom
The appreciation of perfume is, of course, very much a personal thing. Some people like the strong aroma of broom while others hate it. Buy your plants when they're in flower and judge for yourself. *Cytisus praecox* (Warminster broom) carries a huge amount of flower and is very well perfumed. See page 92.

Daphne
The daphnes flower in spring and will fill the garden with perfume. Planting near a path means that you can bury your nose in the blooms, but that's not exactly necessary since the scents are so strong. They prefer light shade and an acid to neutral soil. As well as the varieties suggested on page 101, look out for *Daphne odora* 'Aureomarginata', a useful evergreen which has golden edges to its leaves.

Deutzia
In early summer the deutzias produce a mass of flower, but are of little interest afterwards. *Deutzia compacta* grows to 1.5m (5ft) and is covered in small, star-shaped flowers with a scent of almonds. *D. elegantissima* has a sweet perfume. See page 102.

Dipelta floribunda
A superb spring-flowerer with arching stems carrying clusters of pale pink flowers with yellow throats. It can be grown in part-shade in most soils and reaches about 3m (10ft).

The delicate scent of Californian lilac (Ceanothus) is very attractive to insects.

Hamamelis Witch hazel

A group of deciduous shrubs with small, spidery, very fragrant flowers on bare stems in winter. See page 103.

Lavandula Lavender

Perhaps the favourite perfume in grand-mother's days, often sewn into bags to put in the wardrobe, made into *pot-pourri* and carried as a posy. It has a wonderfully strong, sweet perfume and attracts insects like no other shrub. See page 95.

Winter-flowering mahonia smells deliciously of lily-of-the-valley.

Lonicera Honeysuckle

Among the most fragrant of all climbers and an absolute 'must' for any garden. See page 52.

Lonicera fragrantissima (shrubby honey-suckle) grows to 2.1m (7ft) and bears small, white flowers with a fruity fragrance in winter. It's suitable for most soils in sun or part-shade.

Lupinus arboreus Tree lupin

Growing to about 1.8m (6ft), this forms a large, rounded bush for the back of the border. In summer it's covered in brilliant yellow, highly perfumed flowers. It's not widely grown because it's unfortunately short-lived, but it's easily raised from seed.

Magnolia

See page 85.

Mahonia media

This outstanding evergreen grows in sun or shade in most soils and will reach about 3m (10ft). The varieties 'Lionel Fortescue' and 'Buckland' are particularly good, both with a strong perfume of lily-of-the-valley. See also page 96.

Osmanthus

Osmanthus burkwoodii and *O. delavayi* are quite similar evergreen shrubs growing to about 3m (10ft) but responsive to pruning to size in smaller borders. In spring the small, white flowers will fill the air with a deliciously sweet perfume. They are quite unfussy as to soil and position.

Philadelphus Mock orange

Don't shun this shrub because it's common – you'll miss one of the sights and smells of summer. It's reliably covered in white, saucer-shaped flowers with a perfume that fills the garden. See page 106.

Syringa 'Mme. Lemoine' is superbly scented in late spring and early summer.

Ribes Flowering currant

An easy-to-grow shrub with a good perfume in spring, particularly *Ribes odoratum*, which has a sweet, clove smell. See page 107.

Rosa Rose

There are, of course, hundreds of perfumed roses, both bush types and climbers, but not all varieties are scented, so choose carefully. In my view you miss out on one of the most important assets of the rose if you buy unscented varieties: I'd leave them well alone. See pages 53, 165, 174, 181 and 193.

***Sarcococca hookeriana digyna*
Christmas box**

Out of flower this is not a distinguished shrub, but for the winter months its honey-scented flowers, though small and hardly flamboyant, smell superb. See page 96.

***Syringa* Lilac**

All the lilacs give off superb perfume in spring from large flowers in various striking colours. See page 108.

Viburnum

A large group with many fine, scented shrubs, mainly flowering in spring. *Viburnum burkwoodii, V. bodnantense, V. carlcephalum, V. carlesii, V. juddii, V. farreri* and *V. tinus* are all excellent scented varieties for small gardens. See pages 97 and 110.

HERBACEOUS PLANTS AND BULBS

Adenophora lilifolia Ladybell
A relative of the campanula producing blue, bell-shaped, scented flowers in summer. It grows to 45cm (18in) and prefers sun or partial shade.

Agastache foeniculum
This 90cm (3ft) perennial has foliage which releases a strong aroma of aniseed when rubbed. It has clusters of violet-blue flowers in late summer.

Amaryllis belladonna
A late-autumn-flowering bulb producing large clusters of deep pink or white flowers with a sweet, fruity perfume. It needs a sunny, south-facing wall to flower well and survive the winter. It grows to about 60cm (2ft).

Anthemis punctata cupaniana
Chamomile-scented foliage is just an extra asset of this superb plant. See page 194.

Artemisia
Generally grown for its attractive, aromatic foliage. See page 90. Artemisia schmidtiana is a lower-growing, spreading variety reaching no more than 30cm (1ft).

Clematis
The herbaceous clematis can be grown to scramble through shrubs, giving another period of flower. Clematis heracleifolia davidiana has small, pale violet flowers and a very sweet perfume. It grows to about 1.2m (4ft) or more.

Convallaria majalis Lily-of-the-valley
A well-known spring-flowerer with sweetly perfumed, white flowers. See page 151.

Cosmos atrosanguineus Chocolate plant
A relative of the dahlia, this tender perennial produces deep maroon flowers with a strong scent of chocolate in summer. It grows to 60cm (2ft). Treat it like a dahlia, lifting it in autumn and taking cuttings in spring.

Crambe cordifolia Seakale
The flowers of this plant are honey-scented. See page 195.

Crinum powellii
A fine flowering plant with ugly foliage, so try to hide it among low-growing perennials. In autumn it produces large, pink or white, lily-scented trumpets. It's not reliably hardy, so give it a sheltered, sunny spot and mulch it with straw in winter. It grows to 90cm (3ft).

Crocus
Naturally you'll have to get your nose down to ground level for these, which on the wet soil of early spring may not be easy. Planting in pots or windowboxes could be the answer. Many varieties have a sweet perfume. See page 154.

Cyclamen
Cyclamen hederifolium produces late summer flowers in shades of pink and white with a sweet scent. Plant it in the shade of trees or under shrubs and it will quite quickly colonize by seeding itself. C. purpurascens flowers in summer and autumn and is also scented. Both grow to about 15cm (6in). See page 167.

Dictamnus albus Burning bush
The white flowers of this interesting perennial produce a lemon-scented volatile oil which can be lit when warm. The foliage is also lemon-scented. Dictamnus albus purpureus has purple flowers. Both grow to 60cm (2ft) in sun, but are quite difficult to establish.

Galtonia candicans Summer hyacinth
See page 197.

Geranium Cranesbill
Many species and varieties of this long-flowering plant have a strong rose perfume. See pages 168, 187 and 197.

Hemerocallis Day lily
Many of the day lilies are scented, especially the yellow varieties. See page 176.

Hosta Plantain lily
Hostas produce tall spikes of flowers with a sweet perfume in summer. See page 131.

Hyacinthoïdes non-scripta Bluebell
A well-known, blue-flowered, spring-flowering bulb which will fill the garden with perfume. It is unfortunately a prolific seeder, so it can become a nuisance. If you have an orchard or a bit of woodland, it's invaluable. It grows to 30cm (1ft).

Hyacinthus Hyacinth
A well-known, bulbous plant often grown for indoor decoration and with about the strongest perfume of all the bulbs. Give it a sunny spot in the garden. It's available in a very wide range of colours and looks best planted in drifts of one colour. It grows to about 30cm (1ft).

Iris
Iris germanica (bearded iris) has a subtle, sweet perfume and is well worth growing in a sunny spot near to the edge of the border where it can be appreciated. See pages 188 and 198. In spring you'll be pleased you planted *I. reticulata*, though since it only grows to 15cm (6in) it needs to be elevated to smelling height in a pot or windowbox. See page 155.

Lilium Lily
Most lilies are well scented and easy to grow among herbaceous plants and low shrubs. See pages 155 and 169.

Lunaria rediviva Perennial honesty
The flower heads of the perennial species are similar to those of the well-known biennial honesty. The white or pale lilac flowers are sweetly scented and perfect for the spring border. It grows to 60cm (2ft), preferring sun or light shade and almost any soil.

Grow Iris germanica *where its subtle perfume can be enjoyed.*

Lupinus polyphyllus **Lupin**
The flowers of lupins have an attractive, spicy scent. See page 208.

Muscari **Grape hyacinth**
See page 190.

Nepeta faassenii **Catmint**
Some people love the Mediterranean scent of the leaves of catmint, while others are not so keen. Your cat will certainly love it. See page 190.

Paeonia lactiflora **Peony**
The flamboyant flowers have a sweet, spicy perfume. See pages 190 and 199.

Phlox
Both *Phlox maculata* and the taller *P. paniculata* have a spicy perfume not to be missed. See page 191.

Primula
You need to get your nose at soil level to smell spring-flowering primulas, but most, including cowslips and primroses, have a sweet perfume. See page 133.

Tellima grandiflora 'Rubra'
A plant for a shady border with attractive, scalloped leaves which turn crimson in winter. In spring and early summer it's covered in tiny, greenish, sweetly scented flowers. It grows to about 60cm (2ft) and can be slightly invasive, but is easily pulled out.

Verbena bonariensis
See page 152.

Grow fragrant plants like herbs close to paths where you brush against them and release their scent.

Viola
A few of the larger-flowered violas have an elusive scent, but *Viola odorata* (sweet violet) is well scented. See page 152.

HERBS

You'll want to grow herbs for the kitchen in any case, yet their value as aromatic plants is equally great. You don't necessarily need a special herb bed, because they're quite at home in the borders where both flowers and foliage mix well with herbaceous plants and shrubs. Some herbs have perfumed flowers, but many more are blessed with very aromatic foliage, so they should be planted where you can pick a leaf or two as you pass.

Since most hail from Mediterranean countries, they need a sunny spot and good drainage and, unless otherwise mentioned, all those on my list require these conditions.

Aloysia triphylla **Lemon verbena**
This superbly lemon-scented shrub is not entirely hardy, though it should survive most winters if the roots are protected with a mulch. It'll grow to about 90cm (3ft) with long, green leaves and rather insignificant, white flowers in late summer. I include it because it has the best lemon-scented leaves I know, so it's worth a bit of extra trouble. If you can't keep it outside, grow it in a pot and bring it into a cold greenhouse for the winter.

Anethum graveolens **Dill**
An attractive annual with filigree foliage and flat heads of yellow flowers. The leaves have a spicy perfume. Sow it in spring where it's to grow and thin to 23cm (9in). It reaches a height of 60cm (2ft) and flowers in mid-summer.

*Purple-leafed sage is as aromatic as
the plain green kind.*

Anthriscus cerefolium Chervil

An annual growing to about 45cm (18in). In
summer it produces heads of white flowers
and the foliage has a pleasant, aniseed scent.
Sow it in spring where it's to flower and in
subsequent years it'll do the job for you.

Borago officinalis Borage

A hardy annual with delightful, blue flowers
and a pronounced scent of cucumber. It can
be sown direct in spring and will thereafter
seed itself. It grows to 45cm (18in).

Calamintha grandiflora Calamint

One of my favourite herbs for its delicate,
lilac-pink flowers and the delightful, fresh
perfume of its leaves. It grows to 45cm
(18in) and is often used for edging paths in
herb gardens.

Carum carvi Caraway

A biennial with heads of white flowers in
summer and a pronounced, spicy aroma. Sow
it in mid-summer for flowering the following
summer or buy plants in spring. It grows to
90cm (3ft).

Chamaemelum nobile Chamomile

A prostrate perennial no more than 15cm
(6in) high with fine, scented foliage. The non-
flowering form 'Treneague' is used to make
chamomile lawns and I have used it in the
town garden between the stepping stones
since it will take a little wear, and when
trodden on it releases its aroma of fresh
apples. The flowering form 'Flore Pleno' has
double, cream flowers in summer.

Foeniculum vulgare Fennel

A wonderful herb which should be used in
every garden for its superb ferny foliage
which is imbued with a fresh, aniseed
perfume. Both this and the variety
'Purpureum', which has bronze leaves, grow
to about 1.8m (6ft) if allowed to produce their
heads of yellow flowers. Alternatively cut
them back to the ground just before flowering
to encourage a fresh crop of leaves.

Galium odoratum Woodruff

A low-growing plant 15cm (6in) high that can
become invasive but is easily pulled out. It's
particularly good for growing underneath
shrubs since it appreciates a shady spot. In
early summer it produces small, white
flowers and has been used for centuries to
dry and hang in houses and airing cupboards
to fill the air with the scent of new-mown hay.

Helichrysum italicum Curry plant

A mounded, silver-leaved shrub topped by
heads of yellow flowers in summer. It has an

intriguing smell of hot curry which I find most attractive, though not everyone does. It grows to 60cm (2ft). In cold areas it could be killed by a hard winter.

Mentha Mint

A perennial herb that needs no introduction. There are several varieties offering a range of perfumes, including peppermint from *Mentha piperita*, eau-de-Cologne from *M. piperita citrata*, spearmint from *M. spicata*, apples from the variegated *M. suaveolens* 'Variegata' and, of course, the mint smell most of us associate with roast lamb from the best culinary variety, *M. rotundifolia* 'Bowles'.

Be warned, however: mint is extremely invasive, and once you allow it to root into the soil you'll never get rid of it. Grow it in a pot on the patio (I have often seen it escape from pots in the borders) and revitalize it every two years by taking a few divisions and repotting them.

Monarda didyma Bergamot

A fine herb with late summer flowers of brilliant red, purple, pink or lavender. The leaves have a fresh scent of lemon and are often used to make a herb tea. It grows to 90cm (3ft). See page 170.

Myrrhis odorata Sweet cicely

A relative of cow parsley with the typical heads of white flowers in spring followed by black seeds. The ferny leaves have an aroma of liquorice and are used in salads. It grows to 90cm (3ft) and prefers light shade, so is excellent under trees in a woodland or informal garden.

Ocimum basilicum Sweet basil

A half-hardy annual that should be raised each year in the greenhouse or on the windowsill and planted out in late spring. Its leaves have a

scent of cloves. It grows to 45cm (18in).

Origanum Marjoram

There are several perennial marjorams and oreganos used in the kitchen, all of which have a strong, spicy perfume. *Origanum onites* (French marjoram) is generally most favoured by cooks and is the most aromatic. *O. vulgare* (English marjoram) is less demanding to grow, and the golden form 'Aureum' is a very attractive plant for the front of the border (see page 178). Its aroma is perhaps less marked than the French version. They grow to about 23cm (9in).

Rosmarinus officinalis Rosemary

This shrub is well known for the pronounced fragrance of its greyish leaves. Like lavender, it must be pruned in spring to within a few buds of the previous season's growth without cutting into old wood. See page 181.

Ruta graveolens 'Jackman's Blue' Rue

A fine shrub whose foliage gives off a pungent aroma of orange. See page 183.

Salvia officinalis Sage

An evergreen shrub with aromatic foliage. There are several coloured-leaved versions which are as good in the kitchen as the green-leaved variety and much more attractive. Look out for 'Icterina' with yellow-variegated foliage; 'Purpurascens', which has dark bronze leaves; and 'Tricolor', which is green, white and purple. It does have violet flowers in early summer but is generally grown for its foliage. If you don't harvest it regularly, prune it in spring to keep it compact. It grows to about 90cm (3ft).

Teucrium chamaedrys Wall germander

An evergreen shrub with strongly aromatic leaves. It grows to no more than about 23cm

(9in) and is often used to edge paths. It has red-purple flowers in late summer.

Thymus Thyme

No garden should be without thymes. The prostrate types are excellent growing in cracks in paving where light treading will release their superb Mediterranean scent. The more upright growers are often used to edge paths or for dwarf hedges in knot gardens. They should be clipped annually in spring to ensure that they retain their bushy habit. Bushy varieties grow to about 30cm (1ft), while prostrate ones rarely exceed 12cm (5in).

Thymus serpyllum (English thyme) is the best for paving cracks. It produces lilac-pink flowers and has a strong perfume. There are also red, white and pink forms.

T. citriodorus (lemon thyme) is a bushy variety with a strong perfume of lemons. It has green leaves and lilac flowers, but there are several named varieties too. 'Aureus' has golden leaves (see page 174), while 'Silver Queen' is silver-variegated.

T. herba-barona is a prostrate variety with green leaves scented of caraway.

ANNUALS AND BIENNIALS

Several annuals and biennials have some perfume. I have restricted my list to those strongly perfumed plants that will often fill the garden with sweet scents. Biennials are raised by sowing outside in late spring or early summer and transplanting to nursery rows when the seedlings are large enough to handle. They're put into their permanent positions in the autumn.

Hardy annuals can be sown in early spring, while half-hardy annuals must be raised in gentle heat in early spring and planted out after all danger of frost has passed.

Centaurea moschata Sweet sultan

A hardy annual with large, fluffy flowers on 60cm (2ft) stems in late summer. It's available generally in a mixture of pink, white, purple and yellow and all colours have a strong perfume.

Dianthus caryophyllus Carnation

The half-hardy carnation has flowers with a wonderful clove scent, which come generally in shades of crimson to pink. It grows to around 45cm (18in).

Gilia tricolor Bird's eye

A hardy annual bearing mauve-and-white flowers with beautifully marked throats which give off a scent of chocolate. It grows to 45cm (18in).

Heliotropium arborescens Cherry pie

A half-hardy annual with very dark red leaves, large, flat heads of deep purple flowers and a good vanilla scent. It's also possible to buy cuttings-raised, named, perennial varieties which have a much more pronounced perfume, but these are naturally more expensive. The plant grows to about 45cm (18in).

Hesperis matronalis Sweet rocket

Don't be without this superb plant and certainly don't be put off by the fact that it behaves rather like a biennial (in fact it's a short-lived perennial), since it will seed itself quite freely. It grows to 1.2m (4ft), producing large sprays of white or lilac flowers with a lovely, sweet fragrance, especially in the evening.

Ipomoea alba Moonflower

A half-hardy climber related to morning glory, which can reach 6m (20ft) on a sunny wall. In the evening its large, white flowers release a powerful, sweet perfume.

Lathyrus odoratus **Sweet pea**
An old cottage-garden scrambler that
certainly needs no description. It's available
in a wide range of lovely colours, but be
aware of the fact that some of the newer
varieties in particular are not scented: avoid
them. Raise sweet peas in a coldframe from
an autumn sowing and plant out in the
spring.

Lobularia maritima **Sweet alyssum**
A low-growing, hardy annual reaching about
10cm (4in). It has flowers of white, pink and
purple and a rich, honey scent, most
noticeable in the evening.

Matthiola **Stock**
Matthiola bicornis (night-scented stock) is an
insignificant, little annual, about 30cm (1ft) in
height, with small, lilac flowers. In the
evening it sheds its Clarke Kent image and
becomes Superman! Incredibly it fills the air
with a strong, sweet, clove scent that will
surprise you.

M. incana (ten-week and seven-week
stocks) are half-hardy annuals which bear
short spikes of flowers in white, yellow, pink
and crimson with a very powerful, clove
scent by day and night. They grow to 75cm
(30in).

Brompton stocks are biennials, but similar
to ten-week stocks. They're sown in mid-
summer outside for flowering the following
spring. They grow to 45cm (18in).

Nicotiana **Tobacco plant**
There are several species of this strongly
scented plant that are well worth growing.

Nicotiana alata, the half-hardy annual, has
received the attention of the breeders in
recent years to produce strains with upward-
facing blooms in a range of reds, pinks,
yellows, white and even lime green. Many,

though not all, are well-perfumed. Heights
vary from 25 to 90cm (10in to 3ft).

The large, white-flowered N. alata grandiflora is a disappointment by day, but at night
it becomes almost luminous and fills the air
with sweet perfume: well worth waiting for.
It grows to 90cm (3ft).

The most impressive of all, though, is the
1.5m (5ft), white-flowered N. sylvestris, which
produces an almost overpowering scent in
the evening.

Oenothera **Evening primrose**
Oenothera biennis (common evening primrose)
has large, yellow, saucer-shaped flowers
which release a lovely lemon scent in the
evening. It grows to 90cm (3ft) and will seed
itself freely. O. odorata is a biennial or short-
lived perennial, bearing lemon-yellow
flowers which turn pink as they fade. It too
has a fine lemon perfume and grows toabout
60cm (2ft).

Scabiosa atropurpurea **Sweet scabious**
Bearing well-known pincushion flowers of
purple, pink or white with a sweet perfume,
this grows to about 60cm (2ft).

Tropaeolum majus **Nasturtium**
A so-called hardy annual, in colder districts
this should be treated as if half-hardy. The
Gleam Hybrids come in a range of bright
yellow, orange and scarlet with a pleasant
perfume. They're semi-trailing plants, so are
good in containers and baskets. They grow to
30cm (1ft).

Verbena hybrida **Verbena**
A half-hardy annual producing heads of
starry flowers in blue, pink, violet and white,
all with a fine, fruity fragrance, especially in
the evening. The reds are not so well scented.
It grows to about 30cm (1ft).

Chapter nine

INHABITING ARCADIA

The inspiration for gardens has, since civilized human beings first began cultivating for pleasure, always come from the natural world. Even today, in a setting that could hardly be more different, we share the selfsame dreams and aspirations as those first gardeners of the ancient world as we set out to build our own paradise on earth.

Each and every garden is, or at least attempts to be, the fulfilment of a vision of Arcadia filled with beautiful flowering plants, the cool shade of trees, the soothing babble of moving water, and of course, the hum of insects and the song of birds. It's an inspiration that goes as far back as the Garden of Eden. Without wildlife it may be pretty, but it would be as barren and as lifeless as the desert.

Fortunately we living things all require the same conditions. Our lives depend on the air we breathe, on plants and on water. Plants provide the necessary sustenance even for carnivores, whose food, somewhere down the chain, depends upon them. I believe that one factor which separates us from other, lower forms of life is that we also have a need to surround ourselves with living plants for the succour of our mind and spirit as well as our body. And, as we fill our gardens with plants for our pleasure, we'll automatically attract other living things.

Naturally they don't come to enjoy the freshness, the colour and the perfume as we do, but to sip the nectar, to collect seeds and berries and to fatten themselves on the greenfly that our plants have attracted. But without lifting a finger we'll fill our space with the song of birds, the buzz of bees and the colour of butterflies. For us it's a pretty good arrangement.

Of course, we should go further. We have, by our profligacy, managed to place just about every other species under some degree of threat, so we owe them something. We gardeners can do a lot to redress the balance by putting our gardens at their disposal to create an alternative home. At the same time, I promise you, you'll fill your life with joy.

In my own garden I sat and listened to a nightingale one summer evening not long ago. It had been some time since I'd heard this amazing songsmith and I'd forgotten the range and sheer musicality of the species. I was enthralled for half an hour or so and the

*Share your garden with wildlife
and reap the many rewards.*

feeling of natural magic remained with me long afterwards. It was a small part of my overall enjoyment of the garden, but worth more than money could buy.

This chapter is devoted to methods of attracting and keeping wildlife in your garden. If you live deep in the city's jungle, you may feel you're at a disadvantage. Not a bit of it. It's an amazing fact that there are actually more species now established in urban areas than there are in the country.

You may feel that, because the chap next door, be he a gardener or a farmer, sprays all wildlife out of existence, there's no point in trying to attract it into your plot only a few metres away. Well, surprisingly, that's not true either. I once did an experiment on three very small, adjacent plots with nothing more than a wire fence between them. The central one was treated entirely organically with no chemical fertilizers or pesticides, while the other two were chemically fertilized and sprayed with whatever pesticides were necessary. Astonishingly, while the two chemical plots remained barren of wildlife, the one in the middle was alive with all kinds of birds and insects. No doubt, because the hoverflies fed on the greenfly, the birds ate the hoverflies and so on.

General Recommendations

In my gardens I've not recommended filling the borders with stinging nettles. If you have a large plot and can hide them away in a corner, they really are a superb breeding habitat for several species of butterfly and other insects. But fundamentally I'm a gardener and, with only a small space to grow a garden, I'm blowed if I'm going to allow in anything but the most attractive of plants.

The answer is to concentrate on attracting birds and insects to feed (which generally means growing the brightest and best-scented flowers) and then badger the highways department to stop regularly cutting the verges outside. Growing nettles and other wild plants there is highly beneficial for us all. We'll return to the days of wildflower-strewn roadsides to delight the eye and the insects will have a perfect breeding area safe from the threat of the farmer's sprayer. And it's a darned sight cheaper on the council tax too.

Many native plants are highly attractive. I've detailed methods of growing wildflowers in grass (see page 141), and I've suggested in other chapters quite a few trees, shrubs and herbaceous plants which grow wild in Europe. But you don't necessarily have to stick to natives in order to attract wildlife. Many birds, for example, migrate huge distances, so they'll come across numerous other species on their travels and will be perfectly familiar with them if they encounter them in your garden.

There's also the alternative of using 'near-native' plants. Many of these have simply been selected by nurserymen from the original natives and differ only perhaps in flower colour or size. A perfect example is the range of red and pink flowering thorns, probably derived as hybrids between the white common hawthorn and the white Midland hawthorn, both European natives.

The main planting principle should be to build up as wide a diversity of species as space will allow. And that, of course, is right up every gardener's street.

A pond is a surefire way to attract all kinds of wildlife. Apart from its obvious role as a habitat for aquatic creatures like frogs, newts and toads, all animals need a drink from time to time. If yours is the only hostelry in the area, they'll all come from miles around.

So a pond is highly recommended and you'll find details of how to build one on page 116.

I don't keep fish in my ponds, though, because they tend to eat much of the wildlife. You'll have to make up your mind one way or the other. Fish are certainly attractive and enjoyable to keep, but they can foul the water somewhat, especially if the pond is small, and they do have to be regularly fed when they're not polishing off the tadpoles, the water boatmen and the dragonfly larvae.

If you have no pond, it's a good idea to provide water in pottery containers. As the water evaporates, it leaves a salt deposit on the side of the container, which many insects lick to replace their reserves.

However, by far the most important factor in attracting and keeping wildlife in your garden is a benevolent attitude. It hardly needs saying that all chemical pest control will have to stop. If you recognize that every living thing is entitled to its space and should be killed only as a very, very last resort, you'll soon achieve a wonderful result and a far more contented frame of mind. You can't poison the baddies without killing the goodies too. But if you see sense and don't kill either, you'll find that the baddies become much less of a threat. For although in gardens that have previously been sprayed regularly you may be on the losing side for a while, a balance of pest and predator will soon be built up and spraying will be unnecessary.

Nature has developed, over millions of years, a natural balance where no one species can ever completely dominate – except, of course, for the human species. But we are equipped with the intelligence to know that we do ourselves no favours by driving any other species to extinction. Peoples less 'civilized' than ourselves have always known it and so have developed sensible, sustainable lifestyles. It's time we woke up and did the same.

Frogs are an important ally in controlling pests in the garden.

Attracting Birds

Trees

There are many things you can do actively to encourage birds into the garden. Obviously any tree will provide places to perch, but it's far and away better if the same tree could be used for nesting and even to provide food too. The following are recommended:

Alnus glutinosa Alder
A large tree growing to 25m (80ft) with dark grey bark, especially good for waterlogged sites. The male catkins are yellow and the females small and red. These female catkins attract siskins, goldfinches and redpolls.

Alnus incana (grey alder) is much smaller and more attractive. The variety 'Aurea' has yellow foliage and orange shoots.

Amelanchier June berry
All species have small berries which are much loved by many birds. See page 82.

Betula pendula Silver birch
A large tree growing to 30m (100ft) eventually, but with a delicate tracery of branches that will not exclude too much light. The female catkins are especially good for attracting redpolls. See also page 83.

Conifers
All conifers have dense, leafy growth which make attractive nesting sites. *Taxus baccata* (yew) also produces sticky, red fruits much loved by thrushes.

Crataegus Flowering thorn
An excellent tree for nesting, with its close network of branches, and for providing berries in winter. The more attractive hybrids offer similar advantages. *Crataegus monogya*

(common hawthorn) also makes a superb hedge with the same qualities. It can, of course, be clipped to keep it in bounds. See page 84.

Fagus sylvatica Beech
This tree is much too big for all but huge gardens. The mast (nuts) is eaten by wood-pigeons, jays, woodpeckers and nuthatches as well as grey squirrels.

Ilex Holly
All the hollies produce berries if they're polli-nated and are used extensively for nesting too. If you have room for only one, choose a self-fertile variety like 'J. C. van Tol'. See page 94.

Malus Apple
All the crab apples produce large quantities of fruit which provide lots of food for birds into the winter. Leave it on the ground to rot, since the birds will still be eating it. See page 85.

Eating apples are also a fine food source and here, of course, there's a little animosity between gardener and birds. No gardener is going to encourage them to eat his/her carefully nurtured fruit, so the answer is to grow small trees, especially trained types like fans or espaliers, and to cover them with netting when the fruit ripens. Make sure that you stretch the netting tight and anchor it firmly at the bottom to prevent birds getting trapped inside.

Quercus Oak
Most of the oaks are splendid trees for many birds, providing insects for young tits and other species as well as acorns which are eaten by woodpigeons, jays, woodpeckers, nuthatches and squirrels. Alas, oaks are all big trees, growing from 20 to about 35m (65 to about 115ft).

Rowan berries and rose hips provide food for birds in winter.

Salix Willow

Many species attract caterpillars and other insects which provide food for birds. There are some quite small varieties and all can be controlled by pollarding. See page 107.

Sambucus Elder

The elders produce mountains of black or red berries which form an important food source for birds and for amateur wine-makers too! Some species have very attractive foliage and none grows too high. See page 134.

Sorbus Rowan/mountain ash

All species have attractive berries which are hungrily devoured by a variety of birds. The yellow-berried varieties seem less attractive to them, but as winter wears on even those go eventually. See page 87.

SHRUBS

Many ornamental shrubs provide food in the form of berries, while others attract insects favoured by birds. Some birds, like blackbirds, thrushes, dunnocks, long-tailed tits, blackcaps, chaffinches, bullfinches, greenfinches and linnets, nest in dense garden shrubs. Goldfinches prefer more open-growing plants like fruit trees and tall shrubs. Climbers on walls are also good nesting sites for birds like wrens, blackbirds and house sparrows.

Berberis Barberry

All varieties produce berries which ripen from mid to late summer and so are invaluable, especially in dry weather. The thick, thorny growth also makes the plants excellent for nesting. See pages 90 and 98.

Cotoneaster

All species produce berries which are eaten by many birds. See pages 92 and 101.

Daphne mezereum

An excellent, small shrub with superbly scented flowers and red berries which are attractive to birds. See page 101.

Euonymus europaeus Spindle

A European hedgerow native with bright red fruits in autumn, very attractive to robins in particular. In gardens it's best to grow the selection 'Red Cascade', which eventually makes a small tree with arching branches pulled down by the weight of the copious, red fruits. It gives good leaf colour in autumn too.

Garrya elliptica Silk tassel bush

A wall shrub, ideal for a north-facing wall and providing good nesting sites for thrushes in particular. See page 78.

Hedera **Ivy**

The ivies produce flowers which are very attractive to insects. Their berries are eaten by woodpigeons, thrushes, blackcaps and robins, and they also provide excellent nesting sites. They are thus among the most important plants for wildlife gardens. See page 74.

Ligustrum ovalifolium **Privet**

The dense growth of privet makes it a fine nesting site, though as a hedge it's a bit too hungry for a small garden. If you want to opt for a single plant as a shrub, grow the golden variety 'Aureum'. See page 95.

Lonicera **Honeysuckle**

The small fruits of honeysuckle ripen in late summer and are a good food source for warblers, thrushes and bullfinches among others. The tangled shoots also make excellent nesting sites. See page 52.

Prunus laurocerasus **Cherry laurel**

An evergreen shrub which makes a good nesting site. It grows to about 6m (20ft), but can be kept to size by hard pruning. More attractive are 'Marbled White' with green and grey marbled leaves and 'Magnoliifolia' with huge, imposing, glossy leaves.

Pyracantha **Firethorn**

All varieties produce berries which are very attractive to birds. As usual the red ones seem to go first, but eventually the orange and yellow berries disappear too. See page 78.

Rosa **Rose**

Any roses that bear hips in autumn are an important food source for seed-eaters like greenfinches. Rambling types like *Rosa canina* should be grown through a hedge. Shrub roses like *R. glauca* (*R. rubrifolia*) are also as useful. See pages 53, 165, 174, 181 and 193.

Rubus fruticosus **Bramble**

This is quite a rampant grower but useful if you have a country hedge, perhaps of hawthorn, to grow it through. The fruits are eaten by blackbirds and warblers in particular and the seeds by bullfinches and greenfinches.

HERBACEOUS PLANTS AND ANNUALS

Most herbaceous plants will attract insects which are, of course, food for birds. My list is relatively short, including only those plants that you really shouldn't be without. Otherwise, grow as wide a diversity as possible. It's probably true to say that the more species of plants you grow, the better your chance of attracting a wide spectrum of wildlife. Some plants are especially good as sources of seeds, so it's valuable to leave the seed heads on well into winter.

Aster **Michaelmas daisy**

The flowers are good attractors of insects late in the summer, and birds eat the seeds.

Centaurea cyanus **Cornflower**

A hardy annual with bright blue flowers whose seeds are enjoyed by birds.

Cheiranthus cheiri **Wallflower**

A biennial which makes a terrific display in various colours in spring from an autumn planting. Leave it to set seed if you can.

Helianthus annuus **Sunflower**

Sunflowers produce masses of seeds which are seized upon hungrily by tits, finches, nuthatches and goldcrests.

RIGHT *Blackbirds enjoy the bright red berries of the firethorn.*

Lunaria annua **Honesty**

A lovely biennial with purple-red or white flowers followed by round, silvery seed heads often used for cut-flower decoration. Birds eat the seeds and this is another plant that will seed itself freely.

Myosotis sylvatica **Forget-me-not**

A short-lived perennial grown as an annual. Bullfinches and goldfinches in particular eat the seeds which should be left on anyway since the plant will then reappear the following season.

Oenothera **Evening primrose**

Biennials and perennials with yellow or pink flowers and seeds attractive to several birds. See pages 178 and 217.

Scabiosa caucasica **Scabious**

A well-known cut flower with superb, pincushion blooms in various blues according to variety. Its seeds are much loved by various birds.

The Lawn and Border Soil

Many birds will find insects, worms, snails, slugs and other invertebrates in the lawn and in the soil around the garden. Blackbirds, song thrushes, robins and starlings are especially likely to search the lawn for food, so the less chemical treatment it gets the better.

Certainly you should never try to kill earthworms in lawns, partly because they're a food source and also for the valuable

aeration job they do. The lawn will also yield small flies to feed wagtails, chaffinches, dunnocks and blue tits. Thrushes are well known for their skill and diligence in clearing up the slug and snail population. Leave the lawn a little longer than normal because the grass is home for myriad insects too.

Feeding Birds

One sure way to attract birds to your garden where you can see them is to feed them, especially in winter when there's not much natural food about. In fact my own recommendation would be to feed them *only* during the winter to avoid encouraging dependence and in particular to ensure that they feed their young on the wild food they're designed for.

In winter you could save quite a few lives by feeding, so set up a bird table and make sure it's out of reach of the cat! Birds like bread, but not too much of it, so it's best to put out other feed too. Kitchen scraps are always welcome and you can include almost anything from meat to potatoes, fat to uncooked pastry. However, avoid salt, which can kill small birds, and make sure that your scraps are not in a place where they'll attract rats or foxes.

There are several special mixes available from pet shops, including highly nutritious foods like peanuts and suet mixes. But don't feed when birds are feeding their young or they may be over-generous.

The Guelder rose provides vital food for birds when little else is available.

You can, of course, buy a range of bird feeders from plastic tubes to pottery bells which you fill with suet. Better still, make your own by boring holes in a piece of birch or hazel branch. Hung from a tree in sight of the house, they'll provide hours of entertainment. If you're lucky, you may even attract a woodpecker.

Nest Boxes

Over sixty species of birds use nest boxes including many tits, sparrows, robins, starlings, nuthatches, spotted flycatchers, house martins, kestrels and owls.

Use untreated softwood for a box and never treat the inside or the area round the entrance hole. You can apply a water-based preservative to the outside, but make sure that it has a chance to dry completely before putting the box up.

For small birds the inside of the box must be at least 10cm (4in) square and the front should be roughened on the inside to allow young birds to scrabble up. The entrance hole must be at least 12.5cm (5in) from the floor just in case a cat manages to get its paw inside after the young birds. You should also drill a drainage hole in the base and the lid should be hinged to allow access for cleaning.

The size of entrance hole is quite critical and depends on the species you hope to attract. Make it 25mm (1in) in diameter for coal, marsh and blue tits, 28mm (1⅛in) for great tits and 32mm (1¼in) for nuthatches and house and tree sparrows.

If you make up the same box but remove the upper half of the front, it's likely to attract robins, wrens and pied wagtails. Larger birds like stock-doves and jackdaws can also be attracted to nest in open-fronted boxes, but they naturally need to be considerably bigger.

An assortment of foods attracts different species to the bird table.

Fix the box to a tree using wire or plastic string inside a piece of hosepipe to prevent damage to the tree. Make sure that it's out of the way of cats. It can be allowed to swing from a branch, which won't worry the birds but could make a cat feel insecure.

Ideally site the box where strong sunlight or rain won't beat in, and fix an open-sided box so that it's angled slightly forward. Put them up at any time, because birds may use them for roosting in the summer as well as nesting, but ensure that they're in place well before the early spring when birds go house hunting.

Of course, bird boxes can be bought too and this is probably the best bet for birds like house martins which need a quite specialized shape. Ask at your pet shop or, better still, get in touch with one of the bird protection organizations.

Attracting Butterflies and Other Insects

Butterflies love what we love. They feed on nectar provided by flowers to attract them in so that they can be dusted with pollen. When they visit the next flower, they deposit their pollen and the crop of seeds is started. To ensure that the pollinating insects don't miss their target, flowers put out advertisements in the form of bright colours or strong perfume. So the insects get fed, the flowers get pollinated and we enjoy the beauty and fragrance of the flowers: perfect.

Naturally they also need to breed and that's where our love/hate relationship comes in. Cabbage White butterflies look pretty fluttering about from cabbage to cabbage, but when their offspring chew the leaves to shreds, we gardeners are not exactly over the moon. In the flower garden, on the other hand, they do very little damage; so, while as a gardener I would suggest you take steps to put your cabbages, peas and fruit trees out of bounds to butterflies and moths, there's absolutely no need to worry about them among the flowers.

Indeed, if you have space, try to encourage breeding by growing food plants like nettles, native grasses, clovers and trefoils; most native plants will support some form of insect life, so the more, the merrier. Developing a wildflower meadow or growing wildflowers in your borders will also provide food without decimating your garden (see page 141).

However, in the main, as I've already suggested, lack of space will prevent you from growing food plants, so make sure that you lobby the local council to cut just the outside edges of the roadside verges, leaving the rest to support wildflowers. Many

councils have already adopted this policy. In the area where I live the front metre is cut and the rest is a mass of colour for most of the spring and summer.

There are certain garden plants that are guaranteed to attract butterflies and no garden of this type should be without them. Even in the deepest city environment, butterflies will smell them out. And, of course, those plants that attract butterflies will also tempt bees and other insects beneficial to the garden.

Alyssum maritimum **Yellow alyssum**
A bright yellow perennial growing to about 20–30cm (8in–1ft).

Aster **Michaelmas daisy**
A useful perennial because it flowers in late summer through into early winter.
See page 184.

Aubrieta
A low, spreading, spring rock plant available in various colours.

Buddleia davidii **Butterfly bush**
An attractive shrub available in many colours. See page 99.

Calendula officinalis **Pot marigold**
A showy hardy annual with bright yellow or orange flowers. See page 157.

Callistephus chinensis **Annual aster**
The well-known, late summer-flowering bedding aster is available in a variety of colours.

Centranthus ruber **Valerian**
A red or white perennial. See page 186.

The ice plant (Sedum 'Meteor') is smothered in small tortoiseshell butterflies in late summer.

Cheiranthus cheiri **Wallflower**
See page 224.

Coreopsis verticillata
See page 175.

Dianthus barbatus **Sweet William**
A cottage-garden biennial with flat flower heads of many colours in summer.

Hebe
Most varieties of this small shrub will attract butterflies. See pages 180 and 192.

Hyssopus officinalis **Hyssop**
A culinary and medicinal herb with blue, pink or white flowers.

Iberis **Candytuft**
Several species of this low-growing rock or edging plant are suitable.

Lavandula **Lavender**
An extremely well-known aromatic shrub. See page 95.

Lunaria annua **Honesty**
See page 225.

Nepeta faassenii **Catmint**
See page 213.

Phlox
Most varieties of this hardy perennial will attract butterflies. See page 213.

Scabiosa **Scabious**
See page 217.

This kind of planting provides a haven for insects of all kinds.

Sedum spectabile **Ice plant**
A very effective, perennial attractor of butterflies, which bears flat heads of pink or white flowers in late summer and autumn. See page 171.

Solidago **Golden rod**
There are several good garden hybrids of this yellow-flowered perennial.

Tanacetum parthenium **Feverfew**
A well-known herb with white, yellow-centred daisies over a long period in summer. It seeds itself freely. There's also a golden-leaved form, 'Aureum' (see page 178).

Tropaeolum majus **Nasturtium**
See page 217.

Verbena
A tender annual and perennial flowering all summer long in a variety of colours. See pages 152 and 217.

Attracting Moths

The main difference between attracting butterflies and attracting moths is that moths mostly fly at night. So you need flowers that are perfumed more strongly from the early evening.

Hesperis matronalis **Sweet rocket**
See page 216.

Jasminum officinale
Common white jasmine
See page 52.

Lonicera **Honeysuckle**
Many species of this shrubby climber are

scented during the day but even more so as night approaches. See page 52.

Nicotiana **Tobacco plant**

Several species, some tender perennials, some tender annuals, have scented flowers. See page 217.

Oenothera **Evening primrose**

Several species of this attractive perennial are very well scented in the evenings. See page 178.

Petunia

Many varieties of this highly cultivated, tender annual are scented at night. It flowers in various colours all summer.

Silene **Bladder campion**

A native European perennial with scented, white flowers.

Attracting Bats

Bram Stoker has a lot to answer for. He and other writers of horror fiction have given bats a bad name and it's stuck. They will not suck your blood, they won't become entangled in your hair and they are just about as far from being anything to do with Lucifer as could be. They're actually harmless little mice with wings and a superbly well developed radar. To watch bats flying around at dusk in their quest for insects is an essential part of the summer experience and not to be missed.

Bats are in decline in Europe, largely because of the loss of roosting sites. In many countries it's illegal to disturb them, even if they're roosting in your house, but they'll do absolutely no harm at all apart from leaving a few small, dry, crumbly droppings.

The best way to attract them into your garden is to build a bat box where they can roost. As with bird boxes, make it from untreated softwood. Bats have a highly developed sense of smell and even tarred roofing felt may put them off. Site the box as high as you can, ideally on a tree, fixed with wire or plastic twine run first through a piece of garden hose to avoid damage to the tree. Fixing the box on a building is also acceptable. Ideally keep the box warm by facing it south and avoid cluttered branches to give the bats a clear flight path.

Once the box is in place, it should never be disturbed. It may be difficult to see whether or not it's being used, but a sure way is to look under the box for droppings.

LEFT *The flowers of the white tobacco plant* (Nicotiana) *are most fragrant in the evening.*

Hedgehogs

Hedgehogs are very much the gardener's friends because they eat slugs and other pests like wireworms, cockchafers, crane-fly larvae and caterpillars. Unfortunately they also eat earthworms, ground beetles and spiders, all of which are gardening allies, but never in quantities likely to cause problems.

Hedgehogs are nice, companionable animals and fascinating to watch, but they do have minds of their own. It is, in fact, quite difficult to attract and keep a hedgehog in the garden, since they're inveterate travellers. However, if you provide them with a place to sleep and to bring up a family, they may well stay a while if the fancy takes them.

You can provide housing for hedgehogs simply by leaving a pile of logs, old leaves and so on in a corner of the garden. They're more likely to nest in this kind of habitat than in a home-made job. They may also take a liking to your bonfire pile, so if it's been standing for a while, make sure when you light it that there are no unsuspecting animals curled up inside.

Many hedgehog enthusiasts feed them and they will often get into the habit of coming for an evening meal of dog food which, provided it contains meat rather than fish, is not harmful. However, it's better in the long run either to collect the food that would make up hedgehogs' natural diet or to allow them to hunt for their own.

BELOW *The Hilton for hedgehogs.*
This pile of logs makes an ideal home for them.

233

Chapter ten

A WINTER HIDEAWAY

After a few years, when the garden's established and foliage is lush, it's not too difficult to find corners where you can hide yourself away in complete privacy. In winter, when the leaves have fallen and branches are bare, it's quite a different matter.

However, when the weather's wet and cold, there's not the same need to get outside. After a short stroll round the garden to check out those brave hearts that are still flowering, most of us would prefer to opt for a spot of double digging, a brisk, blood-warming walk or, better still, a deep armchair by the fire. Yet even in the coldest depths of winter you can still enjoy the company of plants and all the flower colour and perfume the finest summer's day has to offer – but it has to be electrified.

A conservatory or a garden room needn't cost the earth to heat and can still be the pleasantest of places to sit, to eat or to dream of spring on a cold but sunny winter day. With a close, lush planting, you can provide a perfectly secluded, private place which can even be double-glazed, if you wish, to eliminate all noise from outside: not just your own private paradise, but a *tropical* paradise to boot.

The Building

First and foremost it's important to buy a conservatory that will blend with and complement the style of your house. Salesmen, anxious for a commission, will try to pressure you into buying their product regardless of its harmony, or otherwise, with your house. Therefore it's best to get all the brochures first and to make your own selection in peace and quiet. Then get out to look at your choice in the flesh, at a show-site. If the buildings are all made to order, the makers will generally be able to tell you where you can see one they've made for someone else.

When I wanted a conservatory for my own house, I decided that none of the models I had seen was remotely suitable. My small, Victorian farmhouse is built very much in 'rustic peasant' style and simply isn't the sort of house that would ever have been grand enough for a conservatory. So I decided on a large, cedarwood greenhouse sited just outside the back door but not fixed to the

An indoor jungle. The lush greenery makes the conservatory a tranquil place to sit.

house at all. For once in my life I got it dead right. It looks just as if it was meant to be there all along and I'm delighted.

Whatever you buy is not going to be cheap, so take your time choosing just the right style for your own house and then look carefully at the specification to make sure that it's suitable for growing plants. That, after all, is what this conservatory is all about. Strangely, most you see these days are actually designed simply as an extra living room and take little or no account of the conditions needed to grow plants.

VENTILATION

The biggest problem with conservatories is that they get quite horrendously hot in summer. It's nothing for the spring temperatures to be down to 7°C (45°F) at night only to soar to 38°C (100°F) during the day, and there aren't many plants that will thank you for that.

The secret of success with indoor plants is to even out the day- and night-time temperatures as much as possible, so very good ventilation is vital. You need roof ventilators running the whole length of the building and opening up at least 30cm (1ft) from the closed position. Add to that side vents and, if you can, even ventilators in the walls. The obvious problem with this is security. In a greenhouse it doesn't matter much, because few burglars are going to bother stealing your tomatoes, but if the conservatory is an extension of the house, it could make a convenient entry point.

If you're away from the house during the day, you might like to consider ventilating with fans instead. They give no opening for burglars however resourceful, and they have the other obvious advantage that they can be thermostatically controlled to come on only

when the temperature rises beyond what you and your plants would like. They can even be linked electronically with the heaters, so that when temperatures are likely to fluctuate wildly, in the spring in particular, it's still possible to control the atmosphere to within 2 or 3 degrees.

SHADING

Whatever measures you take to provide adequate ventilation, you still won't be able to keep the temperature down enough in hot summers, so some form of shading is also necessary.

The cheapest way to create this is to paint the outside of the glass with a shading paint which will comfortably last the season and,

Simple blinds protect plants from too much sun.

These custom-made roller blinds are expensive but very efficient.

effective and look great, but they're expensive and not recommended for very windy sites.

The most popular types are those that fit inside the house. There are obvious difficulties getting over ventilators and any other obstacles, but the manufacturer of the conservatory will be able to supply blinds to fit. They range from fairly cheap, plastic material to very up-market designs, some of them lined with foil to reflect heat very efficiently.

BORDERS

Another way to shade the conservatory is by using climbing plants. You'd need to choose subjects that don't mind being quite hot themselves, but there are lots of those. Vines, bougainvillea, passion flowers and several others will be quite happy up there in the roof, as long as their roots are as cool as possible. The best bet is to grow them in a bed in the floor.

You'll get the most successful results if you can plan your beds before the building's erected. You'll be putting in a concrete floor to take tiles or paving, so before you do, allow for beds to be left, preferably near the back wall. Ideally you could build a low brick or stone wall around them just to keep the floor clean and to stop the water you'll be splashing about in summer from draining into it.

The bed should be filled with a good compost consisting of 5 parts of good garden soil, 3 parts of garden compost or coir compost and 2 parts of coarse grit. If you can add a layer of manure every 15cm (6in) or so, your plants will really romp away. Give the bed a mulch over the top with manure after planting, and every autumn to keep the roots cool and moist, and your plants will reward you well.

If beds are not an option, you'll have to grow your climbers in pots. They'll have to be pretty big and you'll need to repot from time

while remaining weatherproof, can be easily rubbed off when the weather turns cooler in the autumn. Unfortunately it doesn't exactly enhance the outside appearance of the building, so permanent blinds are much to be preferred.

Roller blinds have the added advantage that they can be pulled down and rolled up again at will, depending on the heat of the day, and it's even possible to do that automatically too. So perfect control is within reach, even if you're out at work all day. Mind you, you'll need to be busy earning, because it's not cheap.

Victorian conservatories and greenhouses had the roller blinds on the outside and they're still available today. They consist of rolls of wood, metal or plastic strips which roll down from the ridge. They're very to time (see page 241). The pots should be made of clay, stone or concrete in preference to plastic, which heats up too much.

HEATING

Unless you're in the ranks of the mega-rich, don't even consider growing what the Victorians called 'stove-house' plants. Things like pineapples were grown for fruit in those days, but coal was cheap and wealthy meant *seriously* wealthy. These days it's much better to stick with those plants that will tolerate a minimum night-time temperature of about 7°C (45°F). There are plenty of them that will delight you just as much – and supermarket pineapples are pretty good after all.

Electricity is by far the best form of heating for a conservatory. It's clean, it gives off no toxic fumes, it's no more expensive than other fuels and, above all, it can be thermostatically controlled to come on only when it's needed. That cuts the cost and also evens out the temperatures to make perfect growing conditions.

Ideally spread the heat as much as possible by installing tubular heaters and always get a qualified electrician to fit them. You'll need waterproof fittings throughout and you should never, never skimp. Badly installed electrical equipment can be dangerous stuff in such a moist atmosphere, but if it is properly installed, it's as safe as houses.

A well fitted-out conservatory is the ideal place to relax – and it needn't cost the earth.

FITTING OUT

First consider the floor. If you want to grow plants well, and you do, you'll have to splash a lot of water about. So you'll need a floor that can take it. No fitted carpets here, I'm afraid. Instead the concrete must be covered with quarry tiles or paving slabs.

For the same reason furniture must also be able to withstand a very damp atmosphere, so soft furnishings are out. Wood or, even better, metal chairs and tables are ideal, though for extra comfort you may want to cover cushions in waterproof material or even leave them in the house and bring them out when you want to sit down.

You'll also need somewhere to stand pot plants and a conventional staging running along at least one side is best. If you make it very strong and raise the edges to form a box 15cm (6in) deep, you can fill it with sand to help create the humid atmosphere these plants prefer in summer, and to reduce the amount of watering you have to do.

In some cases that would simply take up too much room, so in smaller buildings I suggest standing pot plants on tables of different heights. I used metal ones, but there's no reason why they shouldn't be made of wood, provided they're protected with polythene. Cover that with a piece of capillary matting which will absorb water. By keeping the matting wet you'll provide a reservoir which the plants will draw on and you'll also surround them with welcome humidity.

You might also want to hang baskets from the cross-struts in the roof or fix wall baskets to the back wall. The more plants you can squeeze in, the better.

A maximum/minimum thermometer is essential to get the growing regime right. This will tell you the extremes of temperature the conservatory has reached while you weren't

Mainly pink flowers look elegant against white, whether in the conservatory or outdoors.

there and will enable you to even out your growing regime.

Many conservatory plants, while not being as demanding as subjects like rhododendrons, will grow better in acid conditions. But even if the plants are potted into an acid compost, watering with limy water will soon change it. So it's best to install a water butt just outside the building so that you can water with rainwater. Better still, have it inside so that the water reaches ambient temperature. That's especially important in the winter and early spring when tender plants, especially young seedlings, can suffer from an icy bath. With no inside tank the last job of the day in winter should be to fill the watering can so that it can warm up overnight.

General Cultivation

WATERING

During the summer, as a general rule, most plants should not be allowed to dry out. However, overwatering is all too easy. As a rule of thumb, water really well and then allow the plant to dry almost, but not quite, to the point of wilting. Then water well again.

In winter, watering should be reduced to a minimum, with most plants needing a drink only about once a month. Even in winter, when you do water, really soak the roots and then leave them to dry out.

*A terracotta tiled floor is
both practical and attractive.*

DAMPING DOWN

In hot weather it's important to damp down with clear water every morning. Sometimes it may even be necessary in the afternoon as well. Soak the floor and the staging and give the plants a light spray over too, to create a really humid atmosphere around them.

FEEDING

Initially mix a slow-release fertilizer with the compost. This will feed the plants as they need it for about six months. Then you may need to liquid-feed. For foliage plants use a high-nitrogen general liquid fertilizer and for flowering plants use one high in potash.

Some plants are hungrier than others, but as a rule it pays to feed at every watering in

the summer except for a flush-through once every four waterings with clear water to avoid a build-up of salts. In winter no feeding is needed unless the plants are flowering.

Potting and Repotting

Plants should initially be potted into a soilless compost. There are several available commercially, but I recommend mixing your own. Use a good coir compost plus about 15 per cent of fine bark and add slow-release fertilizer according to the maker's instructions.

When repotting, always use the next-sized pot. No plants like to be surrounded by cold, wet compost, especially in winter. For the same reason always repot when the plant is growing actively in spring or summer.

It can be difficult to work compost between the rootball and the sides of the new pot when the space is restricted, so I suggest taking the plant out of its old pot first and using this as an aid. Put a little compost in the bottom of the new pot and rest the old one inside it. Fill round with compost, from time to time tapping the new pot down on the bench or the floor to settle it. Remove the inside pot and you'll be left with a lining of compost. Put the rootball inside and water well to settle the compost round the roots.

Training

Climbing plants must be trained on horizontal wires fixed to the back wall or the glazing bars with screw-eyes. If the plants are natural twiners, you'll also need vertical wires twisted round the horizontals to make a mesh. If they're not, you'll have to tie them in with soft string. This should be done regularly to avoid damage.

Pest Control

Inevitably there will be some pest damage. Red spider mite will attack in dry conditions and whitefly is bound to be in evidence from time to time. Deal with them by using biological controls which can now be bought from garden centres. This sets predator against pest in the most natural way possible and means that you'll do no harm to any other living thing except the ones you want to control. This will naturally mean that you can't use insecticides or you'll kill your allies too, but then you won't need to.

Diseases can generally be controlled with plenty of ventilation and by picking off and destroying diseased leaves.

The Plants

All the plants in the following list will survive with a minimum winter temperature of 7°C (45°F). Where no heights are mentioned, you can expect the plant to grow into the roof without difficulty.

Climbers

Araujia sericifera **Cruel plant**
A vigorous climber for a warm wall, freely producing salver-shaped, scented, white flowers in late summer, followed by large pods which split to reveal silky threads and seeds from which new plants can be raised.

Billarderia longiflora **Purple apple berry**
A small climber growing to about 1.8m (6ft) with twining stems, producing cream or greenish yellow, bell-shaped flowers flushed purple inside in summer. These are followed by electric-blue berries.

Bomarea caldasii
A tuberous, twining climber related to
alstroemeria. It grows to 2.4m (8ft) and bears
numerous speckled, orange or yellow bells
for a long period from late winter. Cut off old
stems if they brown and wither.

Bougainvillea
A well-known climber with large, coloured
bracts surrounding small, creamy white
flowers throughout summer and often into
autumn. Prune side shoots back to the main
stems in late winter. Keep the plant fairly dry
in winter and liquid-feed in summer. In low
winter temperatures it may lose its leaves.

There are many attractive hybrids, so a visit
to a specialist nursery is called for. 'Jennifer
Fernie' is pure white; 'Flamingo Pink' is white
with a pink flush; 'Lady Mary Baring' is yellow;
'Camarillo Fiesta' and 'Jamaica Orange' are
orange; 'Purple Robe' and 'Poultonii Special'
are purple; 'Donyo' and 'James Walker' are
pink; and 'Killie Campbell' is coppery red.

Canarina canariensis
Canary Island bellflower
A low climber growing to about 1.8m (6ft)
and producing delicate, light orange bells
with darker veins from autumn to late spring.
It then dies down to its tuberous rootstock
until late summer. Keep it quite dry during its
dormant period.

Clianthus puniceus **Parrot's bill**
A shrub rather than a climber, but it can be
supported to reach about 1.8m (6ft). It has
attractive, evergreen foliage and brilliant red
or white flowers shaped like a parrot's bill in
spring and early summer.

Morning glory (Ipomaea indica) *make a
striking show all summer.*

Gelsemium sempervirens **Carolina jasmine**
A slender evergreen bearing glossy leaves
and fragrant, golden-yellow, funnel-shaped
flowers with dark orange throats in spring
and summer.

Hardenbergia comptoniana
A delightful evergreen twiner with clusters of
pea-like flowers in late winter and early
spring. 'Rosea' is soft pink; 'Violacea' is deep
violet; 'Happy Wanderer' is lavender-violet
with a primrose eye; and 'White Crystal' is
white. Prune back after flowering to retain a
compact shape.

Hoya **Wax flower**
This twining climber produces exotic, waxy
flowers in summer and autumn. It likes
warm, moist conditions in summer and a
cool, dry atmosphere in winter. Keep it a trifle
pot-bound and feed only a little to encourage
flowering. *Hoya australis* bears clusters of
fragrant, red-spotted, white flowers; *H. fusca*
'Silver Knight' is maroon-pink with silver-
blotched leaves; *H. globulosa* has creamy
white flowers from early spring to autumn;
H. imperialis has large, waxy flowers of
maroon with cream centres; and
H. macgillivrayi has reddish leaves and
maroon flowers.

Ipomoea indica **Morning glory**
The perennial morning glory grows fast and
produces masses of large, purple-blue,
trumpet flowers all summer and autumn.
They turn pink-purple with age to produce a
very attractive, two-tone effect. Prune back
hard in spring, even right to the base.

Jasminum **Jasmine**
Popular climbers, most with fragrant flowers.
Jasminum mesnyi is an evergreen with large,
yellow, semi-double flowers in late winter

and spring. They are not perfumed. After flowering, cut back side shoots hard to within a few buds of the main stem. *J. nitidum* has fragrant, white flowers tinged pink; *J. polyanthum* is not to be missed: the pale pink flowers fill the room with perfume all winter. Prune hard after flowering.

Lapageria rosea Chilean bellflower

A superb climber and a 'must' for the cool conservatory. It has waxy, leathery leaves and huge, bell-shaped flowers of rose-pink from late summer to winter. The flowers are followed by edible fruits. Raised from seed, they vary a lot and can be flushed and marbled with white. They need a shady, cool spot, lime-free soil and plenty of water in summer.

Mandevilla laxa Chilean jasmine

An evergreen climber with large, very fragrant, trumpet-shaped, white flowers in summer. Prune in spring by shortening side shoots to one or two buds from the main stem. Keep fairly pot-bound to encourage flowering and avoid overwatering in the winter. *Mandevilla amoena* 'Alice du Pont' produces large, glowing-pink trumpets but no scent.

Pandorea jasminoïdes Bower plant

A showy evergreen with white or pale pink, funnel-shaped flowers with pink-purple throats all summer.

The variety 'Charisma' has yellow-variegated leaves and rose-pink flowers with a crimson throat. *Pandorea pandorana* (wonga wonga vine) has creamy white flowers flushed with yellow and spotted purple, while *Pandorana* 'Golden Showers' has mahogany buds opening to gold trumpets. They can all be pruned after flowering, but will flower well without.

Passiflora Passion flower

There's a range of passion flowers that make superb climbers, best planted in the border but quite possible to grow to reduced heights in pots. Prune in spring to tidy the plants and remove overcrowded wood. Shorten side shoots back to within a bud or two of the main stem and remove some shoots completely to open up the plant. There are many good varieties, so visit a specialist nursery for the widest choice.

Passiflora amethystina is covered with amethyst-blue flowers in late summer and autumn.

P. alata is a vigorous grower with enormous purple-and-white, slightly fragrant flowers and edible fruits.

P. caerulea is the best known with blue-and-white flowers and orange fruits not worth eating.

P. caeruleoracemosa is a hybrid with striking, rose-crimson flowers all summer.

P. citrina has dainty, yellow flowers.

P. edulis 'Crackerjack' is the best edible variety with small, purple-and-white flowers which are not the showiest but are followed by lots of large, purple fruits with an excellent flavour.

P. mollisima (banana passion fruit) has pink flowers followed by large, yellow fruits shaped like small bananas.

Petrea volubilis Purple wreath

A splendid, vigorous climber with long, pendulous wreaths of dark purple flowers in spring and summer. Prune it to within a bud or two of the main stems after flowering.

Rhodochiton atrosanguineum Purple bell vine

A dainty plant, not vigorous enough to grow into the roof but good supported on canes with three plants to a pot. It produces rose-pink and purple, tubular flowers all summer. It's easily raised each year from collected seed if you want to grow it outside in summer.

Solanum Potato vine

The varieties mentioned on page 54 are suitable for growing in the conservatory where they'll generally perform well and give a longer flowering period.

Streptosolen jamesonii Marmalade bush

A magnificent semi-evergreen shrub covered in bright orange flowers in spring. It'll reach a height of about 3m (10ft) or can be grown as a much smaller bush or even a standard if kept in control by regular pinching back.

Thunbergia alata Black-eyed Susan

A well-known plant usually grown as a half-hardy annual climber, though it is in fact a perennial. It can be grown through other climbers or in a pot on its own supported by canes where it'll reach about 1.8m (6ft). The numerous flowers can be orange with a black eye, yellow or white. Grow new plants from seed each year.

Trachelospermum jasminoïdes Star jasmine

An evergreen with masses of fragrant, white flowers all summer. Prune tall plants after flowering.

Vitis Grape

This deciduous climber makes an excellent productive plant and its hanging bunches of fruits are attractive too. It also provides very good shade in the roof of the conservatory. Varieties like 'Black Hamburgh' and the white 'Buckland Sweetwater' can be grown without heat but, for the very best flavour, grow 'Muscat of Alexandria', a white variety with an unsurpassed flavour and

The golden-flowered Pandorea jasminoïdes *is a very showy evergreen.*

'Madresfield Court', a fine black, both of which need a little heat early in the season. Grapes can't really be grown in pots as climbers, because they need the freedom of a border, though plants can be trained as smaller standards.

When growth starts, pinch back laterals at five leaves and sub-laterals at one and tie them in to horizontal wires. In early winter prune back the main stem to remove two-thirds of the previous summer's growth and cut back laterals to one bud.

In the following and subsequent years look for embryo bunches of grapes and pinch back the shoots two leaves past each bunch. Don't allow too many bunches to form. One every 900 sq. cm (1 sq. ft) is about right. Feed every fortnight with a tomato fertilizer.

POT PLANTS

The staging, tables and areas on the floor can be used to grow a wide variety of pot plants. Those listed below are mainly more exotic plants recommended for conservatories, but don't scorn the easier greenhouse pot plants. Things like pelargoniums, fuchsias, strepto-carpus, calceolaria and primulas are all easy to raise from seed or cuttings and can provide colour all year round. In the winter you may be pleased to have some of the easier, more common subjects.

There are, of course, hundreds of plants you could grow, so I've restricted my list to particular favourites and those I think no self-respecting conservatory should be without. However, I would recommend a trip to a specialist nursery to see for yourself.

Once again, all the plants listed here will be happy with a winter temperature of 7°C (45°F).

Abutilon

A shrubby plant that does well in pots and can be stood outside in summer. Most varieties have maple-like leaves and bell-shaped flowers over a very long period in spring and summer. Prune in spring, cutting back side shoots to within one or two buds of the main stem. 'Souvenir de Bonn' has pink flowers; 'Amsterdam' is bright red; 'Cannington Sally' is bright gold; 'Savitzii' is orange with white-splashed foliage; and 'Nabob' is deep plum. They grow to 1.8m (6ft).

Acacia

A tall shrub with beautiful, yellow flowers in late winter and early spring and attractive, ferny foliage. Prune after flowering to restrict its size. It can go outside in summer and some varieties could be hardy in the warmest areas. It can be restricted to 1.8m (6ft).

Acacia baileyana has elegant, pendulous growth with blue shoots and leaflets and rich golden flowers.

A. dealbata is the florist's mimosa with feathery foliage and fluffy, yellow flowers.

A. pravissima can be free-standing or wall-trained. It has deep yellow flowers in spring.

A. retinoïdes 'Lisette' has pale yellow, scented flowers often from autumn right through winter.

Agapanthus African lily

This wonderfully dramatic flower is even more spectacular and a little earlier under glass. It does very well in tubs and pots and should be allowed to become well pot-bound before repotting. See page 183.

Alyogyne heugelii 'Santa Cruz'

A wonderful relative of the hibiscus with soft pink flowers shaded blue. It's rarely out of flower, so prune in late winter, shortening side shoots. It can be restricted to 2.1m (7ft).

Anisodontea capensis

A charming, shrubby plant covered in mid-pink flowers from spring to winter. Prune hard in spring and take cuttings, since old plants become leggy. It grows to 90cm (3ft).

Argyranthemum frutescens Marguerite

An easy-to-grow tender perennial which will flower most of the year. It has white flowers with yellow centres. 'Jamaica Primrose' bears bright yellow flowers and 'Vancouver' is pink. There are many other varieties. Take cuttings in late summer to renew leggy plants. It grows to 90cm (3ft).

Bougainvillea, grown here with mother-in-law's tongues and the purple passion vine, makes a spectacular conservatory climber.

Bidens ferulifolia

An easy-to-grow, trailing plant especially good in a hanging basket or over the edge of a tall pot. It has buttercup-yellow flowers all summer. Take cuttings in late summer each year to renew the plants.

Bletilla striata

An orchid with purple-red flowers in large clusters. Keep it on the dry side and fairly pot-bound. It grows to 60cm (2ft).

Buddleia **Butterfly bush**

Tender relatives of the hardy garden shrub will flower in winter with a delicious, honey scent. Put them outside in summer, prune hard after flowering and pinch back during the season to keep in check. *B. asiatica* is a weeping evergreen with greyish leaves and scented, white flowers in late winter and early spring. *B. auriculata* has fragrant, cream flowers with a yellow throat from autumn to late winter. *B. lindleyana* produces spikes of purple flowers in mid-summer; feed well. They can all be restricted to 3m (10ft).

Callistemon citrinus **Australian bottle-brush**

A large plant, perhaps a bit ungainly but very striking. The bottle-brush flowers are red and the foliage has a lemon fragrance when crushed. It can be restricted to 2.4m (8ft). Prune in autumn by cutting out weak growth. 'Red Cluster' bears crimson flowers with golden stamens and is very free-flowering.

Clivia miniata **Kaffir lily**

A delightful, bulbous plant which is easy to grow in a large pot. Keep it pot-bound for best flowering and feed regularly in summer. The flowers are generally large and orange, but there are also some good, new colours from white through yellow to pale apricot. It grows to 45cm (18in).

Cordyline australis **Cabbage palm**

A dramatic, spiky, foliage plant that needs a lot of space but makes a fine focal point. There are many good varieties which are too tender for outside planting in all but the warmest of gardens. 'Albertii' has cream, green and pink stripes and 'Sundance' has deep red stripes. They grow to about 1.8m (6ft).

Coronilla valentina glauca

This attractive shrub can be grown outside in warmer areas but does well in a pot inside, where it produces yellow, scented flowers continuously through autumn and winter. The variety 'Variegata' has delicately variegated green-and-cream leaves. It grows to 90cm (3ft). Prune it quite hard after flowering to encourage new growth.

Correa

A small, evergreen shrub which does well whether in a pot or planted in the border, producing bell-shaped flowers. It can be grown as a bush or a standard or trained as a fan. *Correa rosea* 'Mannii' is deep pink and flowers over a long period in winter; *C. alba* is white; *C. backhouseana* has cream flowers in the spring and early summer; and 'Marion's Marvel' is a new variety with flowers of rose-pink and jade-green. They grow to around 1.2cm (4ft).

Daphne

In very mild areas many daphnes will survive if given a warm, south-facing wall. In the conservatory they're simply superb, covered in flower with an almost overpowering perfume. *Daphne odora* bears pretty pink-and-white flowers from mid-winter to early spring. The variety 'Aureomarginata' has cream-variegated leaves. They grow to around 90cm (3ft) and are best put outside in summer.

Euryops pectinatus

An easily grown, tender perennial often bedded out in summer. It makes a lovely, evergreen shrub with finely cut, silvery foliage and bright yellow, daisy flowers all summer. *Euryops chrysanthemoïdes* has green foliage and deep golden daisies. Prune hard in spring to encourage new growth and take cuttings in late summer since the plants are relatively short-lived. They grow to 90cm (3ft).

Felicia amelloïdes **Blue daisy**

A delightful, evergreen perennial which flowers for a very long time during winter, spring and summer. It covers itself with sky-blue daisies, and the variety 'Santa Anita' has larger flowers. 'Variegata' has the bonus of pretty cream-and-green leaves and 'Read's White' bears white flowers. Prune them back from time to time to stop them getting leggy. They grow to 23cm (9in).

Hedychium coronarium **Ginger lily**

Tall, showy, fragrant, white flower spikes in summer make this a striking plant for a big pot or for planting in the borders. Look out too for *Hedychium gardnerianum*, with smaller, yellow flowers and orange stamens. They grow to 1.8m (6ft).

Heliotropium peruvianum
Cherry pie

A shrubby plant with a distinct, fruity fragrance which was popular in Victorian times. The flowers are generally deep purple in colour, but they can vary from white through pink, too. They repeat flower all summer long. Cut them back hard after flowering. They can grow to about 45cm (18in).

---

*Clivea is grown for its
superb large orange flowers in spring.*

Impatiens niamniamensis
Congo cockatoo
A striking plant bearing curious flowers of greenish yellow and crimson, looking like a parrot's beak, in summer and autumn. It grows to 60cm (2ft).

Lachenalia **Cape cowslip**
A bulbous plant producing delicate, bell-shaped flowers in profusion on 15–30cm (6in–1ft) stems from mid-winter to spring. *Lachenalia aloïdes* has yellow or orange flowers and the variety 'Luteola' bears mottled leaves and red, yellow and green flowers.

Lantana camara **Yellow sage**
This shrubby plant has verbena-like flowers which will attract butterflies in profusion. It can be put outside in summer. The flowers open yellow and turn red as they age. There are several good named varieties. Look out for the bright red 'Brasier', the golden-yellow 'Mine d'Or', the deep-pink-and-yellow 'Mr Bessieres' and the low-growing 'Carpet Orange'.

Metrosideros excelsus
New Zealand Christmas tree
A compact shrub with glossy, green leaves and bright red flowers for a long period in summer. The variety 'Scarlet Pimpernel' is especially good. Look out too for *Metrosideros kermadecensis* 'Variegatus' with green-and-yellow leaves and showy, scarlet flowers in early summer.

Nerium oleander **Oleander**
A popular shrub in Mediterranean countries and an excellent conservatory plant. Given plenty of light, it flowers from spring to autumn. Prune side branches by about half after flowering.

There are several good named varieties. 'Clare' is pale pink and semi-double; 'Emilie' is double apricot; 'Hardy's Red' is a deep red single; 'Isle of Capri' is a single yellow; 'Soeur Agnes' is a double white; and 'Variegatum' has pink flowers and leaves with creamy white margins. There are many more, so a trip to a specialist nursery is recommended.

Palms
While many palms need higher temperatures in winter and others grow too tall for most conservatories, there are several that are ideally suited. They certainly impart a tropical effect.
Howea forsteriana and *H. belmoreana* (Kentia palm) are ideal with a beautiful, arching habit. Shade and moisture at the roots are essential.
The Chinese *Rhapis excelsa* (lady palm) has elegant, fan-shaped leaves and forms a bamboo-like clump. *R. foliis variegatis* has slender, white-striped leaves and is slow-growing, so will not become a nuisance.

Pittosporum
An evergreen shrub with attractive foliage and often fragrant flowers. It grows to about 1.8m (6ft).
Pittosporum crassifolium has leaves with a brown felt underneath and also coating the young stems. It bears small, fragrant, red flowers in spring followed by white seed capsules. The variety 'Variegatum' has white-edged leaves
P. eugenioïdes has pale green, wavy-edged leaves which smell of lemon when crushed, plus greenish-white, honey-scented flowers in spring.
P. tenuifolium has wavy, green leaves and black stems, making it a popular flower arrangers' plant. The variety 'Atropurpureum' bears bronze foliage.

Evergreen Plumbago auriculata *with sky-blue flowers is a fast-growing climber.*

Plumbago auriculata **Cape leadwort**

This popular plant was formerly known as *Plumbago capensis* and is still often sold as such. It's a shrubby, scrambling evergreen, so it needs some support. It produces brilliant blue flowers in summer and autumn, and the variety 'Alba' is white. In spring prune back shoots that flowered last year to within two buds of the main stems and thin out old wood.

Sparmannia africana **African hemp**

A fine, large-leaved, evergreen shrub that needs controlling since it can grow very tall. Growing it in a pot and pinching out the growths that become too long can restrict it to about 1.8m (6ft). It has clusters of white flowers with yellow stamens tipped red, produced from spring to autumn. When touched, they immediately respond by opening out.

Tibouchina urvilleana **Glory bush**

Sometimes sold as *Tibouchina semidecandra*, this rather straggly shrub needs support and pruning in spring to keep it compact. It has large, brilliant purple flowers and prominently veined leaves. It grows to 2.4m (8ft). The variety 'Jules' is a dwarf form, growing to 90cm (3ft), with smaller flowers tinged with pink.

Tulbaghia violacea

A bulbous plant requiring a well-drained compost. It has grass-like foliage and very attractive, pink-violet, tubular flowers on 60cm (2ft) stems from spring to autumn. The variety 'Pallida' bears white flowers and 'Silver Lace' has leaves striped white and pink.

Index